Favorite Prayers and Novenas

A treasury of best loved
novenas, prayers, litanies
and chaplets for various needs
along with biographical sketches
of patron saints and the history
of these popular devotions

General Editor
Marianne Lorraine Trouvé, FSP

BOOKS & MEDIA

Boston

With ecclesiastical approval.

(This book of novenas has been compiled from various sources. All of the prayers received the appropriate ecclesiastical approval at the time of their original publication.)

The Scripture quotations contained herein are from the *New Revised Standard Version Bible: Catholic Edition,* copyright © 1996 and 1989 by the Division of Christian Education of the National Council of Churches of Christ in the U.S.A. Used by permission. All rights reserved.

Grateful acknowledgment is made to Templegate Publishers, Springfield, Illinois, for the permission granted to reprint quotations from *Thoughts of the Curé of Ars*.

ISBN 0-8198-2664-2

Printed and published in the U.S.A. by Pauline Books & Media, 50 St. Paul's Avenue, Boston, MA 02130.

http://www.pauline.org
E-mail: PBM_EDIT@INTERRAMP.COM

Pauline Books & Media is the publishing house of the Daughters of St. Paul, an international congregation of women religious serving the Church with the communications media.

1 2 3 4   99 98 97

Contents

Prayers to Jesus Master, Way, Truth and Life

Introduction

During the Last Supper, on the night before he died, Jesus told the apostles that he was going to prepare a place for them. He said, "You know the way to the place where I am going."

Thomas was puzzled by this and asked him, "Lord, we do not know where you are going. How can we know the way?"

Jesus replied, "I am the way, and the truth, and the life. No one comes to the Father except through me" (Jn 14:1-6).

In these simple words, Jesus summed up his life and saving mission. As the *way* to the Father, Jesus teaches us how to live. In the Sermon on the Mount and the Beatitudes, Jesus told us what he expects of his followers. It seems demanding—and it is. But the Lord is always there to strengthen us to fulfill his commands.

As the *truth,* Jesus is the master teacher. People marveled at his words: "Now when Jesus had finished saying these things, the crowds were astounded at his teaching, for he taught them as one having authority, and not as their scribes" (Mt 7:28-29). In the world today, many self-proclaimed prophets strive to gain followers. People wonder who they can trust. In the midst of all the confusion, the words of Jesus cut through the babble and ring out as the truth. As Peter declared, "Lord, to whom can we go? You have the words of eternal life" (Jn 6:68).

Yes, Jesus is our *life*. But the life he gives us is not this mortal life, destined to crumble into dust. Jesus gives us the life that will last forever—eternal life with God. Through the sacraments especially, Jesus pours into us the divine life of grace, which enables us to partake of the life of God. "Thus he has given us, through these things, his precious and very great promises, so that through them you may...become participants of the divine nature" (2 Pet 1:4).

As the way to God the Father, the truth to be believed, and the life of our souls, Jesus is our divine Master. To honor him as such is not just to practice a devotion, but to grasp the essence of the Christian life. Jesus is our life and salvation. All other devotional practices take second place to Jesus.

To honor Jesus as our master means to turn our life over to him. We honor him with our mind, believing the truth he teaches through the Church. We honor him with our will, striving to live according to his teachings. We honor him with our heart, offering him our love and seeking to be more closely united to him through prayer and the sacraments. Growing in the Christian life, we will gradually become more and more like Jesus, until we can say with St. Paul, "It is no longer I who live, but it is Christ who lives in me" (Gal 2:20).

First Day

Jesus Master, Way, Truth and Life, have mercy on us.

Novena Prayer
(to be recited every day)

Jesus Master, your life traces the way for me; your teaching guides my steps; your grace sustains and supports me in my walk toward heaven. You are the perfect Master who gives the example and who teaches and strengthens the disciple to follow you. Jesus, you have the words of eternal life. Grant that I may learn your wisdom and knowledge so that following the way of your Gospel, I may attain salvation. If it be according to your holy will, grant me the graces I ask of you now *(mention your request)*. Amen.

Reading

"I am the way, and the truth, and the life. No one comes to the Father except through me. If you know me, you will know my Father also. From now on you do know him and have seen him.... The one who believes in me will also do the works that I do and, in fact, will do greater works than these, because I am going to the Father. I will do whatever you ask in my name, so that the Father may be glorified in the Son" (Jn 14:6-7, 12-13).

Jesus, Divine Master, I adore you as the Word Incarnate sent by the Father to instruct humanity in life-giving truths. You are uncreated Truth, the only Master. You alone have words of eternal life. I thank you for having imparted to me the light of reason and the light of faith, and for having called me to the light of glory. I believe, submitting my whole mind to you and to the Church. Master, show me the treasures of your wisdom; let me know the Father; make me your true disciple. Increase my faith so that I may attain to the eternal vision in heaven.

Jesus Master, sanctify my mind and increase my faith.

Second Day

Jesus Master, Way, Truth and Life, have mercy on us.

(Recite the novena prayer.)

Reading

"Jesus answered him, 'Those who love me will keep my word, and my Father will love them, and we will come to them and make our home with them. Whoever does not love me does not keep my words; and the word that you hear is not mine, but is from the Father who sent me. I have said these things to you while I am still with you. But the Advocate, the Holy Spirit, whom the Father will send in my name, will teach you everything, and remind you of all that I have said to you. Peace I leave with you; my peace I give to you. I do not give to you as the world gives. Do not let your hearts be troubled, and do not let them be afraid'" (Jn 14:23-27).

Jesus, Divine Master, I adore you as the beloved of the Father, the sole Way to him. I thank you because you made yourself my model. You left me examples of the highest perfection. You have invited me to follow you on earth and in heaven. I contemplate you in the various stages of your earthly life. I docilely place myself in your school and I want to follow your teachings. Draw me to yourself so that by following in your footsteps and renouncing myself, I may seek only your will. Increase active hope in me and the desire to be found similar to you at the judgment, and to possess you forever in heaven.

Jesus, Way of sanctity, make me your faithful imitator.

Third Day

Jesus Master, Way, Truth and Life, have mercy on us.

(Recite the novena prayer.)

Reading

"I am the true vine, and my Father is the vine-grower. He removes every branch in me that bears no fruit. Every branch that bears fruit he prunes to make it bear more fruit. You have already been cleansed by the word that I have spoken to you. Abide in me as I abide in you. Just as the branch cannot bear fruit by itself unless it abides in the vine, neither can you unless you abide in me. I am the vine, you are the branches. Those who abide in me and I in them bear much fruit, because apart from me you can do nothing" (Jn 15:1-5).

Jesus, Divine Master, I adore you as the only-begotten Son of God, come on the earth to give life, the most abundant life, to humanity. I thank you because by dying on the cross, you merited life for me, which you gave me in Baptism and nourish in the Eucharist and in the other sacraments. Live in me, Jesus, with the outpouring of the Holy Spirit, so that I may love you with my whole mind, strength and heart, and love my neighbor as myself for love of you. Increase charity in me, so that one day I may be united with you in the eternal happiness of heaven.

Jesus Life, live in me so that I may live in you, and do not permit me to separate myself from you.

Fourth Day

Jesus Master, Way, Truth and Life, have mercy on us.

(Recite the novena prayer.)

Reading

"If you abide in me, and my words abide in you, ask for whatever you wish, and it will be done for you. My Father is glorified by this, that you bear much fruit and become my disciples. As the Father has loved me, so I have loved you; abide in my love.

17

If you keep my commandments, you will abide in my love, just as I have kept my Father's commandments and abide in his love. I have said these things to you so that my joy may be in you, and that your joy may be complete. This is my commandment, that you love one another as I have loved you. No one has greater love than this, to lay down one's life for one's friends" (Jn 15:7-13).

Jesus, Divine Master, I adore you living in the Church, your Mystical Body, the sole ark of salvation. I thank you for having given me this infallible and indefectible mother, in whom you continue to be for humanity the Way, the Truth and the Life. I ask of you that those who do not believe may come to her inextinguishable light, the erring return to her, and all peoples be united in faith, in a common hope, in charity. Assist the Church; sustain the Pope; sanctify the clergy and religious. Lord Jesus, my wish is yours: that there be one fold under one Shepherd, so that we may all be reunited in the Church glorified in heaven.

Jesus, teaching in the Church, draw everyone to your school.

Fifth Day

Jesus Master, Way, Truth and Life, have mercy on us.

(Recite the novena prayer.)

Reading

"You are my friends if you do what I command you. I do not call you servants any longer, because the servant does not know what the master is doing; but I have called you friends, because I have made known to you everything that I have heard from my Father. You did not choose me but I chose you. And I appointed you to go and bear fruit, fruit that will last, so that the Father will give you whatever you ask him in my name" (Jn 15:14-16).

Jesus, Divine Master, I adore you with the angels who sang the reasons for your incarnation: glory to God and peace to all people. I thank you for having called me to share in your own saving mission. Enkindle in me your own flame of love for God and for all people. Fill all my powers with yourself. Live in me so that I may radiate you through my prayer, suffering and work, as well as by word, example and deed. Send good laborers into your harvest. Enlighten preachers, teachers, writers; infuse in them the Holy Spirit with his seven gifts; dispose minds and hearts to receive him. Come, Master and Lord! Teach and reign, through Mary, Mother, Teacher and Queen.

Jesus Way, may my presence bring grace and consolation everywhere.

Sixth Day

Jesus Master, Way, Truth and Life, have mercy on us.

(Recite the novena prayer.)

Reading

"And Jesus came and said to them, 'All authority in heaven and on earth has been given to me. Go therefore and make disciples of all nations, baptizing them in the name of the Father and of the Son and of the Holy Spirit, and teaching them to obey everything that I have commanded you. And remember, I am with you always, to the end of the age'" (Mt 28:18-20).

Jesus, Divine Master, I adore you as the divine Master of humanity, and I thank you for the great gift of the Gospel. You said: "I was sent to evangelize the poor." Your words bring eternal life. In the Gospel, you revealed divine mysteries, taught the way of God in truth, offered the means of salvation. Grant me the grace to preserve your Gospel with veneration, as Mary did. Help me to listen to it and read it according to the spirit of the Church, and to spread it with the love with which you preached it. May it be known, honored, and received by all! May the world conform its life, laws, morals and teachings to it. May the fire brought by you upon the earth inflame, enlighten and warm everyone.

Jesus Master, deliver me from error, from vain thoughts and from eternal darkness.

Seventh Day

Jesus Master, Way, Truth and Life, have mercy on us.

(Recite the novena prayer.)

Reading

"For God so loved the world that he gave his only Son, so that everyone who believes in him may not perish but may have eternal life. Indeed, God did not send the Son into the world to condemn the world, but in order that the world might be saved through him. Those who believe in him are not condemned; but those who do not believe are condemned already, because they have not believed in the name of the only Son of God" (Jn 3:16-18).

Jesus Master I adore you as Emmanuel, God with us. I thank for the great gift of the Holy Eucharist. Your love makes you dwell in the holy tabernacle, renew your passion in the Mass, and give yourself as food for our souls in Holy Communion. May I know you, O hidden God; may I draw life-giving waters from the font of your heart. Grant me the grace to visit you often in this sacrament, to understand and actively participate in Holy Mass, to receive Holy Communion frequently, with faith and love.

Jesus Way, may I be example and model for souls.

Eighth Day

Jesus Master, Way, Truth and Life, have mercy on us.

(Recite the novena prayer.)

Reading

"Standing near the cross of Jesus were his mother, and his mother's sister, Mary the wife of Clopas, and Mary Magdalene. When Jesus saw his mother and the disciple whom he loved standing beside her, he said to his mother, 'Woman, here is your son.' Then he said to the disciple, 'Here is your mother.' And from that hour the disciple took her into his own home" (Jn 19:25-27).

Jesus, Divine Master, Son of Mary, I adore you. I thank you for having given us the Blessed Virgin Mary as our Mother, Teacher and Queen. From the cross you placed us all in her hands. You gave her a great heart, much wisdom and immense power. May all humanity know her, love her, pray to her! May all permit themselves to be led by her to you, the Savior of the world! I place myself in her hands, as you placed yourself. With this Mother I want to live now, in the hour of my death, and for all eternity!

Mary, grant that all people may follow Jesus the Divine Master, Way, Truth and Life.

Ninth Day

Jesus Master, Way, Truth and Life, have mercy on us.

(Recite the novena prayer.)

Reading

"But I say to you that listen, love your enemies, do good to those who hate you, bless those who curse you, pray for those who abuse you. If anyone strikes you on the cheek, offer the other also; and from anyone who takes away your coat do not withhold even your shirt. Give to everyone who begs from you; and if anyone takes away your goods, do not ask for them again. Do to others as you would have them do to you" (Lk 6:27-31).

Jesus, Divine Master, I thank and bless your most gentle Heart, which led you to give your life for me. Your blood, your wounds, the scourges, the thorns, the cross, your bowed head tell my heart: "No one loves more than he who gives his life for the loved one." The Shepherd died to give life to the sheep. I too want to spend my life for you. Grant that you may always, everywhere, and in all things dispose of me for your greater glory and that I may always repeat, "Your will be done." Inflame my heart with holy love for you and for others.

Jesus, Way between the Father and us, I offer you all and await all from you.

Novena by Ven. James Alberione, SSP

Prayers to the Sacred Heart

Morning Offering of
the Apostleship of Prayer

O Jesus, through the Immaculate Heart of Mary, I offer you all my prayers, works, joys and sufferings of this day, for the intentions of your Sacred Heart, in union with the holy sacrifice of the Mass throughout the world, in reparation for my sins, for the intentions of all our associates and for the general intention recommended this month.

Thanksgiving for the Eucharist

Jesus, Divine Master, I thank and bless your most lovable heart for the great gift of the Holy Eucharist. Your love makes you dwell in the tabernacle, renew your passion in the Mass and give yourself as food for our souls in holy Communion.

May I know you, O hidden God! May I draw life-giving waters from the font of your heart. Grant me the grace to visit you every day in this sacrament, to understand and actively participate in holy Mass, to receive holy Communion often and with the right dispositions.

Thanksgiving for the Church

Jesus, Divine Master, I bless and thank your most gentle heart for the great gift of the Church. She is the Mother who instructs us in the truth, guides us on the way to heaven and communicates supernatural life to us. She continues your own saving mission here on earth, as your Mystical Body. She is the ark of salvation. She is infallible, indefectible, catholic. Grant me the grace to love the Church as you loved her and sanctified her in your blood. May the world know her, may all sheep enter her fold, may everyone humbly cooperate in your kingdom.

Thanksgiving for the Priesthood

Jesus, Divine Master, I bless and thank your most loving heart for the institution of the priesthood. Priests are sent by you, as you were sent by the Father. To them you entrusted the treasures of your doctrine, of your law, of your grace and God's people themselves. Grant me the grace to love your priests, listen to them and let myself be guided by them in your ways. Send good laborers into your vineyard, Jesus. May priests be the salt that purifies and preserves; may they be the light of the world. May they be the city placed on the mountain. May they all be formed according to your heart. And one day in heaven may they have around themselves, as a crown of joy, a great throng of souls won for you.

Thanksgiving for the Religious State

Jesus, Divine Master, I thank and bless your most holy heart for the institution of the religious state. As in heaven, so also on earth the mansions are many. You have chosen those whom you wish to follow you in religious life and you have called them to evangelical perfection. You have made yourself their model, their help and their reward. Divine Heart, multiply religious vocations. Sustain them in faithful observance of the evangelical counsels. May they adorn your Church with virtue. May they console you, pray and work for your honor in every apostolate.

Thanksgiving for Mary, Our Mother

Jesus, Divine Master, I thank and bless your most merciful heart for having given us Mary most holy as our Mother, Teacher and Queen. From the cross you placed us all in her hands. You gave her a great heart, much wisdom and immense power. May everyone know her, love her, pray to her. May all permit themselves to be led by her to you, the Savior of the world. I place myself in her hands, as you placed yourself. With this Mother I want to live now, in the hour of my death and for all eternity.

Thanksgiving for the Passion of Jesus

Jesus, Divine Master, I thank and bless your most gentle heart, which led you to give your life for me. Your blood, your wounds, the scourges, the thorns, the cross, your bowed head tell me: "No one loves more than he who gives his life for the loved one." The shepherd died to give life to the sheep. I too want to spend my life for you. May you always, everywhere and in all things dispose of me for your greater glory. May I always repeat: "Your will be done." Inflame my heart with holy love for you and for everyone.

The Nine First Fridays

The writings of St. Margaret Mary mention many promises that the Sacred Heart of Jesus has made in favor of his devoted ones. The principal promises are:

1. I will give them all the graces necessary for their state of life.

2. I will give peace in their families.

3. I will console them in all their troubles.

4. I will be their refuge in life and especially in death.

5. I will abundantly bless all their undertakings.

6. Sinners will find in my heart the source and infinite ocean of mercy.

7. Tepid souls will become fervent.

8. Fervent souls will rise speedily to great perfection.

9. I will bless those places where the image of my Sacred Heart shall be exposed and venerated.

10. I will give priests the power to touch the most hardened hearts.

11. Persons who propagate this devotion will have their names eternally written in my heart.

12. In the abundant mercy of my heart, I promise that my all-powerful love will grant to all those who will receive Communion on the first Fridays of nine consecutive months the grace of final repentance. They will not die in my displeasure, nor without receiving the sacraments, and my heart will be their secure refuge in that last hour.

Conditions required: 1) To make nine holy Communions; 2) on the first Friday of the month; 3) for nine consecutive months, without interruption; 4) with the proper disposition; 5) with the intention of making reparation to the Sacred Heart of Jesus and to obtain the fruit of this great promise.

Act of Reparation to
the Most Sacred Heart of Jesus

A partial indulgence is granted to the faithful who devoutly recite this act of reparation. A plenary indulgence (with the usual conditions) is granted if it is publicly recited on the feast of the Most Sacred Heart of Jesus.

O most loving Jesus, whose immense love for humanity is repaid by so much forgetfulness, negligence and contempt, see us kneeling before your altar. We wish to make a special act of homage in reparation for the indifference and injuries to which your loving heart is everywhere subjected.

We ourselves have taken part in this ill-treatment, and we regret it now from the depths of our hearts. We humbly ask your pardon and declare our readiness to atone by voluntary penance not only for our personal offenses, but also for the sins of those who have strayed from the path of salvation.

We want to atone for those who obstinately refuse to follow you, their shepherd and leader. We want to atone for those who even renounce the vows of their Baptism and cast off the easy yoke of your law.

While we intend to expiate all such sins, we propose to make reparation for each one in particular:

—immodesty in dress and actions,

—the many seductions that ensnare the innocent,

—the violation of Sundays and holydays,

—the blasphemies spoken against you and your saints,

—the insults hurled against your Vicar and your priests,

—the negligence and the sacrileges by which the very Sacrament of your love is profaned,

—and finally the public crimes of all nations who resist the rights and the teaching authority of the Church you have founded.

If only we could wash away such sins with our blood! And now, in reparation for these violations of your divine honor, we offer the satisfaction that you once made on the cross to your Father, which you renew daily on our altars. We offer it in union with the expiation of your Virgin Mother, all the saints and the faithful on earth. With the help of your grace, we promise to make reparation, as much as we are able, for the neglect of your great love and for the sins that we and others have committed in the past. We intend to do this by a firm faith, an innocent life and the observance of the law of charity. We promise to prevent others with all our powers from offending you and to bring as many as possible to follow you.

O loving Jesus, through the intercession of the Blessed Virgin Mary, our model in reparation, accept our voluntary offering of this act of reparation. By the crowning gift of perseverance, keep us faithful until death in our duty and in the allegiance we owe to you, so that one day we may all come to that happy home where you, with the Father and the Holy Spirit, live and reign, God, forever and ever. Amen.

Act of Consecration to the Most Sacred Heart of Jesus

Most loving Jesus, Redeemer of the human race, look on us kneeling humbly before your altar. We are yours, and yours we wish to be. But to be more surely united to you, we freely consecrate ourselves today to your most Sacred Heart. Many people have never known you. Many, too, scorning your precepts, have rejected you.

Have mercy on them all, most merciful Jesus, and draw them to your Sacred Heart.

Be king, O Lord, not only of the faithful who have never forsaken you, but also of the prodigal children who have abandoned you. Grant that they may quickly return to their Father's house.

Lord, grant to your Church freedom and immunity from harm. Give peace and order to all nations. Make the earth resound from pole to pole with one cry: Praise to the divine heart that wrought our salvation. To Jesus Christ be glory and honor forever. Amen.

Consecration of the Family to the Sacred Heart

The consecration of the family to the Sacred Heart is a devotion desired by our Lord, who has promised to bless families consecrated to him. "I will bless," he said, "those homes where an image of my heart shall be exposed and venerated. I shall give peace in their families. I shall abundantly bless all their undertakings. I shall be their secure refuge in life and especially at the hour of death."

In order to make this consecration, one must have a representation of the Sacred Heart of Jesus that has been blessed by a priest. After the image has been set in a place of honor, the consecration of the entire family is made.

Jesus has granted many favors, even extraordinary ones, to those families which have received him into their midst by consecrating themselves to his Sacred Heart. Among the graces may be mentioned help received in critical periods, dangers averted and discords settled. Above all, countless persons have returned to the Faith.

Act of Consecration of the Family to the Sacred Heart

O most loving Heart of Jesus, who gave St. Margaret Mary this consoling promise, "I will bless those homes in which an image of my Sacred Heart shall be exposed and venerated," we ask you to accept today the consecration of our family to you. By this act we intend to solemnly proclaim the dominion that you have over all creatures and over us, recognizing you as our king. Some refuse to acknowledge your dominion and repeat the cry: "We do not want this one to reign over us," thus offending your most loving heart. We, on the other hand, repeat with greater fervor and more ardent love: O Jesus, reign over our family and over each of its members. Reign over our minds, that we may always believe in the truths you have taught us. Reign over our hearts, that we may always follow your divine teachings. O Divine Heart, you alone are our loving king. You have purchased us with your precious blood.

And now keep your promise and let your blessings fall on us. Bless us in our labors, in our undertakings, in our health, in our interests. Bless us in joy and in sorrow, in prosperity and in adversity, now and always. Grant that peace may reign in our midst, as well as harmony, respect, love for one another and good example.

Defend us from dangers, from sickness, from accidents and, above all, from sin. Finally, write our names in your Sacred Heart, and grant that they may always remain there, so that after having been united with you on earth, we may one day be united with you in heaven, to sing the glories and the triumphs of your mercy. Amen.

Aspiration: We want God, who is our Father; we want God, who is our king.

Now recite one Our Father, one Hail Mary and one Glory to the Father, in honor of the Sacred Heart of Jesus, and a Hail, Holy Queen to the Blessed Virgin Mary to obtain her protection.

It is fitting to renew this consecration on great feasts of our Lord, such as Christmas, Easter and Corpus Christi.

Prayer to the Sacred Heart of Jesus

To be said before each action

Adorable Heart, in all you have done and suffered on earth, you have sought the glory of the heavenly Father and the accomplishment of his holy will. Grant that in union with you, I may offer him the action I am about to begin, with the sole desire of pleasing him and doing his will. Grant me the grace to perform it as I ought. Amen.

Litany of the Sacred Heart of Jesus

Lord, have mercy on us.
Christ, have mercy on us.
Lord, have mercy on us.
Christ, hear us.
Christ, graciously hear us.
God, the Father of heaven, have mercy on us.
God the Son, Redeemer of the world,*
God the Holy Spirit,
Holy Trinity, one God,
Heart of Jesus, formed by the Holy Spirit in the
    womb of the Virgin Mother,
Heart of Jesus, substantially united to the Word
    of God,
Heart of Jesus, of infinite majesty,
Heart of Jesus, sacred temple of God,
Heart of Jesus, tabernacle of the Most High,
Heart of Jesus, burning furnace of charity,
Heart of Jesus, abode of justice and love,
Heart of Jesus, full of goodness and love,

_____

* *have mercy on us.*

Heart of Jesus, source of all virtues,
Heart of Jesus, most worthy of all praise,
Heart of Jesus, king and center of all hearts,
Heart of Jesus, in whom are all the treasures
of wisdom and knowledge,
Heart of Jesus, in whom dwells the fullness
of divinity,
Heart of Jesus, in whom the Father was well
pleased,
Heart of Jesus, of whose fullness we have all
received,
Heart of Jesus, desire of the everlasting hills,
Heart of Jesus, patient and most merciful,
Heart of Jesus, enriching all who invoke you,
Heart of Jesus, fountain of life and holiness,
Heart of Jesus, propitiation for our sins,
Heart of Jesus, laden with insults,
Heart of Jesus, bruised for our offenses,
Heart of Jesus, obedient unto death,
Heart of Jesus, pierced with a lance,
Heart of Jesus, source of all consolation,
Heart of Jesus, our life and resurrection,
Heart of Jesus, our peace and reconciliation,
Heart of Jesus, victim for sins,
Heart of Jesus, salvation of those who trust in you,
Heart of Jesus, hope of those who die in you,
Heart of Jesus, delight of all the saints,

Lamb of God, you take away the sins of the world,
spare us, O Lord.

Lamb of God, you take away the sins of the world,
graciously hear us, O Lord.

Lamb of God, you take away the sins of the world,
have mercy on us.

V. Jesus, gentle and humble of heart,

R. Make our hearts like yours.

Let us pray. Almighty and eternal God, look upon the heart of your beloved Son. Behold the praise and satisfaction he offers you in the name of sinners and for all who seek your mercy. Grant us pardon in the name of the same Jesus Christ, your Son, who lives and reigns with you in the unity of the Holy Spirit forever and ever. Amen.

Act of Self-Offering to Be Made before a Representation of the Sacred Heart*

My loving Jesus, out of the grateful love I have for you, and to make reparation for my sins and my lack of correspondence to grace, I give you my heart. I consecrate myself totally to you, and with your help I resolve never to sin again.

---

* *This prayer and the following prayers to the Sacred Heart are reprinted with the kind permission of St. Anthony's Guild, Paterson, New Jersey.*

Act of Consecration by St. Margaret Mary

I give and consecrate to the Sacred Heart of our Lord Jesus Christ my person and my life, my actions, pains and sufferings, not wishing to use any part of my being except to honor, love and glorify that Sacred Heart.

It is my irrevocable will to be entirely his, and to do everything for his love, renouncing with my whole heart whatever might displease him.

I, take you, then, O Sacred Heart, to be the sole object of my love, the protector of my life, the pledge of my salvation, the remedy of my frailty and inconstancy, the repairer of all the sins of my life, and my secure refuge in the hour of death.

Be then, O Heart of goodness, my justification before God your Father, and remove far from me the punishments of sin. O heart of love, I place all my confidence in you. While I fear all things from my malice and frailty, I hope all things from your goodness.

Free me, then, from whatever can displease or be opposed to you, and let your pure love engrave you so deeply upon my heart that it will be impossible for me ever to forget you or be separated from you.

I ask you, by all your goodness, that my name may be written in you, since I desire that all my happiness and glory should consist in living and dying in service to you. Amen.

Prayer of St. Margaret Mary

O Heart of love, I place all my trust in you. Although I fear all things from my weakness, I hope all things from your goodness.

Daily Act of Self-Offering

Lord Jesus Christ, in union with that divine intention with which you offered on earth your praises to God through your Sacred Heart, and now continue to offer them in all places in the Sacrament of the Eucharist, and will do so to the end of the world, I most willingly offer you throughout this entire day, without the smallest exception, all my intentions and thoughts, all my affections and desires, all my words and actions, in imitation of the most pure heart of the Blessed Virgin Mary. Amen.

Prayer to the Sacred Heart

Most Sacred Heart of Jesus, abundantly pour down your blessings upon your holy Church, upon the Supreme Pontiff, and upon all the clergy and laity; give perseverance to the just, convert sinners, enlighten unbelievers, bless our relatives, friends and benefactors, help the dying, free the souls in purgatory, and extend over all hearts the reign of your love. Amen.

Short Prayers

A partial indulgence is granted to the faithful who, in the performance of their duties and in bearing the trials of life, raise their minds with humble confidence to God, adding—even if only mentally—some pious invocation.

An invocation, as far as indulgences are concerned, is no longer considered a work distinct and complete in itself, but as complementing an action by which the faithful raise their heart and mind with humble confidence to God in performing their duties or bearing the trials of life. Hence, a pious invocation perfects the inward elevation; both together are like a precious jewel joined to one's ordinary actions to adorn them, or like salt added to them to season them properly. The following are cited by way of example:

Sacred Heart of Jesus, I trust in you.

Eucharistic Heart of Jesus, have mercy on us.

Sacred Heart of Jesus, your kingdom come!

Divine Heart of Jesus, convert sinners, save the dying, deliver the holy souls in purgatory.

Jesus, gentle and humble of heart, make our hearts like unto yours.

Sacred Heart of Jesus, I believe in your love for me.

Glory, love and thanksgiving be to the Sacred Heart of Jesus.

Act of Consecration

Most loving Jesus, I wholeheartedly consecrate myself again today to your Divine Heart. I consecrate to you my body with all its senses, my soul with all its faculties, and my whole being entirely. I consecrate to you all my thoughts, words and actions, all my sufferings and work, all my hopes, consolations and joys; above all, I consecrate to you my heart, in order that it may love only you, and may be set on fire with your love. Accept, O Jesus, the desire that I have to console your Divine Heart, and to be yours forever. Take possession of me in such a manner that from now on I may have no other liberty than that of loving you, no other life than that of suffering and dying for you. I place in you unlimited trust, and I hope for the pardon of my sins from your infinite mercy. I place in your hands all my cares, especially that of my eternal salvation. I promise to love you and to honor you to the last moment of my life, and to spread, as much as I am able, devotion to your Sacred Heart. Dispose of me, O my Jesus, according to your will; I seek no other reward than your greater glory and your holy love. Grant me the grace to live in your Divine Heart, where I desire to spend every day of my life, where I desire to breathe my last breath. Make my heart your dwelling-place, the chosen spot for your repose, so that we may always remain closely united; thus may I one day praise, love and possess you for all eternity in heaven, where I will sing forever the infinite mercies of your most Sacred Heart.

Short Prayers in Honor of the Eucharistic Heart of Jesus

A partial indulgence is granted to the faithful who visit the Most Blessed Sacrament to adore it; a plenary indulgence (with the usual conditions) is granted if the visit lasts for at least one half hour.

Eucharistic Heart of Jesus, burning with love for us, enkindle our hearts with love for you.

Blessed be the most Sacred Eucharistic Heart of Jesus.

Blessed and praised be the Sacred Heart and Precious Blood of Jesus in the most Holy Sacrament of the altar.

Praised be the most Sacred Heart of Jesus in the most Blessed Sacrament.

Eucharistic Heart of Jesus, increase in us faith, hope and charity.

May the Eucharistic Heart of Jesus be praised, adored and loved at every moment, in all the tabernacles of the world, even to the end of time. Amen.

Eucharistic Heart of Jesus, furnace of divine charity, give peace to the world.

I adore you, most Sacred Eucharistic Heart of Jesus.

Love, honor and glory to the Eucharistic Heart of Jesus.

Prayers to the Infant of Prague

Devotion to the Infant of Prague originated in Bohemia in the 1600s. A Spanish noblewoman gave a statue of the Infant to the Carmelite monks of Prague. When the religious community began to venerate the Infant, they received extraordinary favors, both spiritual and temporal.

The devotion was spread especially by one of the monks named Fr. Cyril. As time went on, innumerable cures and graces were received by those who prayed to the Divine Child. Then in 1642, the Baroness Benigna von Lobkowitz had a beautiful chapel built for the Divine Infant. In 1644, on the feast of the Holy Name of Jesus, the chapel was blessed and the holy sacrifice of the Mass was celebrated in it for the first time. From that time, the feast of the Holy Name remained the principal feast of the Infant of Prague.

Novena to the Infant of Prague

V. God, come to my assistance.

R. Lord, make haste to help me.

(Our Father, Hail Mary, Glory be)

These should be repeated each day before the prayer for the day.

First Day

Dear Child Jesus, who left the heart of the Father and came into the world for our salvation, who was conceived by the Holy Spirit, who did not disdain the Virgin's womb, and who, being the Word made flesh, took upon yourself the form of a servant, have mercy on us.

Have mercy on us, Child Jesus; have mercy.

(Our Father, Hail Mary, Glory be)

Second Day

Dear Child Jesus, who, while in the womb of your Virgin Mother, visited St. Elizabeth and filled your precursor, John the Baptist, with your Holy Spirit, sanctifying him in his mother's womb, have mercy on us.

Have mercy on us, Child Jesus....

(Our Father, Hail Mary, Glory be)

Third Day

Dear Child Jesus, the Virgin Mary and St. Joseph awaited your birth with eager expectation. You who were offered by God the Father for the salvation of the world, have mercy on us.

Have mercy on us, Child Jesus....

(Our Father, Hail Mary, Glory be)

Fourth Day

Dear Child Jesus, born in Bethlehem of the Virgin Mary, wrapped in swaddling clothes and placed in a manger, heralded by angels and visited by shepherds, have mercy on us.

Have mercy on us, Child Jesus....
(Our Father, Hail Mary, Glory be)

Fifth Day

Dear Child Jesus, wounded after eight days in your circumcision, called by the glorious name of Jesus, and at once, by your Body and by your Blood, foreshadowed as the Savior of the world, have mercy on us.

Have mercy on us, Child Jesus....
(Our Father, Hail Mary, Glory be)

Sixth Day

Dear Child Jesus, manifested to the Magi by the star that led them, worshipped in the arms of your Mother, presented with the meaningful gifts of gold, frankincense and myrrh, have mercy on us.

Have mercy on us, Child Jesus....
(Our Father, Hail Mary, Glory be)

Seventh Day

Dear Child Jesus, presented in the temple by your Virgin Mother, taken up in Simeon's arms, and revealed to Israel by Anna, a prophetess, have mercy on us.

Have mercy on us, Child Jesus....
(Our Father, Hail Mary, Glory be)

Eighth Day

Dear Child Jesus, you lived a holy life in the house at Nazareth, obedient to Mary and Joseph. You who increased in wisdom, age and grace and knew the weariness of poverty and toil, have mercy on us.

Have mercy on us, Child Jesus....
(Our Father, Hail Mary, Glory be)

Ninth Day

Dear Child Jesus, you who visited Jerusalem at twelve years of age and were sought by your sorrowing parents and found with joy after three days in the midst of the teachers of the law, have mercy on us.

Have mercy on us, Child Jesus....
(Our Father, Hail Mary, Glory be)

Let us pray. Almighty and everlasting God, Lord of heaven and earth, you reveal yourself to little ones. Grant that by venerating with due honor the sacred mysteries of your Son, the Child Jesus, and imitating them we may enter the kingdom of heaven, which you have promised to those who become like little children. Through the same Christ our Lord. Amen.

Powerful Novena in Times of Distress

The following prayers are to be repeated at the same time every hour for nine consecutive hours.

Divine Infant of Prague, dearest Jesus, you who so lovingly said, "Ask, and it shall be given you; seek, and you shall find; knock, and it shall be opened to you," have mercy on me now. Through the intercession of our most holy Mother, I humbly ask you to grant me the grace I need. *(Name your petition.)*

Divine Infant of Prague, dearest Jesus, you who so compassionately taught, "If you can believe, all things are possible to the one who believes," have pity on me now. I do believe; help me. Increase my weak faith and through the Blessed Mother's intercession, I humbly ask you to answer my request. *(Name your petition.)*

Divine Infant of Prague, dearest Jesus, you who once said to the apostles, "If you have faith even like a mustard seed, you will say to this mulberry tree, 'Be uprooted and be planted in the sea,' and it will obey you," hear my prayer, I humbly ask. Through the intercession of Mary most holy, I feel certain that my prayer will be answered. *(Name your petition.)*

Chaplet of the Holy Infant Jesus

This devotion owes its origin to the zeal of Sister Marguerite of the Blessed Sacrament, a Carmelite religious who died a holy death at Beaune, France, May 26, 1648, at the age of twenty-seven.

The Divine Infant revealed to his faithful servant how pleasing this holy practice is to him. He promised her that he would grant special graces, above all, purity of heart and innocence, to all who carry the chaplet on their person and recite it in honor of the mysteries of his holy infancy. As a sign of his approval, he showed her these chaplets shining with a supernatural light.

On the medal the following invocation is said:

Divine Infant Jesus, I adore your cross, and I accept all the crosses you will be pleased to send me. Adorable Trinity, I offer you for the glory of the holy name of God, all the adorations of the Sacred Heart of the holy Infant Jesus.

This chaplet is recited as follows: Pray the Our Father three times in honor of the Holy Family, and the Hail Mary twelve times in honor of the twelve years of our divine Savior's infancy. Each Our Father and the first Hail Mary are preceded by the words, "And the Word became flesh and lived among us." The prayer at the conclusion of the chaplet is: "Holy Infant Jesus, bless and protect us."

Prayer of Thanksgiving

I thank you, Divine Infant Jesus, for the many graces and favors which you have granted me with so much love. I shall always praise your infinite mercy and love and make you known to everyone I can.

I adore you as the Beloved of the Father, the sole way to him. I thank you because you made yourself my model. You left us examples of the highest perfection. Draw me to you, so that by following in your footsteps and renouncing myself I may seek only your will. Increase active hope in me, and the desire to be found similar to you at the judgment and to possess you forever in heaven. Amen.

Prayer for Perseverance

Divine Infant of Prague, mediator between God and humanity! You carried out your mission as prophet, priest and shepherd. You are our Truth, our Life, our Way to the Father. Live in me and keep me ever in the state of grace.

Prayer for the Afflicted

Divine Infant, I adore you as the Incarnate Word sent by the Father. For us you chose to be born in a stable amid the most squalid poverty; for us you lived a humble and hidden life; for us you died on the cross, shedding the last drop of your precious blood, saying, "Father, forgive them for they know not what they are doing."

In shame, I beg your forgiveness. I too, have caused you much sorrow. I am not worthy that you should listen to me, but if you will not help me, to whom shall I turn for help?

Dearest Infant Jesus, full of confidence and hope, I open my heart to you.... All those who have believed and turned to you with confidence have had their prayers answered. It is with faith, therefore, that I ask this favor. *(Name your petition.)* However, not my will be done, Jesus, but yours, for I firmly believe that you dispose all for the best.

Through the intercession of the Virgin Mary, keep me under your holy protection. Guard my mind, my heart and my senses, that I may never commit sin.

Sanctify my thoughts, desires, words and actions, so that I may please you, my Jesus, and one day join you in heaven. Give me your holy blessing. In the name of the Father, and of the Son, and of the Holy Spirit. Amen.

Prayer to the Infant of Prague

by Rev. Cyril of the Mother of God (the first and most devoted venerator of the Infant of Prague)

Infant Jesus, through the intercession of Mary, your Mother, I beg your help in my needs. I believe that you are all powerful and can protect me. Full of confidence, I come to you, knowing that you will give me the graces I need.

Repenting of my sins and asking you to free me from their effects, I now give my heart entirely to you. I firmly propose to amend my ways and never offend you again. I resolve to patiently suffer everything for you, so as to serve you eternally. For you I will love my neighbor as myself. I ask you, dear Jesus, to help me in my needs, so that I may enjoy you for all eternity with Mary, Joseph and the angels. Amen.

Litany of the Infant of Prague

(For private use)

Lord, have mercy on us.

Christ, have mercy on us.

Lord, have mercy on us.

Christ, hear us.

Christ, graciously hear us.

God, the Father of heaven, have mercy on us.

God, the Son, Redeemer of the world*

God, the Holy Spirit,

Miraculous Child Jesus,

Divine Infant Jesus, true God and true man,

Divine Infant Jesus, Lord of heaven and earth,

Divine Infant Jesus, whose love knows no bounds,

Divine Infant Jesus, who came on earth to show
  us the way to the Father,

Divine Infant Jesus, true light of the world,

Divine Infant Jesus, font of eternal life,

Divine Infant Jesus, patient and loving,

Divine Infant Jesus, source of peace and
  consolation,

Divine Infant Jesus, hope of all humanity,

Divine Infant Jesus, burning furnace of love,

Divine Infant Jesus, lover of justice and truth,

---

* *have mercy on us.*

Divine Infant Jesus, dispenser of all graces,
Divine Infant Jesus, teacher of all virtues,
Divine Infant Jesus, king of all hearts,
Divine Infant Jesus, divine wonder worker,
Be merciful, spare us, O Lord.
Be merciful, graciously hear us, O Lord.
From all sin, O Jesus, deliver us.
From a sudden death,**
From lightning and storms,
From floods and plagues,
From loss of faith in you,
From everlasting hell fire,
Through your birth,
Through your holy life,
Through your passion,
Through your death,
Through your resurrection,
Through your ascension,
Through your infinite love,
Lamb of God, you take away the sins of the world,
    spare us, O Lord.
Lamb of God, you take away the sins of the world,
    graciously hear us, O Lord.
Lamb of God, you take away the sins of the world,
    have mercy on us.

** *O Jesus, deliver us.*

Jesus, hear us.

Jesus, graciously hear us.

(Our Father, Hail Mary, Glory be)

Let us pray. Divine Jesus, miraculous Infant, kneeling before your sacred image, we implore you to hear our prayer. You whose tender heart went out to all, you who gave sight to the blind, healed lepers, made the deaf hear and the mute speak, you who brought the dead back to life, grant us, we beg you, the graces we humbly ask, through your merits, O Lord Jesus Christ. Amen.

Litany of the Holy Name of Jesus

Lord, have mercy on us.

Christ, have mercy on us.

Lord, have mercy on us.

Christ, hear us.

Christ, graciously hear us.

God, the Father of heaven, have mercy on us.

God, the Son, Redeemer of the world,*

God, the Holy Spirit,

Holy Trinity, one God,

Jesus, Son of the living God,

Jesus, splendor of the Father,

---

* *have mercy on us.*

Jesus, brightness of eternal light,

Jesus, king of glory,

Jesus, sun of justice,

Jesus, son of the Virgin Mary,

Jesus, most amiable,

Jesus, most admirable,

Jesus, mighty God,

Jesus, Father of the centuries to come,

Jesus, messenger of the great council,

Jesus, most powerful,

Jesus, most patient,

Jesus, most obedient,

Jesus, gentle and humble of heart,

Jesus, lover of chastity,

Jesus, lover of humanity,

Jesus, God of peace,

Jesus, author of life,

Jesus, example of virtue,

Jesus, zealous seeker of souls,

Jesus, our God,

Jesus, our refuge,

Jesus, Father of the poor,

Jesus, treasure of the faithful,

Jesus, Good Shepherd,

Jesus, true light,

Jesus, eternal wisdom,

Jesus, infinite goodness,

Jesus, joy of the angels,
Jesus, king of patriarchs,
Jesus, leader of the apostles,
Jesus, teacher of evangelists,
Jesus, strength of martyrs,
Jesus, light of confessors,
Jesus, purity of virgins,
Jesus, glory of all the saints,
From all evil, deliver us, O Lord.
From all sin,**
From your wrath,
From the snares of the devil,
From all impurity,
From the neglect of your inspirations,
Through the mystery of your holy Incarnation,
Through your infancy,
Through your divine life,
Through your labors and weariness,
Through your agony and passion,
Through your cross and desolation,
Through your sufferings and pains,
Through your death and burial,
Through your resurrection,
Through your ascension,
Through your institution of the most holy Eucharist,

** *deliver us, O Lord.*

Through your joys,

Through your glory,

From eternal death,

Lamb of God, you take away the sins of the world, spare us, O Lord.

Lamb of God, you take away the sins of the world, graciously hear us, O Lord.

Lamb of God, you take away the sins of the world, have mercy on us.

Jesus, hear us.

Jesus, graciously hear us.

Let us pray. Lord Jesus Christ, who said, "Ask, and you shall receive; seek, and you shall find; knock, and it shall be opened to you," we beg you to grant us the gift of divine love, so that we may sincerely love you with our thoughts, words and actions and never cease to praise you.

Lord, give us a constant reverence and a fervent love for your most holy name; for you never cease to protect those whom you shower with the treasures of your heart, you who live and reign forever and ever. Amen.

Prayers to the Holy Spirit

Prayer to the Holy Spirit

V. Come, Holy Spirit, fill the hearts of your faithful, and enkindle in them the fire of your love.

V. Send forth your Spirit, and they shall be created.

R. And you shall renew the face of the earth.

Let us pray. O God, who by the light of the Holy Spirit instructs the hearts of the faithful, grant that in the same Spirit we may be truly wise, and ever rejoice in his consolation. Through Christ our Lord. Amen.

Come, Holy Spirit

Come, Holy Spirit, Creator, come,
From your bright heavenly throne;
Come, take possession of our souls,
And make them all your own.
You who are called the Paraclete,
Best gift of God above;
The living spring, the living fire,
Sweet unction and true love.
You who are sevenfold in your grace,

Finger of God's right hand,
His promise, teaching little ones
To speak and understand.
Oh! guide our minds with your blest light,
With love our hearts inflame
And with your strength, which ne'er decays,
Confirm our mortal frame.
Far from us drive our hellish foe,
True peace unto us bring;
And through all perils lead us safe
Beneath your sacred wing.
Through you may we the Father know,
Through you, the eternal Son,
And you, the Spirit of them both
Thrice-blessed three in one.
All glory to the Father be,
And to his risen Son,
The like to you, great Paraclete,
While endless ages run. Amen.

Holy Spirit, Lord of Light!

Holy Spirit, Lord of light!
From your clear celestial height,
Your pure, beaming radiance give;
Come, O Father of the poor!
Come, with treasures which endure!

Come, O light of all that live!
You of all consolers best,
Visiting the troubled breast,
Do refreshing peace bestow;
You in toil are comfort sweet;
Pleasant coolness in the heat;
Solace in the midst of woe.
Light immortal! Light divine!
Visit now these hearts of thine,
And our inmost being fill.
If you take your grace away,
Nothing pure in man will stay;
All his good is turned to ill.
Heal our wounds—our strength renew;
On our dryness pour your dew;
Wash the stains of guilt away;
Bend the stubborn heart and will;
Melt the frozen, warm the chill;
Guide the steps that go astray.
You, on those who evermore
Do confess you and adore,
In your sevenfold gifts descend.
Give them comfort when they die;
Give them life with you on high;
Give them joys which never end. Amen.

Consecration to the Holy Spirit

O divine Holy Spirit, eternal love of the Father and of the Son, I adore you, I thank you, I love you, and I ask you pardon for all the times I have grieved you in myself and in my neighbor.

Descend with many graces during the holy ordination of bishops and priests, during the consecration of men and women religious, during the reception of Confirmation by all the faithful; be light, sanctity and zeal.

To you, O Spirit of Truth, I consecrate my mind, imagination and memory; enlighten me. May I know Jesus Christ our Master and understand his Gospel and the teaching of Holy Church. Increase in me the gifts of wisdom, knowledge, understanding and counsel.

To you, O sanctifying Spirit, I consecrate my will. Guide me in your will, sustain me in the observance of the commandments, in the fulfillment of my duties. Grant me the gifts of fortitude and holy fear of God.

To you, O life-giving Spirit, I consecrate my heart. Guard and increase the divine life in me. Grant me the gift of piety. Amen.

Litany of the Holy Spirit

(For private use)

Lord, have mercy on us.

Christ, have mercy on us.

Lord, have mercy on us.

Holy Spirit, hear us.

Holy Spirit, graciously hear us.

God the Father of heaven, have mercy on us.

God the Son, Redeemer of the world,*

God the Holy Spirit,

Holy Trinity one God,

Holy Spirit, who proceeds from the Father and
     the Son,

Holy Spirit, co-equal with the Father and the Son,

Promise of the Father, most loving and most
     bounteous,

Gift of the most high God,

Ray of heavenly light,

Author of all good,

Source of living water,

Consuming fire,

Burning love,

Spiritual unction,

Spirit of truth and power,

---

* have mercy on us.

Spirit of wisdom and understanding,

Spirit of counsel and fortitude,

Spirit of knowledge and of piety,

Spirit of the fear of the Lord,

Spirit of compunction and of penance,

Spirit of grace and of prayer,

Spirit of charity, peace and joy,

Spirit of patience, longanimity and goodness,

Spirit of benignity, mildness and fidelity,

Spirit of modesty, continence and chastity,

Spirit of adoption of the children of God,

Holy Spirit, the Comforter,

Holy Spirit, the Sanctifier,

Who in the beginning moved over the waters,

By whose inspiration spoke the holy prophets of
God,

Who overshadowed Mary,

Who cooperated in the miraculous conception of
the Son of God,

Who descended upon him at his baptism,

Who on the day of Pentecost appeared in fiery
tongues upon the disciples of our Lord,

By whom we also are born,

Who dwells in us,

Who governs the Church,

Who fills the whole world,

Holy Spirit, hear us.

That you shed abroad your light in our hearts,
   we beseech you, hear us.
That you write your law in our hearts,**
That you inflame us with the fire of your love,
That you open to us the treasures of your grace,
That you enlighten us with your heavenly
   inspirations,
That you keep us to yourself by your powerful
   attractions,
That you grant to us the knowledge that alone is
   necessary,
That you lead us in the way of your
   commandments,
That you make us obedient to your inspirations,
That you teach us to pray, and yourself
   pray with us,
That you clothe us with love toward our brethren,
That you inspire us with horror of evil,
That you direct us in the practice of good,
That you give us the grace of all virtues,
That you cause us to persevere in justice,
That you be yourself our everlasting reward,

Lamb of God, you take away the sins of the world,
   spare us, O Lord.

**we beseech you, hear us.

Lamb of God, you take away the sins of the world,
hear us, O Lord.

Lamb of God, you take away the sins of the world,
have mercy on us, O Lord.

Create in us a clean heart, O God, and renew a right
spirit in us.

Let us pray. Grant, O merciful Father, that your divine Spirit may enlighten, inflame and cleanse our hearts, fill us with his heavenly dew, and make us fruitful in good works, through Jesus Christ our Lord. Amen.

Aspirations to the Holy Spirit

Breathe in me, O Holy Spirit,
That my thoughts may all be holy;
Act in me, O Holy Spirit,
That my work, too, may be holy;
Draw my heart, O Holy Spirit,
That I love but what is holy;
Strengthen me, O Holy Spirit,
To defend all that is holy;
Guard me, then, O Holy Spirit,
That I always may be holy.

Divine Praises in Honor of the Holy Spirit

Glory to the Holy Spirit forever and ever.

Glory to the Comforter forever and ever.

Glory to the Spirit of truth forever and ever.

Glory to the Spirit of grace and prayer forever and ever.

Glory to the Spirit of Jesus forever and ever.

Glory to the Spirit of the Father and the Son forever and ever.

Glory to the Third Person of the adorable Trinity forever and ever.

Novena to the Holy Spirit*

The novena to the Holy Spirit for the feast of Pentecost was the first of all the novenas. It was made at the direction of our Lord Himself when he told the apostles to go back to Jerusalem to await the coming of the Holy Spirit on the first Pentecost.

---

*Reprinted with the kind permission of the Director of Publications, Holy Ghost Fathers, from Novena to the Holy Spirit, published by the Holy Ghost Fathers, Washington, D.C.

Act of Consecration to the Holy Spirit

On my knees before the great multitude of heavenly witnesses I offer myself, soul and body to you, eternal Spirit of God. I adore the brightness of your purity and unerring keenness of your justice and the might of your love. You are the strength and light of my soul. In you I live and move and am. I desire never to grieve you by unfaithfulness to grace, and I pray with all my heart to be kept from the smallest sin against you. Mercifully guard my every thought, and grant that I may always watch for your light and listen to your voice and follow your gracious inspirations. I cling to you and give myself to you and ask you, by your compassion, to watch over me in my weakness. Holding the pierced feet of Jesus and looking at his five wounds, and trusting in his precious blood and adoring his opened side and stricken heart, I implore you, adorable Spirit, helper of my infirmity, so to keep me in your grace that I may never sin against you. Give me grace, O Holy Spirit, Spirit of the Father and the Son, to say to you always and everywhere, "Speak, Lord, for your servant is listening." Amen.

(To be recited daily during the novena.)

Prayer for the Seven Gifts of the Holy Spirit

O Lord Jesus Christ, who before ascending into heaven promised to send the Holy Spirit to finish your work in the souls of your apostles and disciples, grant the same Holy Spirit to me that he may perfect in my soul the work of your grace and your love. Grant me the Spirit of wisdom that I may despise the perishable things of this world and aspire only after the things that are eternal, the Spirit of understanding to enlighten my mind with the light of your divine truth, the Spirit of counsel that I may ever choose the surest way of pleasing God and gaining heaven, the Spirit of fortitude that I may bear my cross with you and that I may overcome with courage all the obstacles that oppose my salvation, the Spirit of knowledge that I may know God and know myself and grow perfect in the science of the saints, the Spirit of piety that I may find the service of God sweet and amiable, the Spirit of fear that I may be filled with a loving reverence toward God and may dread in any way to displease him. Mark me, dear Lord, with the sign of your true disciples and animate me in all things with your Spirit. Amen.

(To be recited daily during the novena.)

First Day

Holy Spirit, Lord of light!
From your clear celestial height,
Your pure beaming radiance give!

The Holy Spirit

Only one thing is important—eternal salvation.
Only one thing, therefore, is to be feared—sin. Sin is
the result of ignorance, weakness and indifference.
The Holy Spirit is the Spirit of light, strength and
love. With his sevenfold gifts he enlightens the
mind, strengthens the will, and inflames the heart
with love of God. To ensure our salvation we ought
to invoke the divine Spirit daily, for "The Spirit
helps us in our weakness; for we do not know how to
pray as we ought, but that very Spirit intercedes with
sighs too deep for words" (Rom 8:26).

Prayer

Almighty and eternal God, who has regenerated
us by water and the Holy Spirit, and has given us
forgiveness of all sins, send forth from heaven upon
us your sevenfold Spirit, the Spirit of wisdom and
understanding, the Spirit of counsel and fortitude,
the Spirit of knowledge and piety, and fill us with the
Spirit of holy fear. Amen.

Our Father and Hail Mary (once).
Glory to the Father (seven times).
Act of Consecration, Prayer for the Seven Gifts.

Second Day

Come, Father of the poor!
Come, with treasures which endure!
Come, O light of all that live!

The Gift of Fear

The gift of fear fills us with a sovereign respect for God, and makes us dread nothing so much as to offend him by sin. It is a fear that arises, not from the thought of hell, but from sentiments of reverence and filial submission to our heavenly Father. It is the fear that is the beginning of wisdom, detaching us from worldly pleasures that could in any way separate us from God. "Only fear the Lord, and serve him faithfully with all your heart; for consider what great things he has done for you" (1 Sam 12:24).

Prayer

Come, O blessed Spirit of holy fear, penetrate my inmost heart, that I may set you, my Lord and God, before my face forever; help me to shun all things that can offend you, and make me worthy to appear before the pure eyes of your divine Majesty in

heaven, where you live and reign in the unity of the
ever blessed Trinity, God world without end. Amen.

Our Father and Hail Mary (once).
Glory to the Father (seven times).
Act of Consecration, Prayer for the Seven Gifts.

Third Day

You, of all consolers best,
Visiting the troubled breast,
Do refreshing peace bestow.

The Gift of Piety

The gift of piety begets in our hearts a filial
affection for God as our most loving Father. It inspires us to love and respect, for his sake, persons
and things consecrated to him, as well as those who
are vested with his authority; his Blessed Mother and
the saints; the Church and its visible head, the Pope;
our parents and superiors; our country and its rulers.
Whoever is filled with the gift of piety finds the
practice of religion not a burdensome duty, but a
delightful service. Where there is love, there is no
labor.

Prayer

Come, O blessed Spirit of piety, possess my
heart. Enkindle therein such a love for God, that I

may find satisfaction only in his service, and for his sake lovingly submit to all legitimate authority. Amen.

Our Father and Hail Mary (once).
Glory to the Father (seven times).
Act of Consecration, Prayer for the Seven Gifts.

Fourth Day

You in toil are comfort sweet;
Pleasant coolness in the heat;
Solace in the midst of woe.

The Gift of Fortitude

The gift of fortitude strengthens us against natural fear, and supports us to the end in the performance of duty. Fortitude imparts to the will an impulse and energy which move it to undertake without hesitancy the most arduous tasks, to face dangers, to trample underfoot human respect, and to endure without complaint the slow martyrdom of even lifelong tribulation. "Whoever perseveres to the end shall be saved."

Prayer

Come, O blessed Spirit of fortitude, uphold my soul in time of trouble and adversity, sustain my efforts for holiness, strengthen my weakness, give me courage against all the assaults of my enemies, that I may never be overcome and separated from you, my God and greatest good. Amen.

Our Father and Hail Mary (once).
Glory to the Father (seven times).
Act of Consecration, Prayer for the Seven Gifts.

Fifth Day

Light immortal! Light divine!
Visit now these hearts of thine,
And our inmost being fill!

The Gift of Knowledge

The gift of knowledge enables the soul to evaluate created things at their true worth—in their relation to God. Knowledge unmasks the pretense of creatures, reveals their emptiness, and points out their only true purpose as instruments in the service of God. It shows us the loving care of God even in adversity, and directs us to glorify him in every circumstance of life. Guided by its light, we put first things first, and prize the friendship of God beyond all else. "Wisdom is a fountain of life to one who has it" (Prov 16:22).

Prayer

Come, O blessed Spirit of knowledge, and grant that I may perceive the will of the Father; show me the nothingness of earthly things, that I may realize their vanity and use them only for your glory and my own salvation, looking ever beyond them to you and your eternal rewards. Amen.

Our Father and Hail Mary (once).
Glory to the Father (seven times).
Act of Consecration, Prayer for the Seven Gifts.

Sixth Day

If you take your grace away,
Nothing pure in man will stay,
All his good is turned to ill.

The Gift of Understanding

Understanding, as a gift of the Holy Spirit, helps us to grasp the meaning of the truths of our holy religion. By faith we know them, but by understanding we learn to appreciate and relish them. It enables us to penetrate the inner meaning of revealed truths and through them to be quickened to newness of life. Our faith ceases to be sterile and inactive, but inspires a mode of life that bears eloquent testimony to the faith that is in us; we begin to "lead lives worthy of the Lord, fully pleasing to him, as you bear fruit in every good work and as you grow in the knowledge of God" (Col 1:10).

Prayer

Come, O Spirit of understanding, and enlighten my mind, that I may know and believe all the mysteries of salvation; and may merit at last to see the eternal light in your light; and in the light of glory to have a clear vision of you and the Father and the Son. Amen.

Our Father and Hail Mary (once).
Glory to the Father (seven times).
Act of Consecration, Prayer for the Seven Gifts.

Seventh Day

Heal our wounds—our strength renew;
On our dryness pour your dew;
Wash the stains of guilt away!

The Gift of Counsel

The gift of counsel endows the soul with supernatural prudence, enabling it to judge promptly and rightly what must be done, especially in difficult circumstances. Counsel applies the principles furnished by knowledge and understanding to the innumerable concrete cases that confront us in the course of our daily duty as parents, teachers, public servants and Christian citizens. Counsel is supernatural common sense, a priceless treasure in the quest of salvation. "Above all these things, pray to the Most High, that he may direct your way in truth."

Prayer

Come, O Spirit of Counsel, help and guide me in all my ways, that I may always do your holy will. Incline my heart to that which is good; turn it away from all that is evil, and direct me by the straight path of your commandments to that goal of eternal life for which I long. Amen.

Our Father and Hail Mary (once).
Glory to the Father (seven times).
Act of Consecration, Prayer for the Seven Gifts.

Eighth Day

Bend the stubborn heart and will;
Melt the frozen, warm the chill;
Guide the steps that go astray!

The Gift of Wisdom

Embodying all the other gifts, as charity embraces all the other virtues, wisdom is the most perfect of the gifts. Of wisdom it is written "all good things came to me along with her, and in her hands uncounted wealth" (Wis 7:11). The gift of wisdom strengthens our faith, fortifies hope, perfects charity, and promotes the practice of virtue in the highest degree. Wisdom enlightens the mind to discern and relish things divine, in the appreciation of which earthly joys lose their savor, while the cross of Christ yields a divine sweetness according to the words of the Savior: "Take my yoke upon you, and learn from me; for I am gentle and humble in heart, and you will find rest for your souls" (Mt 11:29).

Prayer

Come, O Spirit of wisdom, and reveal to my soul the mysteries of heavenly things, their exceeding greatness, power and beauty. Teach me to love them above and beyond all the passing joys and satisfactions of earth. Help me to attain them and possess them forever. men.

Our Father and Hail Mary (once).
Glory to the Father (seven times).
Act of Consecration, Prayer for the Seven Gifts.

Ninth Day

You, on those who evermore
Do confess you and adore,
In your sevenfold gifts descend:
Give them comfort when they die;
Give them life with you on high;
Give them joys which never end. Amen.

The Fruits of the Holy Spirit

The gifts of the Holy Spirit perfect the supernatural virtues by enabling us to practice them with greater docility to divine inspiration. As we grow in the knowledge and love of God under the direction of the Holy Spirit, our service becomes more sincere and generous, the practice of virtue more perfect. Such acts of virtue leave the heart filled with joy and consolation and are known as fruits of the Holy Spirit. These fruits in turn render the practice of virtue more attractive and become a powerful incentive for still greater efforts in the service of God, to serve whom is to reign.

Prayer

Come, O divine Spirit, fill my heart with your heavenly fruits, your charity, joy, peace, patience, benignity, goodness, faith, mildness and temperance, that I may never weary in the service of God, but by continued faithful submission to your inspiration may merit to be united eternally with you in the love of the Father and the Son. Amen.

Our Father and Hail Mary (once).
Glory to the Father (seven times).
Act of Consecration, Prayer for the Seven Gifts.

Prayers to Our Lady of Guadalupe

"Am I not your mother?"

Our Lady spoke these words to Juan Diego on Tepeyac Hill near Mexico City in December, 1531. They capture the essence of Mary's maternal mission toward us. Our Lady of Guadalupe reassures us that she is always ready to help us in all our needs.

When she appeared to Juan Diego, Mary asked that a church be built in her honor on that spot. But how could Juan, a poor, simple man, approach the bishop with such a request? Mary provided a sign: a shower of exquisite roses in Juan's tilma, or cloak, and an even more beautiful portrait of herself which appeared on it. When the bishop saw this, he realized that the Blessed Mother had indeed appeared to this humble peasant.

A basilica was built which still attracts thousands of pilgrims each year. Named as the patroness of Mexico, the people of that country have a special devotion to Our Lady of Guadalupe. Her feastday is celebrated on December 12.

Prayer to the Virgin of Guadalupe

O Immaculate Virgin, Mother of God and Mother of the Church! You, who from this place reveal your clemency and your piety to all those who ask for your protection, hear the prayer that we address to you with loving trust, and present it to your Son Jesus, our sole Redeemer.

Mother of mercy, teacher of hidden and silent sacrifice, to you, who come to meet us sinners, we dedicate on this day all our being and all our love. We also dedicate to you our life, our work, our joys, our infirmities and our sorrows.

Grant peace, justice and prosperity to our peoples, for we entrust to your care all that we have and all that we are, our Lady and Mother.

We wish to be entirely yours and to walk with you along the way of complete faithfulness to Jesus Christ in his Church. Hold us always with your loving hand.

Virgin of Guadalupe, Mother of the Americas, we pray to you for all the bishops, that they may lead the faithful along paths of intense Christian life, of love and humble service of God and souls.

Contemplate this immense harvest, and intercede with the Lord that he may instill a hunger for holiness in the whole People of God, and grant abundant vocations of priests and religious, strong in the faith and zealous dispensers of God's mysteries.

Grant to our homes the grace of loving and respecting life in its beginnings, with the same love with which you conceived in your womb the life of the Son of God.

Blessed Virgin Mary, Mother of Fair Love, protect our families, so that they may always be united, and bless the upbringing of our children. Look upon us with compassion, teach us to go continually to Jesus and, if we fall, help us to rise again and return to him, by confessing our faults and sins in the sacrament of Penance, which gives pardon and peace.

We beg you to grant us a great love for all the holy sacraments, which are the signs that your Son left us on earth.

Thus, most holy Mother, with the peace of God in our conscience, with our hearts free from evil and hatred we will be able to bring to all true joy and true peace, which comes to us from your Son, our Lord Jesus Christ, who with God the Father and the Holy Spirit lives and reigns for ever and ever. Amen.

Pope John Paul II

Triduum to Our Lady of Guadalupe

"For now I have chosen and consecrated this house so that my name may be there forever; my eyes and my heart will be there for all time" (2 Chr 7:16).

"Who is this that looks forth like the dawn, fair as the moon, bright as the sun, terrible as an army with banners?" (Cant 6:10).

(Hail Mary)

Mary speaks:

"My soul magnifies the Lord,

and my spirit rejoices in God my Savior,

for he has looked with favor on the lowliness of his servant.

Surely, from now on all generations will call me blessed;

for the Mighty One has done great things for me, and holy is his name" (Lk 1:46-49).

Prayer

O God, you have been pleased to bestow upon us unceasing favors by having placed us under the special protection of the Most Blessed Virgin Mary. Grant us, your humble servants, who rejoice in honoring her today upon earth, the happiness of seeing her face to face in heaven. Through Christ our Lord. Amen.

Novena in Honor of Our Lady of Guadalupe

First Day

Dearest Lady of Guadalupe, fruitful Mother of holiness, teach me your ways of gentleness and strength. Hear my humble prayer offered with heartfelt confidence, and obtain the favor I ask....

(Our Father, Hail Mary, Glory be)

Second Day

O Mary, conceived without sin, I come to your throne of grace to share the fervent devotion of your faithful Mexican children who call to you under the glorious Aztec title of Guadalupe. Obtain for me a lively faith to do always your Son's holy will. May his will be done on earth as it is in heaven.

(Our Father, Hail Mary, Glory be)

Third Day

O Mary, whose Immaculate Heart was pierced by seven swords of grief, help me to walk courageously amid the sharp thorns strewn across my pathway. Obtain for me the strength to be a true imitator of you. This I ask you, my dear Mother.

(Our Father, Hail Mary, Glory be)

Fourth Day

Dearest Mother of Guadalupe, I beg you for a fortified will to imitate your divine Son's charity—to always seek the good of others in need. Grant me this, I humbly ask of you.

(Our Father, Hail Mary, Glory be)

Fifth Day

O most holy Mother, I beg you to obtain for me pardon of all my sins, abundant graces to serve your Son more faithfully from now on, and lastly, the grace to praise him with you forever in heaven.

(Our Father, Hail Mary, Glory be)

Sixth Day

Mary, Mother of vocations, multiply priestly vocations and fill the earth with religious houses which will be light and warmth for the world, safety in stormy nights. Beg your Son to send the Church many priests and religious. This I ask of you, O Mother.

(Our Father, Hail Mary, Glory be)

Seventh Day

O Lady of Guadalupe, I pray that parents may live a holy life and educate their children in a Christian manner; that children may obey and follow the directions of their parents; that all members of the family may pray and worship together. This I ask of you, O Mother.

(Our Father, Hail Mary, Glory be)

Eighth Day

With my heart full of the most sincere veneration, I come before you, O Mother, to ask you to obtain for me the grace to fulfill the duties of my state in life with faithfulness and constancy.

(Our Father, Hail Mary, Glory be)

Ninth Day

O God, you have been pleased to bestow upon us unceasing favors by having placed us under the special protection of the Most Blessed Virgin Mary. Grant us, your humble servants, who rejoice in honoring her today upon earth, the happiness of seeing her face to face in heaven.

(Our Father, Hail Mary, Glory be)

Magnificat

"My soul magnifies the Lord,
and my spirit rejoices in God my Savior,
for he has looked with favor on the lowliness of
his servant.

Surely, from now on all generations will call
    me blessed;
for the Mighty One has done great things for
    me, and holy is his name.
His mercy is for those who fear him from
    generation to generation.
He has shown strength with his arm;
he has scattered the proud in the thoughts of
    their hearts.
He has brought down the powerful from their
    thrones, and lifted up the lowly;
he has filled the hungry with good things, and
    sent the rich away empty.
He has helped his servant Israel, in remembrance
    of his mercy,
according to the promise he made to our
    ancestors,
to Abraham and to his descendants forever"
(Lk 1:46-55).

Prayers to
Our Lady of Perpetual Help

In the 15th century, a wealthy merchant of Crete possessed a beautiful painting of Our Lady of Perpetual Help. He brought it to Rome, where for some time it was hidden in a private home. It was finally enshrined in the Church of St. Matthew the Apostle, where it was publicly venerated. Many people received extraordinary graces, favors and miraculous cures through praying to Our Lady of Perpetual Help.

When Napoleon sacked Rome in 1789, St. Matthew's was destroyed but a priest hid the picture to keep it from being vandalized. It was forgotten for the next sixty-four years. Then the Redemptorists came into possession of the picture and Pope Pius IX commissioned them to make Our Lady of Perpetual Help known everywhere. Through their efforts, this devotion has spread throughout the world and countless persons have received graces through Our Lady's intercession.

Novena to Our Lady of Perpetual Help

See at your feet, O Mother of Perpetual Help, a poor sinner who has recourse to you and confides in you.

O Mother of Mercy, have pity on me! You are called the refuge and the hope of sinners; be my refuge and my hope. Help me, for the love of Jesus Christ; stretch forth your hand to a poor, fallen creature. I recommend myself to you, and I want to devote myself to your service forever. I bless and thank almighty God, who in his mercy has given me this confidence in you, which I hold to be a pledge of my eternal salvation.

Mary, help me. Mother of Perpetual Help, never allow me to lose my God.

(Our Father, Hail Mary, Glory be, three times.)

Prayer for a Happy Death

O Mary, my good Mother, after Jesus you are my hope and consolation. By your protection make me persevere in my firm determination to offend God no more and to prefer a thousand deaths rather than commit one mortal sin! Obtain for me the grace of final perseverance, and grant that I may remember to ask for it during the time of temptation and at the hour of death. You are the refuge of sinners and our perennial help. Our Lady of Perpetual Help, pray for me.

O Mother of Jesus, I offer you the last day, last hour and last moment of my life, and everything that shall take place in me then, in honor of the last moment, hour and day of your life, and of all that occurred in you on that day. If it pleases you, unite me with all the holy dispositions of your maternal heart and your pure soul. Grant that, by your merits and prayers, my last thoughts, words, acts and breaths may be consecrated to the honor of the last thoughts, words, acts and breaths both of your Son and of yourself. Grant that I may die loving him with his holy love; that I may be utterly consumed and sacrificed to his glory; that my life may end with a last act of most pure love of him.

St. John Eudes

Various Prayers to Our Lady of Perpetual Help

Hail Mary, hope of Christians! Hear the request of a sinner who loves you tenderly, who honors you particularly, and who places in you the hope of salvation. I owe you life. You re-establish in me the grace of your divine Son. You are the sure pledge of my eternal happiness. I beg you to deliver me from the burden of my sins. Dispel the ignorance of my mind, destroy the disordered affections of my heart, repulse the temptations of my enemies, and preside over all the actions of my life, so that by your direction I may arrive at the eternal happiness of heaven.

St. John Damascene

O Mother of Jesus, and my Mother, let me dwell with you, cling to you and love you with ever-increasing love. I promise the honor, love and trust of a child. Give me a mother's protection, for I need your watchful care. You know better than any other the thoughts and desires of the Sacred Heart. Keep constantly before my mind the same thoughts, the same desires, that my heart may be filled with zeal for the interests of the Sacred Heart of your Divine Son. Instill in me a love of all that is noble, that I may no longer be easily roused to resentment, easily led to anger, easily turned to selfishness.

Help me, dearest Mother, to acquire the virtues that God wants of me: to forget myself always, to work solely for him, without fear of sacrifice. I shall always rely on your help to be what Jesus wants me to be. I am his; I am yours, my good Mother! Give me each day your holy and maternal blessing until my last evening on earth, when your Immaculate Heart will present me to the heart of Jesus in heaven, there to love and bless you and your divine Son for all eternity.

Cardinal Newman

We ask you, holy Virgin, to help us with your prayers to God—prayers which are more dear and precious to us than all the treasures of the earth; prayers which make God well disposed toward us and obtain for us a great abundance of graces for receiving pardon of our sins and for practicing virtue; prayers which restrain our enemies, confound their designs, and triumph over all their endeavors. We implore the aid of these prayers with the greatest confidence; graciously grant our request.

St. Andrew of Candia

O Virgin most pure and wholly unspotted; O Mary, Mother of God, Queen of the universe, you are above all the saints, the hope of the elect, and the joy of all the blessed. You have reconciled us with God; you are the only refuge of sinners and the safe harbor of those who are shipwrecked; you are the consolation of the world, the ransom of captives, the health of the weak, the joy of the afflicted, and the salvation of all. We have recourse to you, and we ask you to have pity on us.

St. Ephrem

Prayers to
Our Lady of the Miraculous Medal

In 1830, the Blessed Mother appeared to a novice of the Sisters of Charity, Catherine Labouré. Our Lady showed her the design of a medal and asked that copies be made and distributed widely. The medal shows Our Lady standing on a globe, with brilliant rays beaming out from her hands. Mary told Catherine, "Behold the symbol of graces I shed upon those who ask me for them." Around the frame of the medal appear the words, "O Mary conceived without sin, pray for us who have recourse to you." Our Lady commanded, "Have a medal struck upon this model. All who wear it will receive great graces. Graces will be bestowed abundantly on those who have confidence."

The novice confided in her confessor, and after many difficulties, copies of the medal were made and distributed. It was named the medal of the Immaculate Conception. However, so many cures and conversions were reported through the use of the medal that it was called the "miraculous" medal. Under that name it has been spread throughout the world.

Catherine Labouré lived the rest of her life as a humble sister, quietly carrying out the ordinary duties of religious life. She was canonized by Pope Pius XII on July 27, 1947.

Miraculous Medal Novena

Immaculate Mary

Immaculate Mary, your praises we sing;
You reign now with Christ, our Redeemer and king.

Chorus:
    Ave, ave, ave, Maria!
    Ave, ave, ave, Maria!

In heaven the blessed your glory proclaim
On earth we, your children, invoke your fair name.
(Repeat chorus.)

We pray you, O Mother, may God's will be done;
We pray for his glory; may his kingdom come.
(Repeat chorus.)

We pray for our Mother, the Church upon earth;
And bless, holy Mary, the land of our birth.
(Repeat chorus.)

Opening Prayer

In the name of the Father, and of the Son, and of the Holy Spirit. Amen.

Come, Holy Spirit, fill the hearts of your faithful and kindle in them the fire of your love.

Send forth your Spirit, and they shall be created. And you shall renew the face of the earth.

Let us pray. O God, you instructed the hearts of the faithful by the light of the Holy Spirit. Grant that by the same Spirit we may be truly wise and ever rejoice in his consolation, through Jesus Christ our Lord. Amen.

O Mary, conceived without sin, pray for us who have recourse to you. *(Three times)*

Lord Jesus Christ, by countless miracles you have glorified the Blessed Virgin Mary, who was immaculate from the first moment of her conception. Grant that all who devoutly ask her protection on earth may eternally enjoy your presence in heaven. There with the Father and the Holy Spirit, you live and reign, God, forever and ever. Amen.

Lord Jesus Christ, for the accomplishment of your greatest works, you have chosen the weak things of the world, that no one may glory in your sight. For a better and more widespread belief in the Immaculate Conception of your Mother, you wanted the miraculous medal to be shown to St. Catherine Labouré. Grant that we may be filled with a humility like hers and glorify this mystery through our words and actions. Amen.

Memorare

Remember, O most gracious Virgin Mary, that never was it known, that anyone who fled to your protection, implored your help, or sought your intercession, was left unaided. Inspired with this confidence, I fly to you, O Virgin of virgins, my Mother. To you I come, before you I stand, sinful and sorrowful. O Mother of the Word Incarnate, despise not my petitions, but in your mercy hear and answer me. Amen.

Novena Prayer

Immaculate Virgin Mary, Mother of our Lord Jesus and our Mother, we are filled with the most lively confidence in your all-powerful and never-failing intercession, shown so often through the miraculous medal. As your loving and trustful children, we ask you to obtain for us the graces and favors we request during this novena, if these will be to our spiritual benefit.

(Here, privately mention your petitions.)

You know, O Mary, that we want our souls always to be the temples of the Holy Spirit, who hates sin. Obtain for us, then, a deep hatred of sin and that purity of heart which will attach us to God alone, so that our every thought, word and deed may be directed to his greater glory. Obtain for us a spirit of prayer and self-denial, that we may recover by penance what we have lost by sin and eventually enter that heavenly dwelling where you are the Queen of angels and of humanity. Amen.

An Act of Consecration to
Our Lady of the Miraculous Medal

O Virgin Mother of God, Mary Immaculate, we dedicate and consecrate ourselves to you under the title of Our Lady of the Miraculous Medal. May this medal be for each one of us a sure sign of your affection for us and a constant reminder of our duties toward you. Ever while wearing it, may we be blessed by your loving protection and preserved in the grace of your Son. O most powerful Virgin, Mother of our Savior, keep us close to you every moment of our lives. Obtain for us, your children, the grace of a happy death, so that, in union with you, we may enjoy the happiness of heaven forever. Amen.

O Mary conceived without sin, pray for us who have recourse to you. *(Three times)*

Closing Hymn

O Mary, conceived without sin,
Pray for us, pray for us;
O Mary, conceived without sin,
Pray for us who have recourse to you.

Our Lady of the Miraculous Medal

It is only an oval medallion
But it's a symbol of Mary's love.
She gave it for us to St. Catherine
A source of blessings from above.
All graces come to us through Mary;
Jesus himself wills it that way.
He tenderly loves his dear Mother
And will do what she chooses to say.
Mary's love for God is so perfect;
She wants our love for him to be strong,
For love is proved by words and actions
And by courageously singing life's song,
The song of love, of praise, of valorous deeds
For God and for God alone
As we joyously trod the path of duty,
Lifting hearts besides our own.

Mary wants us to pray for our blessings,
To be grateful to God for all things,
And so she gives us a reminder—
A token—a medal—a medal with wings,
For faithfully to wear the medal
Is a symbol of love and of praise
And a silent prayer of intercession
Which to our heavenly Mother does raise.
Her hands are outstretched with blessings
For all of her children so true.
Call on her sincerely today;
She does have countless favors for you.

Sister Mary Francis Le Blanc, O. Carm.

Prayers to Our Lady of Sorrows

In the Middle Ages, Christian theology and worship concentrated greatly on Jesus Christ's passion and death. At the side of the Man of Sorrows, however, the faithful always contemplated the Queen of Martyrs. Devotion to the Crucified Savior and to the Sorrowful Mother grew side by side.

One spiritual writer expressed the sentiments of Christian devotion in this way, "On Calvary we can contemplate two altars: one in the body of Jesus, the other in the heart of Mary. Jesus immolated his own flesh; Mary immolated her own soul."

On September 15, the day following the ancient feast of the Holy Cross, we commemorate the sorrows of Mary. Let us consider Mary's sufferings during the passion of her Son, the Redeemer. Let us consider her as Mother and Queen of all those who suffer. As Queen of Martyrs, Mary gives an admirable example of patience.

Devotions in Honor of the Seven Sorrows of Mary

1. Reading from Scripture: Luke 2:34-35
Reflection

Prayer: Remember, O Virgin Mary, the sword of sorrow that pierced your heart with the prophecy of Simeon who foretold to you the death of Jesus; pierce our hearts with the sword of contrition.

(Hail Mary)

2. Reading from Scripture: Matthew 2:13-14
Reflection

Prayer: Remember, O Virgin Mary, the sorrow you felt when obliged to flee into Egypt; bring us, your exiled children, back from the darkness to the light and lead us to the splendors of our eternal home.

(Hail Mary)

3. Reading from Scripture: Luke 2:45-46
Reflection

Prayer: Remember, O Virgin Mary, your sorrow when you sought Jesus for three days before finding him in the temple; grant that we may thirst for Christ, that we may seek him always and everywhere, and that our search may be crowned with success.

(Hail Mary) .

4. Reading from Scripture: John 19:16-17
Reflection

Prayer: Remember, O Virgin Mary, the sorrow you felt when Jesus was seized and bound, then scourged and crowned with thorns; heed your children's cries and break the bonds of our sins.

(Hail Mary)

5. Reading from Scripture: John 19:25-30
Reflection

Prayer: Remember, O Virgin Mary, your sorrow when Jesus was raised on the cross and, amid unspeakable spasms, gave up his spirit to the Father; grant that we, too, may benefit from the sacrifice of the cross.

(Hail Mary)

6. Reading from Scripture: Luke 23:50-54
Reflection

Prayer: Remember, O Virgin Mary, your sorrow when the sacred body of Jesus was placed in your arms with sentiments of profound devotion; embrace us, too, O Mother, so that we may enjoy your love.

(Hail Mary)

7. Reading from Scripture: Mark 15:46
Reflection

Prayer: Remember your sorrow, O Virgin Mary, when Jesus was wrapped in a sheet and laid in the sepulcher; cleanse our souls with his Most Precious Blood, and at the end of our lives fill us with deep compunction, so that the gates of heaven may be opened to us.

(Hail Mary)

Brief Novena to Our Lady of Sorrows

I grieve for you, O Mary most sorrowful, in the sadness of your heart at meeting Jesus as he carried his cross. Dear Mother, by your heart so troubled, obtain for me the virtue of patience and the gift of fortitude. *(Hail Mary)*

V. Pray for us, O Virgin most sorrowful.

R. That we may be made worthy of the promises of Christ.

Prayer to Our Sorrowful Mother

O Mother of Sorrows, you who beneath the cross of Jesus were given to be our mother, look down with an eye of pity on us, your children, who weep and mourn in this vale of tears. By that sword of sorrow which pierced your heart when you looked upon the face of your dead Son, obtain for us that comfort we so greatly need in our tribulations.

You were given to us as our mother in the hour of your greatest grief that you might be mindful of our frailty and the evils that press upon us. Without your aid, O Sorrowful Mother, we cannot gain victory in this struggle against flesh and blood. Therefore, we seek your help, O Queen of Sorrows, lest we fall prey to the wiles of the enemy. We are orphans in need of the guiding hand of a mother amid the dangers that threaten our destruction. You whose grief was boundless as the sea, whose life was one continued sorrow, grant us by the memory of those sorrows the strength to conquer in the conflict that is forced upon us.

Intercede further, O Mother of Dolors, for us and all who are near and dear to us, that we may ever do the will of your Son, and may direct all our actions to his honor, and to the spread of devotion to your sorrows. Amen.

Virgin most sorrowful, pray for us.
(Our Father, Hail Mary, Glory be)

Prayer of St. Bonaventure to the Mother of Sorrows

O sorrowful Virgin, unite me at least to the insults and wounds of your Son, so that both he and you may find comfort in having someone sharing your sufferings. How happy I would be if I could do this! For is there perhaps anything greater, sweeter or more advantageous for us? Why do you not grant me what I ask? If I have offended you, be just and pierce my heart. If I have been faithful to you, leave me not without a reward: give me your sorrows.

The Stabat Mater

At the cross her station keeping,
Stood the mournful Mother weeping,
Close to Jesus to the last.

Through her heart, his sorrow sharing,
All his bitter anguish bearing,
Now at length the sword had passed.

Oh, how sad and sore distressed
Was that Mother highly blest
Of the sole-begotten one!

Christ above in torment hangs
She beneath beholds the pangs
Of her dying glorious Son.

Is there one who would not weep,
Whelmed in miseries so deep
Christ's dear Mother to behold?

Can the human heart refrain
From partaking in her pain
In that Mother's pain untold?

Bruised, derided, cursed, defiled,
She beheld her tender Child
All with bloody scourges rent.

For the sins of his own nation
She saw him hang in desolation,
Till his spirit forth he sent.

O my Mother fount of love,
Touch my spirit from above;
Make my heart with yours accord.

Make me feel as you have felt,
Make my soul to glow and melt
With the love of Christ my Lord.

Holy Mother, pierce me through;
In my heart each wound renew
Of my Savior crucified.

Let me share with you his pain,
Who for all my sins was slain,
Who for me in torment died.

Let me mingle tears with you,
Mourning him who mourned for me,
All the days that I may live.

By the cross with you to stay,
There with you to weep and pray,
Is all I ask of you to give.

Virgin of all virgins best,
Listen to my fond request;
Let me share your grief divine.

Let me to my latest breath,
In my body bear the death,
Of that dying Son of yours.

Wounded with his every wound,
Steep my soul till it has swooned,
In his very Blood away.

Be to me, O Virgin, nigh,
Lest in flames I burn and die,
In his awful judgment day.

Christ, when you shall call me hence
Be your Mother my defense;
Be your cross my victory.

While my body here decays,
May my soul your goodness praise,
Safe in paradise with you. Amen.

Thirty Days' Prayer
to the Blessed Virgin Mary

Ever glorious and blessed Mary, Queen of Virgins, Mother of Mercy, hope and comfort of the downhearted, through that sword of sorrow which pierced your tender heart, while your only Son,

Christ Jesus, our Lord, suffered agony and death on the cross; through that filial tenderness and pure love he had for you, grieving in your sorrows, while from his cross he recommended you to the care and protection of his beloved disciple, St. John; take pity, I beseech you, on my poverty and necessities. Have compassion on my anxieties and cares. Assist and comfort me in all my needs.

You are the Mother of mercies, the sweet consoler and refuge of the needy and the orphan, of the suffering and the afflicted. Cast an eye of pity on me in my sorrow, and hear my prayer.

Since I find myself surrounded by many troubles, and feel overwhelmed and desperate in this situation, where can I fly for more secure shelter, O Mother of my Lord and Savior Jesus Christ, than under the wings of your maternal protection? With understanding and compassion, listen to my humble and earnest request. I ask it through the mercy of your Son, Jesus Christ, through that love and abasement with which he took on our nature, when, in compliance with the divine will, you gave your consent; and whom, nine months later, you brought forth from your chaste womb, to visit this world and bless it with his presence.

I ask it through the anguish of mind with which your beloved Son, our loving Savior, was overwhelmed on Mount Olivet, when he invoked his eternal Father to remove from him, if possible, the bitter chalice of his future passion. I ask it through the threefold repetition of his prayer in the garden, after which with sorrowful steps and mournful tears you accompanied him to the place of his sufferings and death.

I ask it through the stripes and wounds of his virginal flesh, occasioned by the cords and whips with which he was bound and scourged when stripped of his seamless garment—for which his executioners afterward cast lots. I ask it through the jeers and insults by which he was insulted, the false accusations and unjust sentence by which he was condemned to death, and which he bore with heavenly patience. I ask it through his bitter tears and bloody sweat, his silence and resignation, his sadness and grief of heart. I ask it through the blood which trickled from his royal and sacred head when struck with the scepter of a reed and pierced with his crown of thorns. I ask it through the excruciating torments he suffered when his hands and feet were fastened with large nails to the tree of the cross.

I ask it through his vehement thirst and bitter potion of vinegar and gall; I ask it through his abandonment on the cross, when he exclaimed: "My God, My God, why have you forsaken me?" I ask it through his mercy extended to the repentant thief, and through his recommending his precious soul and spirit into the hands of his eternal Father before he expired, saying, "All is consummated." I ask it through the blood mixed with water, which flowed from his sacred side when pierced with a lance, and from which a flood of grace and mercy has flowed to us. I ask it through his immaculate life, bitter passion, and death on the cross, at which nature itself was thrown into convulsions, by the earthquake, the bursting of rocks, rending of the veil of the temple, and darkness of the sun and moon.

I ask it through his descent into the abode of the dead, where he comforted the saints of the Old Law with his presence.

I ask it through his glorious victory over death, when he arose again to life on the third day, and through the joy which his appearances for forty days after gave you, his Blessed Mother, his apostles, and the rest of his disciples, when, in your presence, he miraculously ascended into heaven. I ask it through the grace of the Holy Spirit, infused into the hearts of the disciples, when he descended upon them in the form of fiery tongues, and by which they were inspired with zeal for the conversion of the world as they went forth to preach the Gospel. I ask it through the awesome appearance of your Son on the last dreadful day, when he shall come to judge the living and the dead, and destroy the world by fire. I ask it through the love he bore you in this life, and the great joy you felt at your assumption into heaven, where you are eternally absorbed in contemplating his divine perfections. O glorious and ever-blessed Virgin, please obtain for me the favor I ask...*(here mention your request).*

Just as Jesus honors you as his beloved Mother—to whom he refuses nothing, because you ask nothing contrary to his honor—so let me speedily experience the efficacy of your powerful intercession and your maternal affection. May he, whose heart is loving toward his children, mercifully grant the requests and fulfill the desires of those who love and fear him.

O most Blessed Virgin, besides my present petition, and whatever else I may need, obtain for me also from your dear Son, our Lord and our God, a lively faith, firm hope, perfect charity, true contrition of heart, a horror of sin, love of God and my neighbor, contempt of the world, patience to suffer affronts and insults, or even, if necessary, a painful death, for love of your Son, our Savior, Jesus Christ. Obtain likewise for me, O holy Mother of God, perseverance in good works, fulfillment of good resolutions, mortification of self-will, a holy life, and, at my last moments, strong and sincere repentance, accompanied by such a lively and attentive presence of mind as will enable me worthily to receive the last sacraments of the Church, and die in your friendship and favor. Lastly, obtain, I beseech you, life everlasting for the souls of my parents, brethren, relatives and benefactors—both living and dead. Amen.

For Vocations

O Mary, Queen of all the angels, full of grace, conceived without sin, blessed among creatures, living tabernacle of God, remember that painful and solemn moment in which the dying Jesus from the cross gave you John as your son, and in him all people and especially all the apostles. What tender love flooded your heart at that moment for those consecrated to the apostolate, to the following of the cross, to the love of Jesus. For your indescribable sufferings and those of your divine Son, for your motherly heart, O Mary, increase the ranks of apostles, missionaries, priests and virgins. May they be resplendent for sanctity of life, integrity of morals, solid piety, the deepest humility, the most firm faith, the most ardent charity. May they all be holy, purifying salt of the earth, and light of the world.

O Afflicted Virgin

O afflicted Virgin, great in virtues as in sorrows, both the one and the other spring from that intense fire of love burning in your heart for God, the only love of your heart! My Mother, have pity on me. I have loved God so little, and have greatly offended him. Your sorrows, it is true, assure me of pardon, but that is not sufficient. I wish to love God. Who could obtain for me that grace if not you, who are the Mother of holy love? Mary, you console everyone; hasten, then, to console me also. Amen.

St. Alphonsus Liguori

O Mother of Grief

O Mother of grief, Queen of Martyrs and of sufferings, you wept so much for your Son, who died for my salvation! By the merits of your sorrows and pains, obtain for me true repentance for my sins, and true renewal of life, with a tender compassion for your sufferings and the sufferings of Jesus Christ. Since Jesus and you, although innocent, suffered so much for me, let me also suffer something for your love. O my divine Mother, I implore you, by the affliction you endured in seeing your Son bow his head and expire on the cross, obtain for me a holy death. Do not fail to aid my afflicted and struggling soul in that great passage to eternity! Perhaps I shall not then be able to invoke with my lips Jesus and Mary. I invoke them now beforehand, and I ask you, my hope, to assist me at that last moment.

St. Alphonsus Liguori

Meditation on the Sorrowful Mother

Standing near the cross of her Son, the pure and immaculate Virgin contemplated his appalling wounds. She thought again of the blows and the scourging, and in tears she exclaimed: "O my Son, why do you bear this cross? My Son and my God, why do you bear spittle, blows and nails? Why the outrages, the insults and the spear? For what reason the crown of thorns, the purple robe, the sponge, the reed, the gall and the vinegar? Why do you hang dead and naked upon the cross—you who cover the sky with clouds? Why do you suffer thirst—you who are the Creator of the universe, who created the seas and all the waters? Why do you, O innocent one, die among ungodly men and thieves? What have you done? Why did they nail you to the cross—they whose lame and sick you cured, whose dead you restored to life?

"And you, O ungrateful people, do you return abuse for benefits, injury for privileges, and evil for good? O Archangel Gabriel, where now is that Ave with which you greeted me? Where is the blessing you promised me when you said to me: 'Blessed are you among women'? And why did you not tell me that I was to be the Mother of the Victim?... I have been in continuous pain and agony; I have always had to suffer. O Simeon, worthy of belief, behold the sword that you predicted for me; it has pierced my soul. Gaze upon my wound, O my Son and my God. Your death has penetrated deep into my heart; my vision is dimmed; my breast has been transfixed. And now where is the beauty of your face? Therefore, look and have pity upon your Mother, a widow, alone and desolate."

St. Ephrem

Prayers to Mary, Queen of Apostles

Introduction

Devotion to Mary as Queen of Apostles is one of the oldest devotions in the Church. After Christ and with Christ, Mary is the Apostle. God continues to give all graces through Mary, just as he willed that Christ should come to us through Mary: "born of a woman" (Gal 4:4). Every apostolate and every true apostle has life and action from Mary. So it was of Christ: "...Jesus, the apostle and high priest of our confession" (Heb 3:1).

Christ began his apostolate through Mary at Cana; the mission of the apostles was begun through Mary in the cenacle. Likewise through the centuries all apostolates have received their origin and strength through Mary. Without God nothing exists; without Mary, nothing in Christ and in the Church.

History

The feast of the Queen of Apostles was established on the first Saturday after the Ascension by the Sacred Congregation of Rites at the request of the Pallottine Fathers. Mary initiated her mission as Queen of Apostles in the cenacle. She gathered the apostles together, comforted them, and assisted them in prayer. Together with them she hoped, desired and prayed; with them her petitions were heeded and she received the Holy Spirit on the day of Pentecost.

Mary is Queen of Apostles because she was chosen to be the Mother of Jesus Christ and to give him to the world; she was made the apostles' Mother and our own by our Savior on the cross; she was with the apostles while awaiting the descent of the Holy Spirit, obtaining for them the abundance of supernatural graces they received on Pentecost. The most holy Virgin was and always will be the wellspring for every apostolate.

She exercised a universal apostolate, one so vast that it embraced all others. The apostolate of prayer, the apostolate of good example, the apostolate of suffering—Mary fulfilled them all. Other people have practiced certain teachings of the Gospel; Mary lived them all. Mary is full of grace, and we draw from her abundance.

Mary attracts the zealous to the various apostolates, then protects and defends all these works. She sheds on each the warmth of her love and the light of her countenance.

She presented Jesus in a manner unparalleled throughout the ages. Her apostolate is of the highest degree—never to be equaled, much less surpassed.

Mary gave Jesus to the world and with Jesus came every other blessing. Thus, because of Mary we have the Church: "Mary is the Mother of the Church not only because she is the Mother of Christ and his most intimate associate in 'the new economy when the Son of God took a human nature from her, that he might in the mysteries of his flesh free man from sin,' but also because 'she shines forth to the whole community of the elect as a model of the virtues' *(Lumen Gentium,* nn. 55, 65). She now continues to fulfill from heaven her maternal function as the cooperator in the birth and development of the divine life in the individual souls of the redeemed" *(The Great Sign,* by Paul VI).

What do we have of value that we have not received through Mary? It is God's will that every blessing should come to us through her.

Because the Blessed Mother occupies a most important position in God's plan of salvation, all humanity should pay homage to her. Whoever spreads devotion to the Queen of Apostles is an apostolic benefactor of the human race, because devotion to Mary is a treasure. Blessed is the person who possesses this treasure! Mary's devotees will never be without grace; in any danger, in every circumstance they will always have the means to obtain every grace from God.

Novena to the Queen of Apostles

First Day

"I will put enmity between you and the woman, and between your offspring and hers; he will strike your head, and you will strike his heel" (Gen 3:15).

Through God's loving foresight, Mary was placed, so to speak, on a path different from that on which all the common children of Eve, born with original sin, entered the world. The new path is that of the redeemed. The light of the cross illumined Mary's conception, infancy and youth. Thus, she was worthy to be blessed among women.

Together let us honor Mary Immaculate, Queen of Apostles, and ask her to give Jesus Master, Way, Truth and Life, to all of us and to all people on earth.

Reflection and Resolution

Prayer: O God, you sent the Holy Spirit upon the apostles as they were united in prayer with Mary, the Mother of Jesus. May the Queen of Apostles, the same Mother of us all, help us to serve your majesty faithfully, and to spread the glory of your name by word and example. Through Christ our Lord. Amen.

(Our Father, Hail Mary, Glory be)

Queen of Apostles, pray for us.

Second Day

"The Holy Spirit will come upon you, and the power of the Most High will overshadow you; therefore the child to be born will be holy; he will be called Son of God" (Lk 1:35).

The grace in a soul is like a root from which a plant develops with its branches, leaves, flowers and fruits. Virtues grow in a soul in proportion to grace. Thus, we understand why Mary reached the highest degree of virtue and holiness: because she was full of grace. She possessed the theological, cardinal and moral virtues, the beatitudes and the fruits of the Holy Spirit to an eminent degree.

Mary is full of grace, the creature most intimate with God, the Blessed Mother who gives Jesus to us and helps us to love him. She makes us conceive a great fear of sin and of dangerous occasions. She inspires in us the desire for purity and for sacrifice.

Reflection and Resolution

Prayer: O God, you sent the Holy Spirit upon the apostles as they were united in prayer with Mary, the Mother of Jesus. May the Queen of Apostles, the same Mother of us all, help us to serve your majesty faithfully, and to spread the glory of your name by word and example. Through Christ our Lord. Amen.

(Our Father, Hail Mary, Glory be)

Queen of Apostles, pray for us.

Third Day

"She gave birth to her firstborn son and wrapped him in bands of cloth, and laid him in a manger, because there was no place for them in the inn" (Lk 2:7).

Mary fulfills her apostolate: to give Jesus to the Father, to humanity, to heaven. She presented Jesus to the Gentiles, represented by the Magi who came to the crib in Bethlehem. Mary always gives Jesus. She is like a fruitful branch. She always carries Jesus and offers him to us: the Way, the Truth and the Life of humanity.

Let us pray to Mary, the Mother of the infant Jesus, that through her maternal intercession we may all welcome the message from the crib: "Glory to God in the highest heaven, and on earth peace among those whom he favors!" (Lk 2:14).

Reflection and Resolution

Prayer: O God, you sent the Holy Spirit upon the apostles as they were united in prayer with Mary, the Mother of Jesus. May the Queen of Apostles, the same Mother of us all, help us to serve your majesty faithfully, and to spread the glory of your name by word and example. Through Christ our Lord. Amen.

(Our Father, Hail Mary, Glory be)

Queen of Apostles, pray for us.

Fourth Day

"This child is destined for the falling and the rising of many in Israel, and to be a sign that will be opposed...and a sword will pierce your own soul too" (Lk 2:34-35).

Jesus Christ saw Mary at the foot of his cross, sharing in his passion. The Christian possesses an inexhaustible strength and is able to endure great sufferings without breaking. In suffering, a person can attain great nobility of character; indeed, suffering becomes a real apostolate.

Let us always trustfully invoke Mary: "Pray for us, now and at the hour of our death." All to Mary, from Mary, with Mary. She shows everyone on earth her Son. Let us pray: "After this our exile, show to us the blessed fruit of your womb, Jesus."

Reflection and Resolution

Prayer: O God, you sent the Holy Spirit upon the apostles as they were united in prayer with Mary, the Mother of Jesus. May the Queen of Apostles, the same Mother of us all, help us to serve your majesty faithfully, and to spread the glory of your name by word and example. Through Christ our Lord. Amen.

(Our Father, Hail Mary, Glory be)

Queen of Apostles, pray for us.

Fifth Day

"His mother treasured all these things in her heart" (Lk 2:51).

The presentation of the Lord enlightens us to live in holiness, detachment from worldly things, and purity of thoughts and actions. The child Jesus enters the temple, takes possession of it and will live in the Eucharist until the end of time. Once we have known our vocation, we must follow it and live it faithfully until we are called to heaven.

Reflection and Resolution

Prayer: O God, you sent the Holy Spirit upon the apostles as they were united in prayer with Mary, the Mother of Jesus. May the Queen of Apostles, the same Mother of us all, help us to serve your majesty faithfully, and to spread the glory of your name by word and example. Through Christ our Lord. Amen.

(Our Father, Hail Mary, Glory be)

Queen of Apostles, pray for us.

Sixth Day

"Standing near the cross of Jesus were his mother, and his mother's sister, Mary the wife of Clopas, and Mary Magdalene" (Jn 19:25).

Let us look at Jesus—he sacrificed himself on the cross. Let us look at Mary—she shared Christ's mission and passion with him. The essence of the redemption is on Calvary—Jesus offers himself; Mary offers herself and her Son, whom she loves more than herself. Jesus is the Redeemer; Mary, the co-redemptrix.

Reflection and Resolution

Prayer: O God, you sent the Holy Spirit upon the apostles as they were united in prayer with Mary, the Mother of Jesus. May the Queen of Apostles, the same Mother of us all, help us to serve your majesty faithfully, and to spread the glory of your name by word and example. Through Christ our Lord. Amen.

(Our Father, Hail Mary, Glory be)

Queen of Apostles, pray for us.

Seventh Day

"When Jesus saw his mother and the disciple whom he loved standing beside her, he said to his mother, 'Woman, here is your son.' Then he said to the disciple, 'Here is your mother'" (Jn 19:26-27).

When human perversity had reached its height and had brought about the death of our Lord; when the Shepherd was smitten and the entire flock of apostles and faithful were dispersed, Jesus Christ offered hope, salvation, his Mother: "Here is your mother" (Jn 19:26).

Reflection and Resolution

Prayer: O God, you sent the Holy Spirit upon the apostles as they were united in prayer with Mary, the Mother of Jesus. May the Queen of Apostles, the same Mother of us all, help us to serve your majesty faithfully, and to spread the glory of your name by word and example. Through Christ our Lord. Amen.

(Our Father, Hail Mary, Glory be)

Queen of Apostles, pray for us.

Eighth Day

"All these were constantly devoting themselves to prayer, together with certain women, including Mary the mother of Jesus, as well as his brothers" (Acts 1:14).

It is clear that we have to consider and follow Mary as our model. She is the most holy Virgin, the co-redemptrix and the Queen of Apostles. She offered Jesus on Calvary, and together with the apostles she prayed in the cenacle to obtain the Holy Spirit.

She took care of the Church, newly born and already persecuted. As Mother of the Church, she became the outstanding member of the Mystical Body of Christ.

Reflection and Resolution

Prayer: O God, you sent the Holy Spirit upon the apostles as they were united in prayer with Mary, the Mother of Jesus. May the Queen of Apostles, the same Mother of us all, help us to serve your majesty faithfully, and to spread the glory of your name by word and example. Through Christ our Lord. Amen.

(Our Father, Hail Mary, Glory be)

Queen of Apostles, pray for us.

Ninth Day

"Mary Immaculate, the ever-virgin Mother of God, having finished the course of her earthly life, was assumed body and soul into heavenly glory" (Pius XII, November, 1950).

After the death of her Son, Jesus, Mary took care of the apostles, especially St. John, the youngest. She accompanied them with her prayers, good example and maternal comfort. Thus, Jesus willed that Mary be with them during their first years of evangelization, as she had accompanied him. After her earthly pilgrimage, her mission fulfilled, she was assumed into heaven. Let us think about the last day of the world. All the elect will gloriously enter heaven, body and soul; thus they will have an eternal reward.

Reflection and Resolution

Prayer: O God, you sent the Holy Spirit upon the apostles as they were united in prayer with Mary, the Mother of Jesus. May the Queen of Apostles, the same Mother of us all, help us to serve your majesty faithfully, and to spread the glory of your name by word and example. Through Christ our Lord. Amen.

(Our Father, Hail Mary, Glory be)

Queen of Apostles, pray for us.

Chaplet to Mary, Queen of Apostles

1. Most amiable Queen of heaven and of earth, favored Daughter of the Father, sublime Mother of the divine Son, illustrious Spouse of the Holy Spirit, I venerate and praise that privilege, unique in the world, whereby—pleasing God in your humility and faith, and preserving your spotless virginity—you became the great Mother of the divine Savior, our Master, true light of the world, uncreated Wisdom, source of all truth and first apostle of truth. You gave the world the book to read: the Eternal Word. For the indescribable joy you felt and for that privilege so sublime, I bless the Holy Trinity. I ask you to obtain for me the grace of heavenly wisdom, to be a humble and fervent disciple of Jesus, a devoted child of the Church, the pillar of truth. Make the light of the Gospel shine to the farthest bounds of the earth,

overcome errors, gather all people around the See of Peter. Enlighten theologians, preachers and writers, O Mother of Good Counsel, O Seat of Wisdom, O Queen of all saints.

Queen of Apostles, pray for us.

2. O Mary, Queen of all the angels, full of grace, conceived without sin, blessed among creatures, living tabernacle of God, remember that painful and solemn moment in which the dying Jesus from the cross gave you John as your son, and in him all humanity and especially all the apostles. What tender love flooded your heart at that moment for those consecrated to the apostolate, to the following of the cross, to the love of Jesus. For your indescribable sufferings and those of your divine Son, for your motherly heart, O Mary, increase the number of apostles, missionaries, priests and virgins. May they be resplendent for sanctity of life, integrity of morals, solid piety, the deepest humility, the most firm faith, the most ardent charity. May they all be holy, purifying salt of the earth and light of the world.

Queen of Apostles, pray for us.

3. O Virgin most pure, noble Queen of Martyrs, Morning Star, safe refuge of sinners, rejoice for the days in which you were teacher, comforter and Mother of the apostles in the cenacle, to invoke and

receive the divine Paraclete, the Spirit with the seven gifts, Love of the Father and of the Son, transformer of the apostles. By your all-powerful intercession and by your humble and irresistible prayers, which always move God's heart, obtain for me the grace to realize the value of every human person, for whom Jesus Christ shed his most precious blood. May each one of us be enthusiastic about the beauty of the Christian apostolate. May the charity of Christ urge us on. May the spiritual misery of poor humanity move us. Grant that we may feel in our hearts the needs of childhood, of adolescence, of adulthood, of old age. Grant that vast Africa, immense Asia, promising Oceania, troubled Europe, the two Americas may exercise a powerful attraction on our souls. Grant that the apostolate of example and word, of prayer and the press, of films, radio and television, of the souls in purgatory, may conquer many generous persons, even to the point of the most heroic sacrifices. O Mother of the Church, O Queen of Apostles, our Advocate, to you we sigh, mourning in this valley of tears.

Queen of Apostles, pray for us.

4. O our tender Mother Mary, gate of heaven, source of peace and happiness, help of Christians, trust of the dying and hope even of the desperate, I

recall the blessed moment for you in which you left the earth to fly to the blessed embrace of Jesus. It was the omnipotent favor of God which assumed you into heaven, beautiful and immortal. I see you exalted above the angels and saints, confessors and virgins, apostles and martyrs, prophets and patriarchs, and even I, from the midst of my sins, dare to add the voice of an unworthy but repentant sinner to praise and bless you. O Mary, convert me once and for always. Give me a repentant life, that I may have a holy death and one day join my voice to that of the saints to praise you in heaven. I consecrate myself to you and through you to Jesus. With full awareness and here in the presence of all the heavenly court, I renew the promises made in holy Baptism. I renew the resolution, which I place in your heart, to fight my self-love and to combat unceasingly against my principal defect, which so often has cast me into sin. O Mary, gain for yourself the greatest glory: change a great sinner into a great saint, O refuge of sinners, O morning star, O comforter of the afflicted.

Queen of Apostles, pray for us.

5. O Mary, Star of the Sea, my gentle sovereign, our life and Queen of Peace, how great and how wonderful the day on which the Holy Trinity crowned you Queen of heaven and earth, dispenser

of all graces, our most lovable Mother—what a triumph for you! What happiness for the angels, for the saints, for the earth, for purgatory! I know, O Mary, that those who love you will be saved, and that those who love you greatly will be holy and will participate one day in your glory in heaven. I do not doubt your clemency nor your power; I fear my inconstancy in praying to you. Obtain for me perseverance. O Mary, be my salvation. I feel my passions, the devil, the world. O Mary, hold me close to you and to your Jesus! Do not permit me to fall; do not leave me even for an instant, O Mother. It is consoling to cast the first glance upon you in the morning, to walk under your mantle during the day, to fall asleep under your gaze at night. You have smiles for innocent children, strength for struggling youth, light for working men and women, comfort for old age awaiting heaven. O Mary, to you I consecrate my entire life; pray for me now and in the final battle at the hour of my death. Receive my soul when it breathes its last, and do not leave me until I kneel before your throne in heaven, to love you for all eternity. O Mary, my Queen, my advocate, my sweetness, obtain for me holy perseverance.

Queen of Apostles, pray for us.

Prayers to Our Lady of Fatima

In 1917, the Blessed Mother appeared to three shepherd children—Lucy, Jacinta and Francis—to bring a message from her divine Son. She warned the world of present and future evils and requested prayer and penance in reparation for sin. Our Lady also asked that devotion to her Immaculate Heart be spread throughout the world. She also specifically asked for the recitation of the rosary for the intention of peace in the world.

Our Lady of Fatima made known the following great promise to Lucy: "Tell all people that I promise to help them at the hour of death with the graces necessary for salvation, if, on the first Saturday of each month for five consecutive months they will go to confession, receive holy Communion, say five decades of the Rosary and keep me company for fifteen minutes, meditating the mysteries of the Rosary with the intention of making reparation to me."

Here are the specific acts requested by Mary to attain this great promise:

1) *Confession,* which must be well done. It is enough to receive Reconciliation within eight days of the First Saturday.

2) *Holy Communion,* received with the best possible dispositions.

3) *A third part of the Rosary,* reciting the mysteries of our own choice: joyful, sorrowful or glorious. The recitation of the Rosary should be accompanied by meditation on the mysteries, for at least fifteen minutes.

4) *Five consecutive months,* without interruption, even involuntary, are needed for the above practices. The five First Saturdays may start on any month.

5) *These five First Saturdays* must be offered to console the heart of Mary saddened by the indifference and ingratitude of so many people.

The feast of Our Lady of Fatima is celebrated on May 13.

The Reward for Those Who Make Known the Great Promise of Mary

The Blessed Virgin revealed to Sister Lucy that all persons practicing the Five First Saturdays of consecutive months will be placed by our Lady as flowers before the throne of the almighty Lord. If so great is the reward of those who practice this devotion, what consolation, what joy and glory will those persons experience who spread this devotion in their parish? Many persons will one day be grateful to you for your efforts to introduce them to the Five First Saturdays devotion.

Remember that if your zeal will help in establishing this devotion, you will have put in many hands the golden key that will open the gates of heaven.

In this sad and tragic hour, when humanity is more and more plunging itself into evil, the holy Virgin is longing for those who will understand the desire of her Immaculate Heart, and will work with zeal for the spread of this most efficacious devotion.

Act of Reparation for the First Saturday of the Month

Most holy Virgin and our beloved Mother, we listen with grief to the complaints of your Immaculate Heart surrounded with the thorns which ungrateful people place therein at every moment by their blasphemies and ingratitude. Moved by the ardent desire of loving you as our Mother and of promoting a true devotion to the Immaculate Heart, we come before you to express the sorrow we feel for the grievances that people cause you. We want to atone, by means of our prayers and sacrifices, for the offenses with which many return your tender love.

Obtain for them and for us the pardon of so many sins. A word from you will obtain grace and amendment for us all.

Hasten, O Mary, the conversion of sinners, that they may love Jesus and cease to offend the Lord, already so much offended, and thus not fall into hell.

Turn your eyes of mercy toward us, that henceforth we may love God with all our heart while on earth and enjoy him forever in heaven. Amen.

Prayers of the Angel

The following prayers were taught to the children of Fatima by the angel who appeared to them.

My God, I believe, I adore, I hope and I love you. Pardon those who do not believe, do not adore, do not hope in and do not love you.

Most Holy Trinity, Father, Son and Holy Spirit, I humbly adore you. I offer you the most precious body, blood, soul and divinity of our Lord Jesus Christ present in all the tabernacles of the world, in reparation for the outrages with which he himself is offended. Through the infinite merits of his most Sacred Heart and the intercession of the Immaculate Heart of Mary, obtain the conversion of sinners. Amen.

Prayer Taught by the Blessed Virgin

The Blessed Mother taught the children of Fatima to say this prayer.

O my Jesus, forgive us our sins; save us from the fires of hell. Lead all souls to heaven, especially those most in need of your mercy.

O Jesus, this is for your love, for the conversion of sinners, in reparation for the sins committed against the Immaculate Heart of Mary and for the Holy Father.

Novena to Our Lady of Fatima

Most holy Virgin, who came to Fatima to reveal to the three shepherd children the treasures of graces hidden in the recitation of the Rosary, inspire our hearts with a sincere love of this devotion, so that by meditating on the mysteries of our redemption that are recalled in it, we may gather their fruits and obtain the conversion of sinners, the conversion of Russia, and *(here name the other favors you are praying for),* which we ask of you in this novena, for the greater glory of God, for your own honor, and for the good of people. Amen.

(Our Father, Hail Mary, Glory be)

Our Lady of the Rosary of Fatima, pray for us!

How to Say the Rosary

The complete rosary consists of fifteen decades, traditionally divided into three distinct parts, each containing five decades: the joyful mysteries, which are ordinarily recited on Mondays and Thursdays; the sorrowful mysteries, which are said on Tuesdays and Fridays; the glorious mysteries, usually recited on Wednesdays, Saturdays and Sundays.

To pray the rosary as the blend of contemplative and vocal prayer that it is meant to be, and to gain the indulgences attached to the rosary, we must meditate on the individual mysteries during the recitation of the decades. Prayed in this way, the rosary will bring us closer to Jesus and Mary, help us to love them more and give us the desire to imitate them.

We begin the rosary by blessing ourselves with the crucifix. Then we may recite the Apostles' Creed, one Our Father, three Hail Marys and one Glory to the Father on the small chain. Then pray one Our Father, ten Hail Marys and one Glory to the Father. This completes one decade, and all the other decades are recited in the same manner with a different mystery meditated during each decade. At the end of the rosary, the Hail Holy Queen and the Litany of the Blessed Virgin may be recited.

The Sign of the Cross

In the name of the Father, and of the Son, and of the Holy Spirit. Amen.

Apostles' Creed

I believe in God, the Father Almighty, Creator of heaven and earth; and in Jesus Christ, his only Son, our Lord; who was conceived by the Holy Spirit, born of the Virgin Mary, suffered under Pontius Pilate, was crucified, died and was buried. He descended into hell; the third day he arose again from the dead; he ascended into heaven, sits at the right hand of God, the Father Almighty; from thence he shall come to judge the living and the dead. I believe in the Holy Spirit, the Holy Catholic Church, the communion of saints, the forgiveness of sins, the resurrection of the body, and life everlasting. Amen.

The Lord's Prayer

Our Father, who art in heaven, hallowed be thy name; thy kingdom come; thy will be done on earth as it is in heaven. Give us this day our daily bread; and forgive us our trespasses as we forgive those who trespass against us; and lead us not into temptation, but deliver us from evil. Amen.

Hail Mary

Hail Mary, full of grace! The Lord is with you; blessed are you among women, and blessed is the fruit of your womb, Jesus. Holy Mary, Mother of God, pray for us sinners, now and at the hour of our death. Amen.

Glory to the Father

Glory to the Father, and to the Son, and to the Holy Spirit, as it was in the beginning, is now and will be forever. Amen.

Hail, Holy Queen

Hail, holy Queen, Mother of mercy, our life, our sweetness, and our hope! To you we cry, poor banished children of Eve; to you we send up our sighs, mourning and weeping in this valley of tears. Turn then, most gracious advocate, your eyes of mercy toward us, and after this our exile, show unto us the blessed fruit of your womb, Jesus. O clement, O loving, O sweet Virgin Mary.

The Joyful Mysteries

First Joyful Mystery
The Annunciation to the Blessed Virgin

Consideration: The archangel Gabriel announces to the holy Virgin the incarnation of our Lord Jesus Christ and her elevation to Mother of God. Mary accepts, declaring herself to be the handmaid of the Lord. Let us imitate her and ask the virtue of humility.

Intention: For non-believers

Let us ask that the light of the Gospel may soon reach all people. We pray for non-believers, for non-Catholics, for all those who waver in their faith. For ourselves we ask the faith of the saints.

One Our Father, ten Hail Marys, one Glory to the Father

O my Jesus, forgive us our sins, save us from the fires of hell. Lead all souls to heaven, especially those most in need of your mercy.

Second Joyful Mystery
The Visitation of the Blessed Virgin to St. Elizabeth

Consideration: Mary hastens with concern to visit and serve St. Elizabeth. Let us ask for Mary's love toward our neighbor.

Intention: For mothers

Let us pray for the sanctity of Christian families. We pray that mothers may be holy, may imitate our Blessed Mother in her virtues, and give their children a good Christian education.

One Our Father, ten Hail Marys, one Glory to the Father

O my Jesus, forgive us our sins, save us from the fires of hell. Lead all souls to heaven, especially those most in need of your mercy.

Third Joyful Mystery
The Nativity of Jesus at Bethlehem

Consideration: Born in a stable in Bethlehem, Jesus is placed in a manger in the most squalid poverty. Kneeling before the crib, let us praise the virtue of poverty and ask it of Jesus and Mary.

Intention: For children.

Let us pray to Jesus that all children may receive the gift of Baptism and remain innocent and close to him. Let us recommend to him all the children who are deprived of the loving care of their parents.

One Our Father, ten Hail Marys, one Glory to the Father

O my Jesus, forgive us our sins, save us from the fires of hell. Lead all souls to heaven, especially those most in need of your mercy.

Fourth Joyful Mystery
The Presentation of Jesus in the Temple

Consideration: Although not bound by duty, Mary presents Jesus in the temple and perfectly fulfills what was prescribed for her purification. Let us consider and ask for the obedience of the Blessed Virgin.

Intention: For priests

Let us pray that priests may be holy, the true salt that keeps the world from corruption and sin; that they may all be fervent, conformable to the heart of Jesus, full of wisdom and the Holy Spirit.

One Our Father, ten Hail Marys, one Glory to the Father

O my Jesus, forgive us our sins, save us from the fires of hell. Lead all souls to heaven, especially those most in need of your mercy.

Fifth Joyful Mystery
The Finding of the Child Jesus in the Temple

Consideration: Jesus is lost, diligently sought for three days and found in the temple. We lose Jesus by committing sin. Let us ask the grace to avoid and detest sin.

Intention: For teachers

Let us pray for all those who teach and especially for those who teach religion, that they may instill sound doctrine in their students.

One Our Father, ten Hail Marys, one Glory to the Father

O my Jesus, forgive us our sins, save us from the fires of hell. Lead all souls to heaven, especially those most in need of your mercy.

Sorrowful Mysteries

First Sorrowful Mystery
The Agony in the Garden

Consideration: In the Garden of Gethsemane, Jesus sweats blood and prays with humility, confidence and perseverance. The angel comforts him. Let us ask for the spirit of prayer.

Intention: For those who are tempted

Let us ask light and comfort for all those who are groaning under the weight of their trials and beg for them the grace to know how to draw strength from prayer as Jesus did.

One Our Father, ten Hail Marys, one Glory to the Father

O my Jesus, forgive us our sins, save us from the fires of hell. Lead all souls to heaven, especially those most in need of your mercy.

Second Sorrowful Mystery
The Scourging of Jesus at the Pillar

Consideration: Jesus is tied to the pillar and cruelly scourged in reparation for sins of impurity. Let us ask for the virtue of chastity.

Intention: For those who are obstinate in sin

Let us recommend to Jesus those who are in danger of falling into sin, and those who have already fallen. Let us pray that the spread of errors through the evil use of the media of social communications may cease, and that these media may be used at the service of truth.

One Our Father, ten Hail Marys, one Glory to the Father

O my Jesus, forgive us our sins, save us from the fires of hell. Lead all souls to heaven, especially those most in need of your mercy.

Third Sorrowful Mystery
The Crowning of Jesus with Thorns

Consideration: Jesus is crowned with thorns and mocked in reparation for our evil thoughts and sentiments. Let us ask for purity of mind and heart.

Intention: For those who govern

St. Paul says: "First of all, then, I urge that supplications, prayers, intercessions, and thanksgivings be made for everyone, for kings and all who are in high positions, so that we may lead a quiet and peaceable life in all godliness and dignity" (1 Tim 2:1-2). Let us pray that all civil leaders will govern their nations with justice.

One Our Father, ten Hail Marys, one Glory to the Father

O my Jesus, forgive us our sins, save us from the fires of hell. Lead all souls to heaven, especially those most in need of your mercy.

Fourth Sorrowful Mystery
Jesus Carries His Cross to Calvary

Consideration: Condemned to death, Jesus carries the heavy cross to Calvary. Let us admire our Savior's patience and ask for patience to bear our crosses.

Intention: For those who suffer

Let us ask for a generous heart that will embrace the needs of all people, and that will be moved by their sufferings to try and alleviate them.

One Our Father, ten Hail Marys, one Glory to the Father

O my Jesus, forgive us our sins, save us from the fires of hell. Lead all souls to heaven, especially those most in need of your mercy.

Fifth Sorrowful Mystery
The Crucifixion

Consideration: Jesus is crucified, suffers for three hours and dies for our salvation. Let us ask for devotion to the holy Mass, which renews Jesus' sacrifice on the cross.

Intention: For the dying

How many at this moment are suffering the pains of their last agony and are at the point of presenting themselves before the tribunal of God to give an account of their life. Let us recommend them to God with all our heart and pray that God may grant them the grace of a happy death.

One Our Father, ten Hail Marys, one Glory to the Father

O my Jesus, forgive us our sins, save us from the fires of hell. Lead all souls to heaven, especially those most in need of your mercy.

Glorious Mysteries

First Glorious Mystery
The Resurrection of Jesus

Consideration: Our Lord Jesus Christ rises gloriously from the sepulcher. This resurrection represents our personal resurrection from our sins and defects. Let us ask this of the Blessed Virgin.

Intention: For those who do not believe in Christ

"The number of those who do not know Christ and do not belong to the Church is constantly on the increase.... When we consider this immense portion of humanity which is loved by the Father and for whom he sent his Son, the urgency of the Church's mission is obvious" (Pope John Paul II).

Let us assist and pray for the work of missionaries the world over.

One Our Father, ten Hail Marys, one Glory to the Father

O my Jesus, forgive us our sins, save us from the fires of hell. Lead all souls to heaven, especially those most in need of your mercy.

Second Glorious Mystery
The Ascension of Our Lord into Heaven

Consideration: Forty days after his death, Jesus ascends into heaven with wonderful glory and triumph. Let us ask for detachment from the honors and pleasures of this world and to desire heavenly joys, glory and goods alone.

Intention: For religious

Let us pray for all religious so that they may be true salt of the earth and may be formed according to the heart of Jesus.

One Our Father, ten Hail Marys, one Glory to the Father

O my Jesus, forgive us our sins, save us from the fires of hell. Lead all souls to heaven, especially those most in need of your mercy.

Third Glorious Mystery
The Descent of the Holy Spirit upon the Apostles

Consideration: The Holy Spirit descends upon the apostles to enlighten, comfort and sanctify them. Let us ask for the gifts of the Holy Spirit, especially heavenly wisdom, fortitude and zeal.

Intention: For the Church

Let us pray for the sanctification of the whole people of God and for the mission of the Church.

One Our Father, ten Hail Marys, one Glory to the Father

O my Jesus, forgive us our sins, save us from the fires of hell. Lead all souls to heaven, especially those most in need of your mercy.

Fourth Glorious Mystery
The Assumption of the Blessed Virgin into Heaven

Consideration: The most holy Virgin Mary is taken into heaven with admirable glory at the end of her earthly life. Let us ask for a holy life and the grace to die in the love of God.

Intention: For the dead

Let us pray for all the holy souls in purgatory, who are undergoing purification and need the help of our prayers.

One Our Father, ten Hail Marys, one Glory to the Father

O my Jesus, forgive us our sins, save us from the fires of hell. Lead all souls to heaven, especially those most in need of your mercy.

Fifth Glorious Mystery
The Coronation of the Blessed Virgin Mary

Consideration: Mary is crowned Queen of heaven and earth, dispenser of all graces, our most powerful and loving Mother. Let us promise to be devoted to the most holy Virgin and ask for the gift of perseverance in the Faith until death.

Intention: For the apostolate of the media

To the one who is the Mother, Teacher and Queen of the apostles, let us recommend that the apostolate of the Catholic social communications media may spread throughout the world.

One Our Father, ten Hail Marys, one Glory to the Father

O my Jesus, forgive us our sins, save us from the fires of hell. Lead all souls to heaven, especially those most in need of your mercy.

Hail, Holy Queen

Hail, holy Queen, Mother of mercy, our life, our sweetness and our hope, to you do we cry, poor banished children of Eve. To you do we send up our sighs, mourning and weeping in this valley of tears. Turn then, most gracious advocate, your eyes of mercy toward us, and after this our exile, show unto us the blessed fruit of your womb, Jesus. O clement, O loving, O sweet Virgin Mary.

The Litany of the Blessed Virgin

Lord, have mercy on us.
Christ, have mercy on us.
Lord, have mercy on us.
Christ, hear us.
Christ, graciously hear us.
God the Father of heaven, have mercy on us.
God the Son, Redeemer of the world, have mercy
    on us.
Holy Trinity, one God, have mercy on us.
Holy Mary, pray for us.
Holy Mother of God,*
Holy Virgin of virgins,
Mother of Christ,

---

* *pray for us.*

151

Mother of the Church,
Mother of divine grace,
Mother most pure,
Mother most chaste,
Mother inviolate,
Mother undefiled,
Mother most amiable,
Mother most admirable,
Mother of good counsel,
Mother of our Creator,
Mother of our Redeemer,
Virgin most prudent,
Virgin most venerable,
Virgin most renowned,
Virgin most merciful,
Virgin most faithful,
Mirror of justice,
Seat of wisdom,
Cause of our joy,
Vessel of honor,
Singular vessel of devotion,
Mystical rose,
Tower of David,
Tower of ivory,
House of gold,
Ark of the covenant,
Gate of heaven,

Morning star,

Health of the sick,

Refuge of sinners,

Comforter of the afflicted,

Help of Christians,

Queen of angels,

Queen of patriarchs,

Queen of prophets,

Queen of apostles,

Queen of martyrs,

Queen of confessors,

Queen of virgins,

Queen of all saints,

Queen conceived without original sin,

Queen assumed into heaven,

Queen of the most holy rosary,

Queen of families,

Queen of peace,

Lamb of God, you take away the sins of the world,
spare us, O Lord.

Lamb of God, you take away the sins of the world,
graciously hear us, O Lord.

Lamb of God, you take away the sins of the world,
have mercy on us.

R. Pray for us, O holy Mother of God.

V. That we may be made worthy of the promises
of Christ.

Let us pray. O God, whose only-begotten Son by his life, death and resurrection, has purchased for us the rewards of eternal salvation, grant, we pray, that meditating upon these mysteries in the most holy rosary of the Blessed Virgin Mary, we may imitate what they contain and obtain what they promise. Through Christ our Lord. Amen.

Prayers to St. Michael the Archangel

Patron of France and Helper
in Times of Temptation

"And war broke out in heaven; Michael and his angels fought against the dragon. The dragon and his angels fought back, but they were defeated, and there was no longer any place for them in heaven. The great dragon was thrown down, that ancient serpent, who is called the Devil and Satan, the deceiver of the whole world—he was thrown down to the earth, and his angels were thrown down with him" (Rev 12:7-9).

This Scripture passage is the basis for devotion to the archangel Michael. In speaking of the fall of the angels, the *Catechism of the Catholic Church* states: "We find a reflection of that rebellion in the tempter's words to our first parents: 'You will be like God'" (n. 392). Michael, instead, chose to worship and adore God alone. The very name *Mi-cha-el* means "Who is like God?"

Michael is invoked as a special protector against the power of Satan. Foreseeing something of the evil that would occur in the 20th century, Pope Leo XIII decreed that the prayer to St. Michael be recited by all the faithful at the end of the Mass. Although this public practice has been discontinued, we can still pray privately that St. Michael will crush the head of Satan. Michael's feast is celebrated on September 29.

Prayer to St. Michael the Archangel
(Promulgated by Pope Leo XIII)

St. Michael, the archangel, defend us in the battle. Be our defense against the wickedness and snares of the evil. May God rebuke him, we humbly pray. O prince of the heavenly host, by the power of God cast into hell Satan and the other evil spirits who roam through the world seeking the ruin of souls. Amen.

Glorious St. Michael, prince of the heavenly hosts, you are ever ready to assist the people of God. You fought with the dragon, the ancient serpent, and cast him out of heaven. Now you valiantly defend the Church of God so the gates of hell may never prevail against her. I earnestly entreat you to assist me also in the painful and dangerous conflict I must sustain against the devil. Be with me, O mighty prince, that I may courageously fight and wholly vanquish that proud spirit, whom you, by the divine power, have overthrown, and whom our powerful king, Jesus Christ, so completely overcame. Then, triumphing over the enemy of my salvation, I may, with you and the holy angels, praise the mercy of God, who has granted repentance and forgiveness to fallen humanity.

Prayer for Perseverance

O God, you made blessed Michael, your archangel, victorious over proud Lucifer and all the evil spirits. I beseech you that, combating under the cross and ever adopting his maxim, "Who is like unto God," I may be victorious over all obstacles, and be delivered from all evils. Regulate my life according to your will and commandments. Through Jesus Christ, our Lord. Amen.

For Assistance at the Hour of Death

Glorious archangel St. Michael, by your protection, enable my soul to be so enriched by grace as to be worthy to be presented by you to Jesus Christ, my judge, at the hour of my death. As you conquered Satan and expelled him from heaven, conquer him again, and drive him far away from me at the hour of my death.

O Mary, Queen of heaven, obtain for me the assistance of St. Michael at the hour of my death!

For the Reign of the Sacred Heart

O Mary Immaculate, great Queen of heaven and earth and our gentle advocate, we beg you to intercede for us. Pray God to send St. Michael and the holy angels to ward off all the obstacles contrary to the reign of the Sacred Heart in ourselves, our families, our country and in the whole world.

And you, O holy Michael, prince of the heavenly hosts, from our hearts we beg you to come to our aid. Defend us against Satan. Through the divine power bestowed on you by God, after securing victory for the Church here below, guide us to our eternal home. Amen.

St. Michael, first champion of the kingship of Christ, pray for us!

Novena to St. Michael

Prayer to St. Michael

Glorious prince of the heavenly hosts and victor over rebellious spirits, be mindful of me who am so weak and sinful and yet so prone to pride and ambition. Give me, I pray, your powerful aid in every temptation and difficulty, and above all do not forsake me in my last struggle with the powers of evil. Amen.

The Angelic Trisagion

Holy, Holy, Holy, Lord God of hosts, heaven and earth are full of your glory.

St. Michael, the archangel, defend us in the battle, that we may not perish in the dreadful judgment.

Prayer for Protection of the Church and Her Members

O glorious St. Michael, guardian and defender of the Church of Jesus Christ, come to the assistance of this Church, against which the powers of hell are unchained. Guard the Pope with special care, and obtain the graces he desires for the Church. O glorious archangel St. Michael, watch over us during life; defend us against the assaults of the demon; assist us especially at the hour of death. Obtain for us a favorable judgment and the happiness of beholding God face to face for endless ages. Amen.

Angelical Crown or Chaplet

Before or after each salutation, one our Father and three Hail Marys are prayed.

V. O God, come to my assistance.

R. O Lord, make haste to help me.

Glory be to the Father, etc.

First Salutation. At the intercession of St. Michael and the heavenly choir of seraphim, may it please God to make us worthy to receive into our hearts the fire of his perfect charity. Amen.

Second Salutation. At the intercession of St. Michael and the heavenly choir of the cherubim, may God grant us grace to abandon the ways of sin and follow the path of Christian perfection. Amen.

Third Salutation. At the intercession of St. Michael and the heavenly choir of the thrones, may it please God to infuse into our hearts a true and earnest spirit of humility. Amen.

Fourth Salutation. At the intercession of St. Michael and the heavenly choir of the dominations, may it please God to grant us the grace to have dominion over our senses, and to properly regulate our passions. Amen.

Fifth Salutation. At the intercession of St. Michael and the heavenly choir of the powers, may God keep our souls from the wiles and temptations of the devil. Amen.

Sixth Salutation. At the intercession of St. Michael and the choir of the admirable celestial virtues, may our Lord keep us from falling into temptations and deliver us from evil. Amen.

Seventh Salutation. At the intercession of St. Michael and the heavenly choir of the principalities, may it please God to fill our hearts with the spirit of true and loving obedience. Amen.

Eighth Salutation. At the intercession of St. Michael and the heavenly choir of archangels, may it please God to grant us the gift of perseverance in the Faith and in all good works, that we may thereby be enabled to attain unto the glory of paradise. Amen.

Ninth Salutation. At the intercession of St. Michael and the heavenly choir of holy angels, may God grant that they may protect us during life, and after death may lead us into the everlasting glory of heaven. Amen.

Then say the Our Father four times in conclusion: the first in honor of St. Michael, the second in honor of St. Gabriel, the third in honor of St. Raphael, and the fourth in honor of your guardian angel. End as follows:

St. Michael, glorious prince, chief and champion of the heavenly host, guardian of the human race, conqueror of the rebellious angels, steward of the palace of God under Jesus Christ, our worthy leader, endowed with superhuman excellence and virtue, with full confidence we have recourse to you. Free us from every ill. By your incomparable protection enable us to make progress every day in the faithful service of our God. Amen.

V. Pray for us, most blessed Michael, prince of the Church of Jesus Christ.

R. That we may be made worthy of his promises.

Let us pray. Almighty and eternal God, in your goodness and compassion for the salvation of the human race, you chose the glorious archangel Michael to be the prince of your Church. Make us worthy, we beg you, to be delivered by his protection from all our spiritual foes so that at the hour of our death none of them may approach to harm us. Rather, grant that by the same archangel Michael we may come into the presence of your most high and divine majesty. Through the merits of the same Jesus Christ our Lord. Amen.

Litany of St. Michael

(For private use)

Lord, have mercy on us.

Christ, have mercy on us.

Lord, have mercy on us.

Christ, hear us.

Christ, graciously hear us.

God the Father of heaven, have mercy on us.

God the Son, Redeemer of the world, have mercy on us.

God the Holy Spirit, have mercy on us.

Holy Trinity, one God, have mercy on us.

Holy Mary, Queen of Angels, pray for us

St. Michael,*

St. Michael, filled with the wisdom of God,

St. Michael, perfect adorer of the Incarnate Word,

St. Michael, crowned with honor and glory,

St. Michael, most powerful prince of the armies of the Lord,

St. Michael, standard-bearer of the Most Holy Trinity,

St. Michael, guardian of paradise,

St. Michael, guide and comforter of the people of Israel,

St. Michael, splendor and fortress of the Church on earth,

St. Michael, honor and joy of the Church in heaven,

St. Michael, light of angels,

St. Michael, bulwark of orthodox believers,

St. Michael, strength of those who fight under the standard of the cross,

St. Michael, light and confidence of souls at the hour of death,

St. Michael, our most sure aid,

St. Michael, our help in all adversities,

St. Michael, our help in the hour of death,

---

pray for us.

163

St. Michael, consoler of souls being purified in
    purgatory,

St. Michael, whom the Lord has charged to receive
    souls after death,

St. Michael, our prince,

St. Michael, our advocate,

Lamb of God, you take away the sins of the world,
    spare us, O Lord.

Lamb of God, you take away the sins of the world,
    graciously hear us, O Lord.

Lamb of God, you take away the sins of the world,
    have mercy on us.

Christ, hear us.

Christ, graciously hear us.

    V. Pray for us, O glorious St. Michael, prince of
the Church of Jesus Christ.

    R. That we may be made worthy of his promises.

    Let us pray. Sanctify us, we beseech you, O
Lord Jesus, with your holy blessing, and grant us, by
the intercession of St. Michael, that wisdom which
teaches us to store treasures in heaven by exchanging the goods of this world for those of eternity, you
who live and reign world without end. Amen.

Prayer for the Church and for the Human Race

Recommended for frequent recitation in the present critical times

O glorious prince of the heavenly host, St. Michael the archangel, defend us in the battle and in the fearful warfare we are waging against the principalities and powers, against the rulers of this world of darkness, against the evil spirits. Come to the assistance of all people, whom Almighty God created immortal, making them in his own image and likeness and redeeming them at a great price from the tyranny of Satan. Fight this day the battle of the Lord with your legions of holy angels, even as of old you fought against Lucifer, the leader of the proud spirits and all his rebel angels, who were powerless to stand against you. Neither was their place found anymore in heaven. And that apostate angel, transformed into an angel of darkness who still creeps about the earth seeking our ruin, was cast headlong into the abyss together with his followers. But that first enemy of the human race, who was a murderer from the beginning, has regained his confidence. Changing himself into an angel of light, he goes about with the whole multitude of wicked spirits to invade the earth and blot out the name of God and of his Christ, to plunder, to slay and to try to lure into hell those whom God desires to have everlasting life. This evil spirit tries to corrupt persons with the poison of his malice, the spirit of lying, godlessness and blasphemy, and the deadly breath of impurity and every form of vice and iniquity. The evil spirits also desire to corrupt the Church with sin and a lukewarm spirit. O invincible prince, hasten to help the people of God against the inroads of the lost spirits and grant us victory. Amen.

Prayers to St. Raphael the Archangel

Patron of Travelers and Bearers of the Good News

The archangel Raphael is mentioned in the Old Testament book of Tobit. He appears as an important character who brings healing and help to his human charges. Raphael also appears in a non-Scriptural Jewish writing, the book of Enoch, where he also heals human ills. Thus, devotion to Raphael has deep roots in tradition.

Raphael is considered the angel of joy, the angel of healing, the patron of travelers and bearers of the Good News. His feast is celebrated on September 29, along with Michael and Gabriel.

Prayer to St. Raphael

St. Raphael, archangel, you protected young Tobiah as he journeyed to a distant land. Protect all travelers and most especially those who go about near and far preaching the Gospel. Guide and inspire modern apostles who use the communications media to bring the Good News of Christ to many people.

You also brought healing and joy to all you met. Help those who bring the Word of God to others, that they may be as instruments in God's hands to draw many to lives of Christian holiness.

We ask this through Christ our Lord. Amen.

Prayer to St. Raphael
for the Choice of a Good Spouse

St. Raphael, you were sent by God to guide young Tobiah in choosing a good and virtuous spouse. Please help me in this important choice which will affect my whole future. You not only directed Tobiah in finding a wife, but you also gave him guidelines which should be foremost in every Christian marriage, telling him to pray together with his wife to ask God's blessings. If through prayer we keep God as the "third partner" in our marriage, we will have the strength and grace we need to always accept and do his will.

(Our Father, Hail Mary, Glory be)

Short Novena to St. Raphael

Antiphon: O St. Raphael, bearer of holy joy and messenger of peace, intercede for us before God's holy throne.

V. You who are one of the seven before the throne of God.

R. Be our model and inspiration in purity.

Prayer: O God, you brought joy of spirit and health in mind and body into the lives of Tobit, Sarah and Tobiah by means of your holy angel, Raphael. Grant, we beg you, the grace we ask through St. Raphael's intercession. Amen.

(Our Father, Hail Mary, Glory be)

Prayers to the Guardian Angels

"The whole life of the Church benefits from the mysterious and powerful help of angels.... From infancy to death human life is surrounded by their watchful care and intercession. 'Beside each believer stands an angel as protector and shepherd leading him to life.' Already here on earth the Christian life shares by faith in the blessed company of angels and men united in God" (*Catechism of the Catholic Church,* nn. 334, 336).

1. Heavenly Father, I thank your infinite goodness for having entrusted me from the moment my soul came forth from your creative hands to an angel to "light and guard, rule and guide" me. I also thank you, my guardian angel, for accompanying me daily on my return journey to my heavenly Father. Your holy inspirations, your continual protection against spiritual and material dangers, and your powerful prayers to God give me great comfort and sure hope.

Angel of God, my guardian dear, to whom God's love entrusts me here, ever this day be at my side, to enlighten and guard, to rule and guide me. Amen.

2. My guardian angel, you contemplate the Lord at all times and you want me as your fellow citizen in heaven. I beseech you to obtain for me pardon from the Lord because I have so often been deaf to your advice, have sinned in your presence, and recall so seldom that you are always near me.

Angel of God...

3. My guardian angel, faithful and strong in virtue, you are one of the angels led by St. Michael who overcame Satan and his followers. That battle which one day took place in heaven now continues on earth: the prince of evil and his followers oppose Jesus Christ, and try to ensnare souls. Pray to the Immaculate Queen of the Apostles for the Church, the city of God which fights against the city of Satan. St. Michael the archangel, together with your followers defend us in the battle; be our protection against the malice and snares of the devil. May the Lord subdue him! And you, prince of the heavenly host, thrust back into hell Satan and the other evil spirits who roam through the world seeking the ruin of souls.

Angel of God...

4. Angels of heaven, watch over those who write, produce and distribute audiovisual media and all those who use them. Defend them from evil,

guide them in the truth, and obtain for them true charity. For the apostolate of the audiovisual media, ask of God the necessary vocations and be with them in their delicate mission. Inspire everyone to contribute to the apostolate of social communications media with deeds, prayer and offerings. Enlighten and guide the world of audiovisual media, that it may serve to uplift the level of this present life and direct all peoples toward eternal goods.

Angel of God...

5. All you angels of the Lord, you are called to pay noble homage, give praise and incessantly bless the Holy Trinity, to make reparation for our negligence. You are true lovers of God and of humanity, and you continue to sing "Glory to God in the highest and peace on earth to those of good will." We ask you on behalf of humanity that all may know the one true God, his Son whom he sent, and the Church, the pillar of truth. Pray that the name of God may be held sacred, the kingdom of Jesus Christ may come, and his will be done on earth as it is in heaven. Extend your protection over civil authorities, working people and those who suffer. Obtain blessings and salvation for all those who seek truth, justice and peace.

Angel of God...

Prayers to St. Anthony
(1195-1231)

Patron of the Poor and
of Finding Lost Articles

Anthony was born in Lisbon, Portugal, and baptized Fernando. As a teenager he wanted to become a priest and joined the Augustinians. Not long after, he met a group of five Franciscan friars who were on their way to Morocco to preach to the Moslems. They stirred his interest in their new order, and when those friars were later martyred, Fernando felt a great desire to imitate them. So he transferred to the Franciscans and was ordained soon after.

Changing his name to Anthony, he quickly became famous for his preaching ability. Anthony traveled throughout Italy and crowds flocked to hear his sermons. He had a gift for touching hearts through his preaching and as a result many people came to a conversion of life. Worn out by travel and fatigue, Anthony became ill and died at a young age. Many favors were reported through his intercession, and his fame grew even more after his death. His feastday is June 13.

Thirteen Tuesdays in Honor of St. Anthony

First Tuesday

Prayer for Every Day

Prostrate before your divine presence, O my God, I adore you with my whole heart. I am sorry for having offended you. I recognize my own sinfulness. Inflame my heart, O Lord, so that I may imitate the example of your faithful servant, St. Anthony, under whose patronage I place my soul and body. Amen.

Meditation: Pure intention

Those devoted to St. Anthony should ask favors of him only with a pure intention, because the great saint is not willing to listen to those whose aims are not directed to their own spiritual welfare. St. Anthony will be your protector only under this condition.

Are you a sinner? Cry out for help. The saint will aid you immediately. Ask his intercession and he will help you to break and destroy the chain of your sin.

Here make your request.

Prayer: O glorious St. Anthony, obtain from Jesus the grace that the darkness of error may disappear from the hearts of so many unfortunate sinners.

Do so in such a manner that the light of truth taught by the Catholic Church may always appear as a brilliant torch to them and to us. We hope through your intercession to enjoy God forever in your company.

Glory be... (5 times) and the Responsory

The Responsory of St. Anthony of Padua

If then you ask for a miracle,
Death, error, all calamities,
The leprosy and demons fly,
And health succeeds infirmities.

> The sea obeys and fetters break,
> And lifeless limbs you do restore;
> While treasures lost are found again
> When young or old your aid implore.

All dangers vanish at your prayer,
And direst need does quickly flee.
Let those who know your power proclaim,
Let Paduans say these are of you.

> The sea obeys, and fetters break,
> And lifeless limbs you do restore;
> While treasures lost are found again,
> When young or old your aid implore.

To Father, Son may glory be,
And Holy Spirit eternally.

The sea obeys and fetters break,
And lifeless limbs you do restore;
While treasures lost are found again,
When young or old your aid implore.

V. Pray for us, blessed Anthony.

R. That we may be made worthy of the promises of Christ.

Let us pray. O God, let the commemoration of blessed Anthony, your confessor, bring joy to your Church, that we may be fortified by spiritual assistance and may deserve to possess eternal joy, through Jesus Christ our Lord. Amen.

Second Tuesday

Prayer: Prostrate...

Meditation: Death

Everyone must die. Sooner or later we will pass from this world. We do not know when, but we may be sure that when death comes no one can escape. One day the thread of our life will be cut off forever. Do we know where death will find us? No. Will it come to us suddenly? After a long illness? Will we be prepared? Why not resolve now to prepare ourselves for it? Let us imitate the example of St. Anthony who dedicated himself to God as a youth to prepare himself for a happy death.

Here make your request.

Prayer: Glorious St. Anthony, obtain for us the grace to imitate your example in faithfully observing our duties according to our particular state of life.

Glory be... (5 times) and the Responsory

Third Tuesday

Prayer: Prostrate...

Meditation: Fight the devil

Since the creation of the first human beings, the devil has come to interfere with the great work of God. Temptation came for the angels. Many fell and were cast into hell, while the faithful ones were confirmed in grace.

The same thing happened to the human race. Our first parents did not resist temptation and they fell away. The devil has received from God a certain amount of freedom to tempt us, to spread error and heresy in the world so that through these evils we may prove our obedience to the Creator and merit heaven. Imitate the example of St. Anthony; fight against error, against passion. Let us pray for our own sanctification and that of our neighbor.

Here make your request.

Prayer: Glorious St. Anthony, destroy all heresy and schism in the world. Pray for us so that we may always sing the glory of God, and one day come to heaven to enjoy our eternal reward.

Glory be... (5 times) and the Responsory

Fourth Tuesday

Prayer: Prostrate...

Meditation: Work for eternal salvation

"A mortal, born of woman, few of days and full of trouble, comes up like a flower and withers, flees like a shadow and does not last" (Job 14:1-2).

At last death comes and knocks, calling us to appear before the eternal judge. Begin a new life now. Imitate St. Anthony, working day and night for your eternal salvation.

Here make your request.

Prayer: Glorious St. Anthony, who led your soul to the port of celestial glory, obtain for us the grace that our soul may be guided by the light of faith, hope and charity which leads to the port of eternal love. Then the kingdom of heaven one day shall be our possession.

Glory be... (5 times) and the Responsory

Fifth Tuesday

Prayer: Prostrate...

Meditation: Watch and pray

St. Peter urged the early Christians to watch and pray because the devil stands before us; as a roaring lion he does not remain still a single moment, but is always on the lookout for new prey among the children of God (cf. 1 Pet 5:8).

Satan, as a keen general, is helped by his faithful attendants: the world, the devils and human passions. Who will be a sure guide for us against such a dreadful enemy? We must look with St. Anthony at Jesus Christ hanging from the cross and learn from him.

Here make your request.

Prayer: Glorious St. Anthony, obtain for us from Jesus Christ abundant graces, so that we may conquer the three great enemies—the world, the devil, and our own passions, and thus enter the kingdom of heaven.

Glory be... (5 times) and the Responsory

Sixth Tuesday

Prayer: Prostrate...

Meditation: Sin

Infirmity, leprosy and diseases oppress our body, but how much more should we feel the leprosy of sin, which affects and destroys the beauty of the most noble part of our being, our soul?

As the world deprived of the sun remains in deep darkness, so persons deprived of divine grace by mortal sin remain in spiritual darkness, unable to know themselves and their Creator.

Arise from your sinful life; beg God to help you turn away from all sin. Place yourself in the loving hands of St. Anthony. He will take care of you.

Here make your request.

Prayer: Glorious St. Anthony, who worked zealously for the conversion of sinners, we beg you to obtain for us the grace of a true conversion, so that we may give ourselves entirely to God.

Glory be... (5 times) and the Responsory

Seventh Tuesday

Prayer: Prostrate...

Meditation: Human life is exposed to many dangers

We may become the owners of all the things God created for us, but many dangers and difficulties must be conquered to improve the condition of our life. We can be exposed to danger on land, but the danger of the seas is much worse. On many occasions St. Anthony made himself a protector of those who lead a seafaring life. The waves of the sea are a perfect image of the moral sea of our life. We have many obstacles to overcome before reaching the safe port of our eternal salvation. If St. Anthony will take care of us, we may be perfectly sure to end our life in the hands of God.

Here make your request.

Prayer: Glorious St. Anthony, obtain for us that better days may come to enlighten the minds of all.

Glory be... (5 times) and the Responsory

Eighth Tuesday

Prayer: Prostrate...

Meditation: Our passions

The many favors obtained by St. Anthony while he was living as a poor prisoner should encourage us to invoke his protection. We must beg him to come and break the chains of our disordered passions. When properly regulated, passions can become a powerful force for good; when allowed to get out of control, they can do great damage.

Here make your request.

Prayer: Glorious St. Anthony, obtain for us that all children may be educated in the holy fear of God, and adults may proclaim with their works the faith of their Baptism, so that the eternal judge will call all of them to his right hand at the final judgment.

Glory be... (5 times) and the Responsory

Ninth Tuesday

Prayer: Prostrate...

Meditation: St. Anthony helps his devotees

St. Anthony spent the nine years of his apostolate doing good and healing the sick. He has a remedy for all human misfortunes.

Here make your request.

Prayer: Glorious St. Anthony, obtain for us the great privilege of receiving Jesus Christ in our hearts to remain forever as king of all our affections.

Glory be... (5 times) and the Responsory

Tenth Tuesday

Prayer: Prostrate...

Meditation: St. Anthony's protection

The Christian way of life often comes under attack in our secular society. "We are facing an enormous and dramatic clash between good and evil, death and life, the 'culture of death' and the 'culture of life'" (Pope John Paul II). St. Anthony faced similar dangers in his day. He persevered in preaching the Gospel despite all opposition. He will take care of his devout followers and bring them safely home to heaven.

Here make your request.

Prayer: Glorious St. Anthony, obtain for us from Jesus Christ that we may all be united in the love of God, so that one day we may all together enjoy the eternal glory of heaven.

Glory be... (5 times) and the Responsory

Eleventh Tuesday

Prayer: Prostrate...

Meditation: Help the poor

The poor are God's beloved. Jesus said, "Just as you did it to one of the least of these who are members of my family, you did it to me" (Mt 25:40).

The poor are the living image of Jesus Christ. The wealthy have an obligation to share their wealth with the needy. Give to everyone who asks in the name of charity. Do good, hoping for nothing in return, and your reward shall be great.

St. Anthony faithfully carried out the orders of our Lord. He can obtain for his devotees material goods and spiritual blessings.

Here make your request.

Prayer: Glorious St. Anthony, inspire the hearts of the rich that they may, with generous hands, help the poor in their necessities, and through this charity obtain for us the grace that we may all one day see him, who for us made himself poor in this world. Amen.

Glory be... (5 times) and the Responsory

Twelfth Tuesday

Prayer: Prostrate...

Meditation: The Most Holy Trinity

The devotees of St. Anthony have always had a special devotion toward the Most Holy Trinity, due to the many special gifts which God has granted through Anthony. St. Bonaventure exhorts us to say often: "Glory be to the Father, glory be to the Son, glory be to the Holy Spirit." Let us repeat this prayer frequently, and turn away from everything evil, because, by so doing, we shall never merit the rebuke of God: "These people...honor me with their lips, while their hearts are far from me" (Is 29:13). Say often to God: "There is no one I love as I love you."

Here make your request.

Prayer: Glorious St. Anthony, I give thanks to the Most Holy Trinity for all the privileges granted to you. Obtain for us light to know the divine will and strength to follow it, so that our soul may come up to heaven and contemplate forever the Most Holy Trinity in your company.

Glory be... (5 times) and the Responsory

Thirteenth Tuesday

Prayer: Prostrate...

Meditation: The name of Jesus

No one can be saved except through the merits of Jesus Christ, whose name is most holy and causes our prayer to be heard before the eternal Father's throne. Jesus said to his disciples before he left this world: "I will do whatever you ask in my name, so that the Father may be glorified in the Son" (Jn 14:13).

In the name of Jesus, the crippled walked, the dead came back to life, the diseased were cured, and the tempted received the strength to practice virtue. In the power of Jesus' name St. Anthony performed many wonders. Let us beg St. Anthony to intercede for us before the eternal Father, through our Savior Jesus Christ.

Here make your request.

Prayer: Glorious St. Anthony, faithful lover of Jesus Christ, beg him that his most holy name be always a light for us, so that our life may be continually in harmony with his divine will. At the end of our life, tell him to bring us soon to his kingdom to enjoy with you his eternal bliss forever. Amen.

Glory be... (5 times) and the Responsory

Prayer to St. Anthony

I salute you with all my heart; I salute you a thousand times, O St. Anthony. You are a chosen vessel of divine grace. Jesus is with you. You are blessed as the most admirable son of the Seraphic Father, Francis. Remember, O miraculous saint, that you never fail to help and console those who invoke you in their need. Animated with great confidence and the certitude my prayer will be heard, I turn to you, who are so rich in grace, and the most fortunate friend of the Infant Jesus.

O St. Anthony, saint of miracles, saint of help, I

too need your assistance. Please obtain for me this special favor *(mention it)*.

Console me in my present necessity and give me the help that I hope for with full confidence. I promise an offering for St. Anthony's bread for the poor.

Bless me, O great saint, in the name of the Father, and of the Son, and of the Holy Spirit. Amen.

St. Anthony, you are generally called the saint of Padua, but you are worthy to be called the saint of the world, because the whole world invokes you and blesses you.

Accept the homage of my devotion and receive me under your protection. So often you held in your arms the child Jesus. Obtain for me the grace necessary to keep him always in my heart. Pray that I might receive the grace of perseverance.

(Our Father, Hail Mary, Glory be)

For a Special Favor

O holy St. Anthony, gentlest and kindest of saints, your great virtues and your charity toward your fellow creatures made you worthy when on earth to possess most extraordinary miraculous powers. The afflicted never sought your help in vain. To the sick you gave back health; you restored what was lost; the grieving were the objects of your tender compassion; you even raised the dead to life, when the wounded heart cried to you from the depths of its anguish. While on earth, nothing was impossible to you, except not to have compassion on those in distress and sorrow. Encouraged by this thought and convinced of the power of your intercession, I kneel before your holy image, and full of confidence I implore you to obtain my request *(mention it)*.

The answer to this prayer may require a miracle. Even so, are you not the saint of miracles? When on earth, you had only to speak and the mightiest wonders were wrought. O gentle and loving St. Anthony, you whose heart was ever full of human sympathy, whisper my prayer into the ears of the infant Jesus.

One word from you and my prayer will be granted. Speak that word and the gratitude of my heart will ever be yours.

(Our Father, Hail Mary, Glory be)

For Each Tuesday

O glorious St. Anthony, safe refuge of the afflicted and distressed, by miraculous revelation you have directed all those who seek aid to come to your altar with the promise that whoever visits it and there devoutly invokes you, for nine consecutive Tuesdays, will feel the power of your intercession. Encouraged by this promise, I, a poor sinner, come to you, O powerful saint. With a firm hope I implore your aid, your protection, your counsel and your blessing. Obtain for me, I beseech you, my request in this necessity *(mention it)*.

But if it should be opposed to the will of God and my spiritual welfare, obtain for me other graces that will be helpful to my salvation. Through Christ our Lord. Amen.

(Our Father, Hail Mary, Glory be)

V. Pray for us, Blessed Anthony.

R. That we may be made worthy of the promises of Christ.

Let us pray. Almighty and eternal God, you glorified your faithful confessor, Anthony, with the perpetual gift of working miracles.

Graciously grant that what we confidently seek through his merits we may surely receive through his intercession. Through Christ our Lord. Amen.

Litany of St. Anthony

(For private use)

Lord, have mercy on us.
Christ, have mercy on us.
Christ, hear us.
Christ, graciously hear us.
Holy Mary, pray for us.
Holy Father Francis,*
St. Anthony of Padua,
Glory of the Order of Friars Minor,
Martyr in desiring to die for Christ,
Pillar of the Church,
Worthy priest of God,
Apostolic preacher,
Teacher of truth,
Hammer of heretics,
Terror of evil spirits,
Comforter of the afflicted,
Helper in necessities,
Deliverer of captives,
Guide of the erring,
Restorer of lost things,
Chosen intercessor,
Continuous worker of miracles,
Be merciful to us, spare us, O Lord.

---

* *pray for us.*

Be merciful to us, hear us, O Lord.

From all evil, O Lord, deliver us.

From all sin,*

From all dangers of body and soul,

From the snares of the devil,

From pestilence, famine and war,

From eternal death,

Through the merits of St. Anthony,

Through his zeal for the conversion of sinners,

Through his desire for the crown of martyrdom,

Through his fatigues and labors,

Through his preaching and teaching,

Through his penitential tears,

Through his patience and humility,

Through his glorious death,

Through the number of his prodigies,

In the day of judgment,

We sinners,

That you bring us to true penance, we beseech you, hear us.

That you grant us patience in our trials,**

That you assist us in our necessities,

That you grant our petitions,

That you kindle the fire of divine love within us,

---

* *deliver us.*

* * *we beseech you, hear us.*

That you give us the protection and intercession of
    St. Anthony,

Son of God,

Lamb of God, you take away the sins of the world,
    spare us, O Lord.

Lamb of God, you take away the sins of the world,
    graciously hear us, O Lord.

Lamb of God, you take away the sins of the world,
    have mercy on us.

Christ, hear us.

Christ, graciously hear us.

    V. Pray for us, St. Anthony.

    R. That we may be made worthy of the promises
of Christ.

Prayers to St. Dymphna

Patroness of Those Who Suffer
with Mental or Emotional Problems

Sometimes called the "Lily of Eire," Dymphna was born in Ireland sometime in the early 600s. Her father was a pagan king, but her mother was a devout Christian and raised Dymphna in the Faith. From a young age, Dymphna was attracted to religion, and desired to consecrate herself entirely to Jesus Christ through a life of virginity.

When Dymphna was still a teenager, her mother died. Her father then decided to marry Dymphna. Horrified at the idea of incest, Dymphna escaped and fled to Gheel, Belgium, with her confessor, Fr. Gerebran. Dymphna's father pursued them and when he found them, he ordered his men to kill the priest. He tried to persuade Dymphna to return with him, but she steadfastly refused. Infuriated, the father drew a dagger from his belt and with his own hand struck off the head of his child.

After some time people recognized Dymphna's holiness and began to invoke her. Many healings were reported as a result of her intercession, especially for those troubled with psychological and emotional problems. Dymphna's fame grew, and Gheel developed into a town famous for its care of the mentally ill.

St. Dymphna is still popular today as the patroness of those afflicted with mental and emotional problems. Her feastday is May 15.

Litany in Honor of St. Dymphna

(For private use)

Lord, have mercy on us.

Christ, have mercy on us.

Lord, have mercy on us.

Christ, hear us.

Christ, graciously hear us.

God the Father of heaven, have mercy on us.

God the Son, Redeemer of the world,*

God the Holy Spirit,

Holy Trinity, one God,

Holy Mary, Virgin and Mother of God, pray for us.

Health of the sick,**

Comforter of the afflicted,

Help of Christians,

St. Dymphna, virgin and martyr,

---

* *have mercy on us.*

** *pray for us.*

St. Dymphna, daughter of royal parents,

St. Dymphna, child of great beauty of soul and
body,

St. Dymphna, docile to the lessons of your
holy mother,

St. Dymphna, obedient to your saintly confessor,

St. Dymphna, who abandoned the court of your
father to escape the danger of impurity,

St. Dymphna, who chose a life of poverty on earth
so that you might store treasures in heaven,

St. Dymphna, who sought strength and consolation
in Holy Mass, Holy Communion and prayer,

St. Dymphna, ardent lover of the divine bridegroom,

St. Dymphna, devoted to the Mother of God,

St. Dymphna, beheaded by your own father,

St. Dymphna, martyr of holy purity,

St. Dymphna, brilliant example of Christian youth,

St. Dymphna, renowned for many miracles,

St. Dymphna, glory of Ireland and Belgium,

St. Dymphna, full of compassion for those in need,

St. Dymphna, protector against all mental and
psychological disorders,

St. Dymphna, consoler of the afflicted,

St. Dymphna, friend of the helpless,

St. Dymphna, comforter of the despondent,

St. Dymphna, light of those in mental darkness,

St. Dymphna, patroness of those who suffer with
    mental or emotional problems,

That we may love the Lord our God with all our
    hearts and above all things, we beseech you,
    hear us.

That we may hate sin and avoid all occasions of
    sin,***

That we may carefully preserve the virtue of purity
    according to our state,

That we may receive the sacraments frequently,

That we may obtain the spirit of prayer,

That we may be humble and obedient, surrendering
    ourselves to God's holy will,

That we may learn to have confidence in God
    during our afflictions,

That we may obtain the grace of final perseverance,

In times of sickness, disease, war and persecution,

In our last illness,

At the hour of death,

Lamb of God, you take away the sins of the world,
    spare us, O Lord.

Lamb of God, you take away the sins of the world,
    graciously hear us, O Lord.

Lamb of God, you take away the sins of the world,
have mercy on us.

*** *we beseech you, hear us.*

V. Pray for us, St. Dymphna,

R. That we may be made worthy of the promises of Christ.

Let us pray. O God, since you gave St. Dymphna to your Church as a model of all virtues, especially holy purity, and willed that she should seal her faith with her innocent blood and perform numerous miracles, grant that we who honor her as patroness of those afflicted with mental or emotional problems, may continue to enjoy her powerful intercession and protection and attain eternal life. Through Christ our Lord. Amen.

Prayer for Abandonment to God's Will

O God, who led the holy virgin and martyr St. Dymphna through danger and trial to her glorious crown in heaven, help me through her intercession to trust in you in all the afflictions and trials of my own life, and by accepting your will, to ascend from the sorrows of this life to the eternal glory of heaven. Through Christ our Lord. Amen.

Prayer in Any Affliction

Compassionate St. Dymphna, who restored health and soundness of mind to so many through the power of your heavenly Bridegroom, Jesus Christ, behold me *(or mention the person afflicted)* in this suffering. Trusting in your powerful intercession, I beg you to ask Jesus, the merciful healer of the sick, to restore me *(or N.)* that, helped by his grace, I *(he/she)* may serve God better and promote devotion to you, together with the many others who have experienced your help. Amen.

(Our Father, Hail Mary, Glory be)

Prayer for Purity

St. Dymphna, holy virgin and martyr, for the love of Jesus Christ you faithfully preserved the robe of innocence and purity, valiantly resisting all the allurements of evil passions. Help me, too, to overcome all temptations against purity and to remain steadfast in the love of Christ, in order to preserve this great gift of God. Implore for me the grace of perseverance in prayer, distrust of myself, and flight from the occasions of sin, and finally the grace of a good death, so that in heaven I may be happy with God for all eternity. Amen.

Prayer for Those Afflicted with
Mental or Emotional Problems

Lord Jesus Christ, you have willed that St. Dymphna should be invoked by thousands of devotees as the patroness of those who suffer with mental or emotional problems. You have brought about that her interest in these persons should be an inspiration to and an ideal of charity at her great shrine and throughout the world. Grant that, through the prayers of this youthful martyr of purity, those who suffer from psychological and emotional problems everywhere on earth may be helped and consoled. I recommend to you in particular...*(here mention those you wish to pray for).*

Be pleased to hear the prayers of St. Dymphna and of your Blessed Mother, health of the sick and comforter of the afflicted, in behalf of those whom I recommend to the love and compassion of your Sacred Heart. Give them the consolation they need and especially the cure they so much desire, if it be your will. May we all serve your suffering members with a charity that may merit for us the reward of being united forever in heaven with you, our divine Head, who lives and reigns with the Father in the unity of the Holy Spirit forever and ever. Amen.

O God, we beg you through your servant, St. Dymphna, who sealed with her blood the love she had for you, her eternal Spouse, to grant relief to those in our midst who suffer from psychological or emotional problems. Through Christ our Lord. Amen.

Prayers to St. Francis
(1182-1226)

Patron of Italy, of Merchants, of Ecologists and of Animals

Probably one of the most popular saints of the Catholic Church, Francis has attracted countless followers for over eight centuries. Born in Assisi in 1182, he was raised in a wealthy family. As a young man, Francis enjoyed a good time and his cheerfulness and generosity attracted many friends. The glamour of knighthood lured him to go off to war. He was soon captured and spent a year in prison. This experience made him ponder life more deeply. Soon after, he experienced a profound conversion and sought to live the Gospel radically.

Others were attracted to his ideal and soon the group began to take shape as a religious order. Francis emphasized radical poverty and evangelical simplicity, sending the friars out as poor men to preach the Gospel to the masses. More and more young men joined them, and the Franciscans grew rapidly. Along with another new mendicant order, the Dominicans, they helped to bring about a great spiritual renewal in the Church.

Toward the end of his life, Francis received the stigmata, or the wounds of Christ. Hard work, poverty and suffering weakened Francis' health, and he died on October 2, 1226. His feastday is celebrated on October 4.

Begging God's Gifts and Thanking Him

By choice and vow St. Francis was the "beggar saint," and before God we are all beggars who need divine aid. St. Francis knew that we must ask with faith if we wish to receive, and he will help us to do so.

Above all, St. Francis is the saint of gratitude for the favors God gives us, and will help us imitate him by making our sense of thanksgiving manifest.

We invoke the aid of St. Francis of Assisi because in his time and place he was a perfect mirror of Christ, our Lord.

Various Prayers

St. Francis of Assisi, help us. By your example may we learn that life does not consist in the pursuit of wealth nor in the abundance of our possessions.

St. Francis of Assisi, come to our aid. Because we live at a time when people glorify ease and seek after luxuries, and when many wish only the gratification of fleshly desires, we especially need your single-minded dedication to Christ in the narrow way that leads to life.

St. Francis of Assisi, assist us now. May we appreciate as you did the beauties of God's wonderful creation, and the glory of the world he made for us. Help us to enjoy and appreciate God's bounty without spoiling or defacing his gifts by our heedlessness and greed.

Teach us, seraphic Father Francis, to value all things as Christ did and to be imitators of him as you were. May we thus enjoy the good things of life, but always prefer the blessings of the endless life to come. Amen.

V. God forbid that I should glory—

R. Save in the cross of our Lord, Jesus Christ.

St. Francis, the little poor man of Assisi, we invoke you as the admirable mirror you were of our Divine Master.

You imitated Christ the Lord in your humility and obedience. You faithfully followed him in poverty and weakness. With joy you accepted suffering, contempt and trials for the sake of his name.

In your goodness help us, then, to imitate your example. By your power with God obtain for us the special favor we now seek through your intercession.

Please pray for us, gentle and happy saint of the poor, that we may always be loyal followers of our Savior, Jesus Christ, and filled with divine riches. Amen.

Jeffrey Keefe, OFM Conv.

Prayer of St. Francis

Lord,
make me an instrument of your peace.
Where there is hatred let me sow love;
where there is injury, pardon;
where there is doubt, faith;
where there is despair, hope;
where there is darkness, light;
and where there is sadness, joy.

O Divine Master, grant that I may not so much seek to be consoled as to console; to be understood as to understand; to be loved as to love; for it is in giving that we receive, it is in pardoning that we are pardoned, and it is in dying that we are born to eternal life.

The Testament Prayer

We adore you, Lord Jesus Christ, in all your churches in the whole world, and we bless you, because by your holy cross you have redeemed the world.

Prayer Before the Crucifix

Most high, glorious God, enlighten the darkness of my heart. Instill in me a correct faith, a certain hope and a perfect love; a sense and a knowledge, Lord, so that I may do your holy and true command.

Song of St. Francis

Since God is love,
I'll sing his song.
With God above
I will be strong.
With God within,
What else need I?
While God shall reign
Can my song die?

—Attributed to St. Francis of Assisi

Prayers to St. Francis Xavier
(1506-1552)

Patron of Missionaries

As a young man, this fiery Spaniard's main interest was in having a good time. But at the University of Paris, he met Ignatius Loyola—and before long, Ignatius persuaded Francis that he was meant for greater things.

Francis joined the newly-forming group of Jesuits, and some time later Ignatius sent him to the East Indies as a missionary. Throughout Goa, India, Japan and other lands of the East, St. Francis made thousands of converts. In fact, he baptized so many people that at times he became too weak to raise his arms. His goal was to reach China, but he died on an island outside that country before realizing the final stage of his dream. St. Francis is the patron saint of missionaries. His feastday is December 3.

Novena of Grace to St. Francis Xavier

St. Francis Xavier, well loved and full of charity, in union with you, I reverently adore the majesty of God. And since I rejoice greatly in the special gifts of grace given to you during your life, and your gifts of glory after death, I give him thanks for them.

I beg you with all my heart's devotion to obtain for me, by your powerful intercession, above all things, the grace of a holy life and a happy death. Moreover, I ask you to obtain for me *(mention the favor you desire).*

But if what I ask does not tend to the glory of God and the greater good of my soul, I pray that you obtain for me what is more profitable to both these ends. Amen.

(Our Father, Hail Mary, Glory be)

Prayers to St. Gemma Galgani
(1878-1903)

As a young girl, Gemma received mystical graces and was especially attracted to the passion of Christ. She lived a heroic life of great suffering. Her mother died when Gemma was eight, and her father also died soon after. The family was penniless, and Gemma was placed in the home of the Giannini family, who took good care of her. She endured illness and physical sufferings, which increased when she received the stigmata. She offered everything in expiation for sin, and especially for priests. Consumed with suffering, she died on Holy Saturday, 1903. Her feastday is April 11.

Novena Prayer to St. Gemma Galgani to Obtain a Special Favor

O St. Gemma, how compassionate was your love for those in distress, and how great your desire to help them. Help me, also, in my present necessity and obtain for me the favor I humbly implore, if it be profitable for my soul.

The numerous miracles and the wonderful favors attributed to your intercession instill in me the confidence that you can help me. Pray to Jesus, your Spouse, for me. Show him the stigmata which his love has given you. Remind him of the blood which flowed from these same wounds, the excruciating pain which you have suffered, the tears which you have shed for the salvation of souls. Place all this as your precious treasure in a chalice of love, and Jesus will hear you. Amen.

(Our Father, Hail Mary, Glory be)

Msgr. G. Bardi

Prayers to St. Gerard Majella
(1726-1755)

Patron of Mothers

A humble Redemptorist brother, Gerard distinguished himself for great virtue, despite his short life. He centered his spirituality on trust in divine Providence, and always sought to surrender himself to the holy will of God.

His greatest trial came when he was calumniated by a vindictive girl who accused him of sexual misconduct. Instead of defending himself, Gerard chose to accept the penance imposed on him by St. Alphonsus, the founder of the Redemptorists. Gerard was later vindicated when the girl admitted she had lied.

Blessed with extraordinary spiritual gifts, Gerard also had the gift of healing. In particular, he worked many miracles to aid expectant mothers and their unborn children. For this reason, he is invoked as the patron saint of mothers.

After contracting tuberculosis, Gerard died in 1755 at the age of 29. Pope St. Pius X canonized him on December 11, 1904. Gerard's feastday is October 16.

Novena to St. Gerard Majella

First Day

St. Gerard's Love for Prayer

"Ask, and it will be given you; search, and you will find; knock, and the door will be opened for you. For everyone who asks receives, and everyone who searches finds, and for everyone who knocks, the door will be opened" (Lk 11:9-10).

St. Gerard, you understood so well this invitation of our Divine Master. Your great devotion to prayer led you to a very close union with God during your life here on earth, and has gained for you the unending happiness of heaven. Help me to pray with humility, confidence and perseverance, so that my prayer will always be pleasing and acceptable to the Lord.

Make me realize more and more the great value of the holy Mass and the sacraments, and keep me faithful in my practices of worship. Remind me to turn to God often during the day in praise of his majesty and goodness, in thanksgiving for his countless blessings, in petition for the graces I need most and in sorrow and resolution to do better when I have offended him. Amen.

Novena Prayer

St. Gerard, you loved God and served him faithfully as a humble Redemptorist brother. Now, from heaven, teach me to have great confidence in the Lord. Instill in me that same love which you had for his holy will.

I come to you now to ask your help. Trusting in your powerful intercession before the most Blessed Trinity, I ask you to obtain for me, if it be God's will, the following grace.... *(Here mention your request.)* I promise you in return, that I will try my best to live a holy life until the day when I will be united with you and all the angels and saints in heaven to praise God for all eternity. Amen.

(Our Father, Hail Mary, Glory be)

St. Gerard, pray for us.

Second Day

St. Gerard's Simplicity

"For where your treasure is, there your heart will be also" (Lk 12:34).

St. Gerard, you had the grace of always keeping God as the center of your life. So many times I do not leave room for God in my life because of my own selfishness, pride and failures in charity. Pray for me that I may put aside all the useless worries and ambitions which hinder my growth in holiness, so that I may concentrate on the only thing which really matters: loving God and doing everything to please him alone. Amen.

(Recite the novena prayer.)

Third Day

St. Gerard's Patience

"I therefore, the prisoner in the Lord, beg you to lead a life worthy of the calling to which you have been called, with all humility and gentleness, with patience, bearing with one another in love" (Eph 4:1-2).

St. Gerard, help me to be patient with myself and with others. You have given a practical example of this virtue by your willing acceptance of the crosses which God allowed you to carry during your life. Please ask our Lord to give me the strength to take my own sufferings and trials from his hands as a means of my personal sanctification. Remind me to repeat often, "May your will and not mine be done, Lord." Amen.

(Recite the novena prayer.)

Fourth Day

St. Gerard's Perseverance

"So let us not grow weary in doing what is right, for we will reap at harvest time, if we do not give up" (Gal 6:9).

St. Gerard, I know you understand what disappointment and discouragement can mean. You had to struggle to obtain admission into the religious life even though you knew so clearly that this was what God wanted of you. Help me, in my own particular state in life, in my family circle, at work and in my community, to strive always to imitate Jesus and to obey the voice of his Church no matter how many pressures tempt me to do otherwise. If I fail to live up what God expects of me, intercede for me before the Lord, that I may repent and never give in to discouragement. Make me turn instead with renewed hope and confidence to my Divine Master who is always ready with his grace to lift me up again. Amen.

(Recite the novena prayer.)

Fifth Day

St. Gerard's Devotion to the Holy Eucharist

"While they were eating, he took a loaf of bread, and after blessing it he broke it, gave it to them, and said, 'Take; this is my body.' Then he took a cup, and after giving thanks he gave it to them, and all of them drank from it. He said to them, 'This is my blood of the covenant, which is poured out for many'" (Mk 14:22-24).

In the Eucharist Jesus feeds us with his body and blood. But sometimes I almost take our Lord's Real Presence in the tabernacle for granted. Stir up within me a profound and living faith in this great mystery. Remind me that when I kneel before the Blessed Sacrament I am in the company of my Lord and my God; I am with Jesus, my Divine Master who is entirely present in this sacrament—body, blood, soul and divinity—and is waiting to listen to me and speak to me. Renew my spirit of gratitude for this wonderful gift and help me to appreciate the Holy Eucharist more each day. Amen.

(Recite the novena prayer.)

Sixth Day

St. Gerard's Spirit of Forgiveness

"For if you forgive others their trespasses, your heavenly Father will also forgive you; but if you do not forgive others, neither will your Father forgive your trespasses" (Mt 6:14-15).

St. Gerard, help me to live, as you did, the spirit of the Our Father. Remind me that I must not only forgive injuries but forget them, following your example in the face of false accusations. Ask God to make me an instrument of his peace, and obtain for me from the Lord the grace to be the first one to apologize whenever there has been a misunderstanding. Amen.

(Recite the novena prayer.)

Seventh Day

St. Gerard—Molder of Upright Consciences

"If you forgive the sins of any, they are forgiven them; if you retain the sins of any, they are retained" (Jn 20:23).

St. Gerard, during your lifetime you helped many people to sincerely examine their lives and to single out points for improvement.

Obtain for me from Jesus and his holy Mother Mary the grace of having a good conscience. Assist me in my preparation for and reception of the sacrament of Reconciliation. Teach me to approach this sacrament with great confidence in the Lord's mercy and with a humble recognition of my own sinfulness and need of forgiveness. Never allow me to conceal any sin out of shame or embarrassment, but remind me of Jesus' promise that whoever humbles himself will be exalted. Amen.

(Recite the novena prayer.)

Eighth Day

St. Gerard's Love for Our Blessed Mother

"Standing near the cross of Jesus were his mother, and his mother's sister, Mary the wife of Clopas, and Mary Magdalene. When Jesus saw his mother and the disciple whom he loved standing beside her, he said to his mother, 'Woman, here is your son.' Then he said to the disciple, 'Here is your mother.' And from that hour the disciple took her into his own home" (Jn 19:25-27).

St. Gerard, you found in Mary the Mother of Jesus and our own Mother, a safe refuge and sure guide in every circumstance of your life. Lead me now to a trusting and true devotion to my Mother, Teacher and Queen, and remind me often that the safest, quickest and easiest way to union with Jesus is always to go to him through Mary.

Teach me, also, St. Gerard, the beauty and great value of the rosary, that scriptural prayer which helps me to meditate on the main events in the life of Jesus and Mary. Amen.

(Recite the novena prayer.)

Ninth Day

St. Gerard's Reward

"Come, you that are blessed by my Father, inherit the kingdom prepared for you from the foundation of the world" (Mt 25:34).

St. Gerard, God has exalted you in his Church that you may be for all of us a friend who will aid us on our way to heaven. Because you have already reached this goal, I am confident that you will pray for me now to the Lord so that I, too, may live in a way that will merit for me the eternal joys of heaven. Amen.

(Recite the novena prayer.)

Novena by Patricia Edward Jablonski, FSP

To St. Gerard for Motherhood

Glorious St. Gerard, powerful intercessor before God, I call upon you and seek your help. You who always fulfilled God's will on earth, help me to do God's holy will. Beseech the Master of life that I may conceive and raise children who will please God in this life, and be heirs to the kingdom of heaven. Amen.

Traditional

To St. Gerard for a Mother in Danger

Almighty God, through the work of the Holy Spirit, you prepared the body and soul of the glorious Virgin Mary, Mother of God, to be worthy of your Son. Listen to my prayer through the intercession of St. Gerard, your faithful servant. Protect me *(her)* during pregnancy and childbirth, and safeguard against the evil spirit the tender fruit you have given me *(her),* in order that, by your saving hand, this child may receive holy Baptism. Grant also that, after living as good Christians on earth, both mother and child may attain everlasting happiness in heaven. Amen.

Traditional

Prayers to Saints Joachim and Ann

Patron and Patroness of Parents

According to popular tradition, Joachim and Ann were the parents of the Blessed Virgin Mary. Their names are found in a second-century work called *The Protoevangelium of James*. According to this source, the couple was childless for many years and they promised God that if they had a child, they would dedicate the baby to God. When Mary was born, they fulfilled the promise by bringing her to the Temple at a young age.

Joachim and Ann are the patron and patroness of parents. Their feastday is July 26.

Novena in Honor of
Saints Joachim and Ann

Saints Joachim and Ann, grandparents of Jesus and parents of Mary, we seek your intercession. We beg you to direct all our actions to the greater glory of God and the salvation of souls. Strengthen us when we are tempted, console us during our trials, help us when we are in need, be with us in life and in death. O divine Savior, we thank you for having chosen Saints Joachim and Ann to be the parents of our Blessed Mother Mary and so to be your own beloved grandparents. We place ourselves under their patronage this day. We recommend to them our families, our children and our grandchildren. Keep them from all spiritual and physical harm. Grant that they may ever grow in greater love of God and others. Saints Joachim and Ann, we have many great needs. We beg you to intercede for us before the throne of your divine grandson. All of us here have our own special intentions, our own special needs, and we pray that through your intercession our prayers may be granted. Amen.

(Here mention your own intentions.)

Prayer of a Family

God of goodness and mercy, through the intercession of Saints Joachim and Ann, we commend our family, our household and all that belongs to us to your loving protection. We entrust all to your love and keeping. Fill our homes with your blessings. Above all else keep far from us the stain of sin. Help each one of us to keep your holy laws, to love you sincerely and to imitate your example, the example of Mary, and that of the saints whose intercession we seek. Lord, preserve our homes from all evils and misfortunes. May we always surrender to your holy will, even when crosses and sorrows come to us. Give all of us the grace to live in perfect harmony and love toward each other and our neighbor. Grant that each one of us may receive the comfort of your sacraments at the hour of death. Bless our homes, God the Father who created us, God the Son who suffered for us on the cross, and God the Holy Spirit, who fills our hearts with inspirations. Amen.

(Answer each of the following petitions with the words: "Lord, hear our prayer.")

That all members of our family may ever lead lives pleasing to God, let us pray to the Lord.

That we may have a truly holy, happy and peaceful home without discord, let us pray to the Lord.

That our home may be truly Catholic and Christ may rule as its head, let us pray to the Lord.

That bickering, nagging and disagreement may not mar our home life and scar the lives of our children, let us pray to the Lord.

That the love of parents for each other and the love of children for their parents may daily increase, let us pray to the Lord.

That our homes may be protected from fires and storms and every other calamity, let us pray to the Lord.

For good health for everyone in the family, let us pray to the Lord.

Fathers' Prayer

O God, through the intercession of Saints Joachim and Ann, we fathers come to beg your help. Ours is an awesome and heavy responsibility. By your own command, you have placed us at the head of the family. By your command too, we must love our wives with the same love Christ has for his Church. We know that it is our solemn duty to instruct our children and bring them up to love you. It is our responsibility to train them in the observance of your commandments and in the practice of their faith, as well as to supply their every spiritual and physical need to the best of our ability. Above all, we are bound constantly to give good example and to go before our children as a shining light in word and deed. How can we do this, O Lord, unless you bestow your special graces and blessings upon us. Grant us the gift, O God, to live up fully to our state in life, so that our children may be justly proud of us. We ask this through the intercession of Saints Joachim and Ann, and through St. Joseph, the foster father of Jesus Christ our Savior. Amen.

Mothers' Prayer

O God, through the intercession of Saints Joachim and Ann, we mothers come to seek your help. We pray that the love we bestow upon our children, our care for them in sickness and in health, may not go unrewarded. May it induce them to love us more and more each day of their lives. We plead for peace in our homes, joy and contentment in our families. Teach us, O Lord, to find constant happiness in the work of our homes and in our duties as wives and mothers. We beg that all our families be ever united in love. Grant that we may always be a source of inspiration and joy to our children. Help us to bring them up in the love of God and others. Let our lives be spent in giving good example, and make us worthy of the trust you and our children have placed in us. Grant that through our efforts it may be said of our children as was said of the Christ child: "[He] was obedient to them....and...increased in wisdom and in years, and in divine and human favor" (Lk 2:51-52). Finally, O Lord, having served you in this life, may all our families be united again in heaven where there shall be no more tears and no more parting, but everlasting happiness.

We ask this, O God, through Jesus Christ your Son, through Mary the greatest of all mothers, and through her parents Joachim and Ann. Amen.

Parents' Prayer

O God, our loving Father, through your goodness we have received the precious gift of our children. You have also given us the responsibility to bring them up in your love and service. We realize that some day we must account to you, O God, for their upbringing. Grant us, O Lord, the many graces we so much need to lead them along the path of justice and holiness. We plead with you that our example may never lead them astray. Help us to give them a good Christian upbringing. Give us the strength to govern them with a loving and firm heart. Do not permit us to become blind to their faults, but grant us the grace to reprove and correct them whenever there is need. Should it ever happen, O God, that our children go astray, may our love and our prayers bring them back again and so, like the father of the prodigal son, we may rejoice that those who were lost are found again. For these and all the graces which we need to rightly fulfill our duties as parents, we ask through Christ our Lord and through the intercession of Saints Joachim and Ann. Amen.

Closing Prayers

O blessed parents of the Queen of Heaven, take our families under your special protection. Models of saintly parenthood, may we imitate your examples in our homes and families. Guardians of the childhood of Mary, obtain graces for those living in the married state; sanctify our homes and lead those entrusted to our care to eternal glory. Amen.

God our Father, you honored Saints Joachim and Ann by making them the parents of Mary, the Mother of your beloved Son. Through their prayers and intercession may we attain the salvation you have promised your people. We ask this through Christ our Lord. Amen.

Novena by Rev. Nicholas Schneiders, C.P.

Prayers to St. John Vianney
(1786-1859)

Patron of Parish Priests

Generally known as the Curé of Ars, St. John Vianney was born at Dardilly, France, in 1786. After overcoming many difficulties in his studies, he was ordained to the priesthood and was appointed pastor of the remote village of Ars. With prayer, penance, sermons, catechism classes and countless hours in the confessional, the holy Curé transformed his parish into a haven of holiness. His reputation spread throughout France, and Ars became a place of pilgrimage for the thousands of people who wanted St. John to hear their confessions. A railroad had to be built to Ars to accommodate the penitents who flocked to this holy priest. Worn out by labor and a life of extreme penance, St. John died in 1859 and was canonized in 1925. The patron of parish priests, his feastday is August 4.

Novena to St. John Vianney

First Day

St. John Vianney, who accepted the cross

"If any want to become my followers, let them deny themselves and take up their cross and follow me" (Mt 16:24).

O holy priest of Ars, as a young seminarian you met many obstacles on the road to the priesthood, but you realized that to suffer was to suffer with Christ on Calvary, and so, if following our Lord meant taking up his cross, you lovingly embraced it. Your motto in life became loving while suffering and suffering in order to love. You did not get discouraged, but your strong faith united you closer to Jesus every day of your life.

O great St. John Vianney, you know what is needed for my salvation—a strong faith able to accept the will of God in all things. If I want to serve Christ, I too must take up my cross and follow him. By your prayers, obtain for me a heart full of courage and strength; obtain for our priests, religious and seminarians that same courage and strength to follow Jesus wholeheartedly even if it means following him to Calvary. Intercede for me before the Lord that

I may do the will of God, obey the commandments, and loyally love the Church, the Bride of Christ.

(Recite the novena prayer.)

Novena Prayer

O holy priest of Ars, St. John Marie Vianney, you loved God and served him faithfully as his priest. Now you see God face to face in heaven. You never despaired but persevered in your faith until you died. Remember now the dangers, fears and anxieties that surround me and intercede for me in all my needs and troubles, especially.... *(Here mention your request.)* St. John Vianney, I have confidence in your intercession. Pray for me in a special way during this novena.

Second Day

St. John Vianney, full of zeal for souls

"For what will it profit them if they gain the whole world but forfeit their life? Or what will they give in return for their life?" (Mt 16:26).

O holy priest of Ars, you taught people to pray daily: "O my God, come to me, so that you may dwell in me and I may dwell in you." In your life you lived out this prayer. The divine life of grace abided in you. Your zeal for the salvation of souls was manifested by your total self-surrender to God, which was expressed in your selfless service to others. You gave of yourself unreservedly in the confessional, at the altar, in the classroom, in fact, in every action you performed.

O great St. John Vianney, obtain for me the realization that God also dwells in me when I am free of sin. I know that the salvation of my soul is the fulfillment of my existence. Awaken in me a sense of self-giving for the salvation of souls. By your intercession obtain for all priests, religious and seminarians a zeal for souls like your zeal. May they see that God dwells in them and in other people. Obtain for them from our Lord, the grace to lead all people to salvation. Let your prayer be theirs: "If you really love God, you will greatly desire to see him loved by all the world."

(Recite the novena prayer.)

Third Day

St. John Vianney, adorer of the Blessed Sacrament

"Very truly, I tell you, unless you eat the flesh of the Son of Man and drink his blood, you have no life in you.... Those who eat my flesh and drink my blood abide in me, and I in them" (Jn 6:53, 56).

O holy priest of Ars, you had such an overwhelming love for Christ in the Blessed Sacrament that you prayed for hours in his presence. You said that "...when our Lord sees them coming eagerly to visit him in the Blessed Sacrament, he smiles upon them. They come with that simplicity which pleases him so much."

O saint of the Eucharist, may your example enkindle in me a love for Jesus in the Blessed Sacrament. By your prayers, never let me doubt Christ's Real Presence, but obtain for me a firm faith rooted in him. Help me not to be afraid to defend or preach Christ's Real Presence in the Blessed Sacrament. Obtain for me the grace to approach our Lord with simplicity of heart as I place my soul's innermost thoughts before his Sacred Heart. Keep priests, religious and seminarians under your continual protection, that they may be supported by your example and assistance and be faithfully devoted to Christ in the Blessed Sacrament. May their lives reflect their belief in our Lord's abiding presence with us. O St. John Vianney, by the power of your intercession, give us priests devoted to the holy sacrament of the altar.

(Recite the novena prayer.)

Fourth Day

*St. John Vianney, greatly devoted
to our Blessed Mother*

"O daughter, you are blessed by the Most High God above all other women on earth; and blessed be the Lord God, who created the heavens and the earth" (Judith 13:18).

O holy priest of Ars, your life was consecrated to the Blessed Mother. You prayed earnestly to her, entrusting your priesthood to her care.

You begged all the faithful to pray the rosary, the favorite prayer of Mary, our Mother. You summed up the reason for your great love of our Lady by saying: "We have only to turn to the Blessed Mother to be heard. Her heart is all love."

O great St. John Vianney, I ask you with all my heart, through the merits of Jesus and the intercession of Mary, the Virgin Mother, to make my life patterned after that of our heavenly Mother, full of love for God and my neighbors. Obtain for me a deep love for our Lady and a filial confidence in her. I can turn to her in times of distress, when lonely or upset, or in times of temptation. Inspire priests, religious and seminarians to consecrate their lives to their Mother in heaven. May priests throughout the world never desert the cross of Christ, but remain, as Mary did, at the foot of the cross.

(Recite the novena prayer.)

Fifth Day

St. John Vianney, lover of sinners

"Come to me, all you that are weary and are carrying heavy burdens, and I will give you rest. Take my yoke upon you, and learn from me; for I am gentle and humble in heart, and you will find rest for your souls. For my yoke is easy, and my burden is light" (Mt 11:28-30).

O holy priest of Ars, you spent many long hours daily in the confessional. People came to you from far off places for forgiveness of their sins. Although you despised sin, you always received the sinner with much love and forgiveness.

O holy confessor of the Lord, St. John Vianney, awaken in me a sense of my sinfulness before the eyes of God. By your priestly example and prayers, grant me a love of the sacrament of Reconciliation. Help me to realize that in confessing my sins God's mercy is poured out upon me and I draw closer to Christ. Obtain for me a deep hatred of sin and the grace to resist temptation. Teach me the value of frequent confession, where I meet Jesus my Savior, the source of all mercy and consolation. Pray that all priests, religious, and seminarians may always love the sacrament of Reconciliation. Pray that they may call sinners to repentance by their good example and lives given in complete service to our Lord.

(Recite the novena prayer.)

Sixth Day

St. John Vianney, model of purity

"Let no one despise your youth, but set the believers an example in speech and conduct, in love, in faith, in purity" (1 Tim 4:12).

O holy priest of Ars, your life was a model of purity. Your chastity edified everyone. You said that when a soul is pure the whole court of heaven looks upon it with great joy. Today we are experiencing a great disregard for the virtue of purity; our secular society often scorns and ridicules it.

O great St. John Vianney, more than ever before, I need your prayers and help in avoiding sins of impurity. I ask you to help me keep pure in mind and in body and to give good example in my speech, conduct and in my faith. Obtain for me the strength necessary to combat temptations against the virtue of purity. Unite your prayers with those of Mary Immaculate to implore God that all priests, religious and seminarians be pure in mind and heart, and preserve them from those sins which are so displeasing to God.

(Recite the novena prayer.)

Seventh Day

St. John Vianney, humble in all things

"All who exalt themselves will be humbled, and all who humble themselves will be exalted" (Mt 23:12).

O holy priest of Ars, your life was filled with humility. You wore an old cassock and ate meager meals. You realized that before the throne of God you were one of his creatures, made to glorify God and praise him in all things. You said that the "first virtue is humility; the second, humility; and the third, humility." You counseled people to remain humble, remain simple, and the more one is so, the more good one will do. Your simplicity of soul and your uncluttered way of life led you to sanctity.

O humble St. John Vianney, when I forget that I am totally dependent on God for everything, intercede for me with Almighty God, to allow me to see that without my Creator nothing is possible and that I must rely on God for everything. He is my Creator, who keeps me in existence at every moment. Obtain for all priests, religious and seminarians the grace of humility. May their lives exemplify your humility and simplicity, a life uncluttered, a life totally dependent on God.

(Recite the novena prayer.)

Eighth Day

*St. John Vianney, lover of penance
and mortification*

"If the world hates you, be aware that it hated me before it hated you" (Jn 15:18).

O holy priest of Ars, you led a life of detachment from worldly pleasures. Your meals consisted of a boiled potato each day; you slept a few hours each night. But you did all of this so that you would be able to serve God to the best of your ability. Your life was portrayed by this saying: "We complain when we suffer. We have much more reason to complain when we do not suffer, since nothing so likens us to our Lord as the bearing of his cross."

O great St. John Vianney, in these days when we are surrounded by so many comforts and pleasures, it can be so difficult for us to do penance for our sins and live a life of detachment. I resolve to offer some sacrifice today for the expiation of my sins and the sins of all humanity. I resolve to lovingly accept the cross God chooses to send me. May all priests, religious and seminarians become men and women of sacrifice. May they willingly offer their whole lives to God! Obtain for them the grace to liken their lives to that of Christ by the bearing of his cross.

(Recite the novena prayer.)

Ninth Day

St. John Vianney, good and holy priest

"As you therefore have received Christ Jesus the Lord, continue to live your lives in him, rooted and built up in him and established in the faith, just as you were taught, abounding in thanksgiving" (Col 2:6-7).

O holy priest of Ars, you lived in an age of much upheaval, in a time when people turned their backs on God. Your bishop told you he wished to send you to a parish where there was no love. He assigned you to Ars and said that you would be the priest who would enable the people to know the love of God. Not only did you draw these people back to God, but your saintly reputation soon spread and many people were converted to a life of holiness.

You said that a good priest, a priest after

Christ's own heart, is the greatest treasure that God can give a parish. Give us such priests!

O great St. John Vianney, once again we are living in days of upheaval. Evil abounds in the world. Obtain for me the grace to persevere in my faith and never to despair. May I walk with the Lord and trust in him all the days of my life. Obtain through your heavenly intercession, for all priests, religious and seminarians, the grace of modeling their lives after that of Jesus Christ. More than ever, we need priests full of the love of God, able to bring the world to Christ. Pray for good priests, O great priest of Ars.

(Recite the novena prayer.)

Novena by Rev. Anthony Manuppella

Prayers to St. Joseph

Patron of the Universal Church, of Workers, of the Dying and of Providing for Spiritual and Material Needs

The Gospels do not tell us much about Joseph—just enough to make us realize his special place in God's plan of salvation. God selected this "just man" (cf. Mt 1:19) to be the foster father of Jesus and the guardian of the Blessed Mother. A humble laborer, Joseph worked hard to support his family. He reached great holiness by faithfully fulfilling the ordinary duties of life.

Generations of Christians have received great favors through St. Joseph's powerful intercession. He is venerated as a model for laborers, the saint of divine providence, and the patron of a holy death. In 1870 Pope Pius IX proclaimed him patron of the universal Church. St. Joseph's feastday is March 19, and the feast of St. Joseph the Worker is May 1.

Devotion of the Seven Sundays

An excellent means to obtain special favors through St. Joseph's intercession is to honor his seven sorrows and seven joys on seven consecutive Sundays. This devotion may be practiced at any time of the year, but fervent followers of St. Joseph like to venerate him especially on the seven Sundays preceding his feast. In this season they have more confident hope of obtaining some particular favor.

St. Teresa tells us that St. Joseph frequently obtained for her far greater favors than those for which she had asked.

The seven Sundays in honor of St. Joseph are observed as follows: on each Sunday Holy Communion is received in St. Joseph's honor and the prayers commemorating his seven sorrows and seven joys are recited.

Persons seeking a special favor may also have seven Masses offered in honor of St. Joseph or take part in seven Masses, give seven donations or fast seven times, pay seven visits to a chapel or to an image of the saint. The prayers of the seven sorrows and seven joys of St. Joseph may be said for nine days, as a novena, or for thirty days, concluding with the reception of the sacraments. It is very pleasing to St. Joseph to aid those souls in purgatory who during life practiced special devotion to him. We might promise St. Joseph that if he comes to our aid we will have one or more Masses said for the poor souls or offer Holy Communion for them.

St. Teresa, who experienced the power and help of St. Joseph in an astonishing manner, urged everyone, for love of God, to try practicing devotion to this glorious saint. She tells us that she cannot remember ever having asked St. Joseph for anything without receiving it.

Prayers in Honor of the Seven Sorrows and Joys of St. Joseph

1. O glorious St. Joseph, chaste spouse of Mary most holy, what anguish filled your heart when you thought of putting your spouse away privately. Yet your joy was unspeakable when the stupendous mystery of the incarnation was made known to you by the angel.

By this sorrow and joy of yours, we ask you to comfort us with the joy of a good life, followed by a holy death, patterned after your own, in the arms of Jesus and Mary.

(Our Father, Hail Mary, Glory be)

2. O glorious St. Joseph, chosen to be the foster father of the Word made flesh, your sorrow at seeing the child Jesus born in such poverty was changed into heavenly exultation when you heard the angelic hymn and beheld the glories of that resplendent night.

By this sorrow and joy, we beg you to obtain for us the grace to one day hear the angelic songs of praise and rejoice in the shining splendor of heavenly glory.

(Our Father, Hail Mary, Glory be)

3. O glorious St. Joseph, you faithfully obeyed the law of God. Your heart was pierced at the sight of the precious blood shed by the Infant Savior during his circumcision, but the name "Jesus" gave you new life and filled you with quiet joy.

By this sorrow and joy, obtain for us the grace to be freed from all sin during life, and to die rejoicing, with the holy name of Jesus in our hearts and on our lips.

(Our Father, Hail Mary, Glory be)

4. O glorious St. Joseph, most faithful saint who shared the mysteries of our redemption, the prophecy of Simeon regarding the sufferings of Jesus and Mary caused you to shudder with fear. But at the same time it filled you with blessed joy over the salvation which Simeon foretold would be attained by countless persons.

By this sorrow and joy, obtain for us the grace to be numbered among those who, through the merits of Jesus and the intercession of Mary, are destined to enjoy eternal salvation.

(Our Father, Hail Mary, Glory be)

5. O glorious St. Joseph, most watchful guardian of the incarnate Son of God, how you toiled and struggled, caring for the Son of the Most High, especially during the flight into Egypt! Yet at the same time, how you rejoiced to have God himself always near you amid the idols of Egypt.

By this sorrow and joy, obtain for us the grace to keep ourselves safe from the evil one, especially by fleeing spiritual dangers; may every idol of earthly affection be recognized and rejected by us; may we become wholly engaged in serving Jesus and Mary, and for them alone may we live and happily die.

(Our Father, Hail Mary, Glory be)

6. O glorious St. Joseph, you marveled to see the king of heaven obedient to your commands, but your consolation in bringing Jesus out of the land of Egypt was troubled by your fear of Herod's successor; nevertheless, being reassured by the angel, you lived happily at Nazareth with Jesus and Mary.

By this sorrow and joy, obtain for us deliverance from harmful fears, so that we may rejoice in peace of conscience and live in safety with Jesus and Mary, and like you, may die in their company.

(Our Father, Hail Mary, Glory be)

7. O glorious St. Joseph, pattern of all holiness, when you lost the child Jesus through no fault of

yours, you sorrowfully sought him for three days until with great joy you found him in the temple, sitting in the midst of the teachers.

By this sorrow and joy, we beg you to keep us from ever having the misfortune of losing Jesus through mortal sin. But if this grave misfortune should befall us, grant that we may seek Jesus with sorrow until we find him again, ready to show us his mercy, especially at the hour of death. Thus may we enjoy his presence in heaven, and there, in company with you, sing the praises of his divine mercy forever.

(Our Father, Hail Mary, Glory be)

Antiphon: When he began his work, Jesus was about thirty years of age, being—as it was supposed—the son of Joseph.

V. Pray for us, O holy Joseph.

R. That we may be made worthy of the promises of Christ.

Let us pray. O God, who in your providence chose blessed Joseph to be the spouse of your most holy Mother, grant that we may desire the heavenly intercession of him whom we honor on earth as our protector. You live and reign forever and ever. Amen.

Novenas

To St. Joseph, Protector

.St. Joseph, please hear my prayer. You are my glorious protector, and shall ever be, after Jesus and Mary, the object of my deepest veneration and most tender trust. You are the most hidden, though the greatest saint, and are the special patron of those who serve God with great purity and fervor. In union with all those who have ever been devoted to you, I now dedicate myself to your service, begging you, for the sake of Jesus Christ, who condescended to love and obey you as a son, to become a father to me and to obtain for me filial respect, confidence and a child's love for you. O powerful intercessor for all Christians, whose mediation, as St. Teresa assures us, has never been found to fail, please intercede for me now, and obtain for me the particular intention of this novena. *(Specify it.)*

Present me, O great saint, to the Holy Trinity, with whom you have such intimate communication. Obtain that I may never mar by sin the sacred image in whose likeness I was created. Beg for me that my divine Redeemer may enkindle in my heart and in all hearts the fire of his love and infuse therein the virtues of his infancy: his purity, simplicity, obedience and humility. Obtain for me also a fervent devotion to your virgin spouse, and protect me so powerfully in life and death that I may have the happiness of dying, as you did, in the friendship of my Creator, and under the immediate protection of the Mother of God.

O Glorious St. Joseph

O glorious St. Joseph, faithful follower of Jesus Christ, to you we raise our hearts and hands to ask your powerful intercession in obtaining from the compassionate heart of Jesus all the helps and graces necessary for our spiritual and temporal welfare, particularly the grace of a happy death, and the special grace for which we now ask. *(Name it.)*

O guardian of the Word Incarnate, we feel animated with confidence that your prayers for us will be graciously heard at the throne of God.

(Then the following is to be said seven times in honor of the seven joys and seven sorrows of St. Joseph.)

V. O glorious St. Joseph, through the love you bear for Jesus Christ, and for the glory of his name,

R. Hear our prayers and obtain our petitions.

Prayer in Any Difficulty

With childlike confidence I present myself before you, O holy Joseph, faithful foster father of Jesus. I beg your compassionate intercession and support in my present need. I firmly believe that you are most powerful before the throne of God, who chose you to be the foster father of his well beloved Son, Jesus Christ. O blessed saint, you saved that treasure of heaven, with his virginal Mother, from the rage of his enemies. With tireless energy you supplied his earthly needs, and with a father's care you accompanied and protected him in all the journeys of his childhood. Take me also, for the love of Jesus, as your child. With your prayers before God assist me in my present difficulty. The infinite goodness of our Savior, who loved and honored you as his father on earth, cannot refuse you any request now in heaven.

How many people have sought help from you in their needs and have experienced how good, how ready you are to help. How quickly you turn to those who call upon you with confidence! How powerful you are in bringing help and restoring joy to anxious and dejected hearts!

Therefore, I fly to you, most worthy father of Jesus, most chaste spouse of Mary. Good St. Joseph,

I ask you, by the burning love you had for Jesus and Mary on earth, to console me in my distress and present my petition, through Jesus and Mary, before the throne of God! One word from you will cheer my afflicted spirit. Then most joyfully I shall praise and thank both God and you. Amen.

Bless Me, St. Joseph

Bless me, O my dearly beloved father St. Joseph. Bless my body and my soul. Bless my resolutions, my words and deeds, all my actions, my every step. Bless all that I possess, all my interior and exterior goods—that all may redound to the great honor of God. Bless me for time and eternity and preserve me from every sin.

Obtain for me the great grace to atone for all my sins by love and contrition here on earth, so that after my last breath I may without delay, meet you in heaven and thank you for all the love and goodness you have shown me here below. Amen.

(Now pray the Our Father, Hail Mary, *and* Glory be *three times, in thanksgiving to God for the graces and privileges given by him to St. Joseph.)*

O Jesus, Mary and Joseph, accept these prayers from me, a poor sinner. Please look on me with compassion and grant my petition.

I beg you by the faithful love which you had for one another, and by all the mercy you have shown to those in distress, to show your love also to me in my present need and grant my earnest request.

To St. Joseph, Spouse of the Blessed Virgin Mary and Patron of the Church

O glorious St. Joseph, you were chosen by God to be the foster father of Jesus, the chaste spouse of Mary ever Virgin, and the head of the Holy Family. You were then appointed by the Vicar of Christ to be the heavenly patron and defender of the Church founded by Jesus. Most confidently I ask your powerful help for the pilgrim Church. Shield especially with your fatherly love the Holy Father and all the bishops and priests in union with the See of Peter. Defend all who labor for the Gospel amid the trials and tribulations of this life. May all the peoples of the earth find a spiritual home in that Church which is the ark of salvation for all.

St. Joseph, please also accept this dedication of myself which I now make to you. I dedicate myself wholly to you, that you may ever be my father, my patron and my guide in the way of salvation. Obtain for me great purity of heart and a fervent devotion to the interior life. Grant that, following your example,

I may direct all my actions to the greater glory of God, in union with the Sacred Heart of Jesus, the Immaculate Heart of Mary and your own heart. Finally, pray for me that I may partake in the peace and joy which were yours at the hour of your holy death. Amen.

Prayer to St. Joseph, Patron of the Universal Church

Most powerful intercessor, St. Joseph, patron of the universal Church, which has always invoked you in anxiety and trouble, cast a loving glance upon the whole Catholic world. Let your fatherly heart be touched at the sight of Christ's mystical spouse and his vicar overwhelmed with sorrow and persecuted by powerful enemies. By the sorrows and trials you experienced on earth, comfort and defend the Holy Father; intercede for him with the giver of peace and charity, so that in peace and unity, the entire Church may serve God in perfect liberty. Amen.

To You, Blessed Joseph

To you, blessed Joseph, we come in our trials, and having asked the help of your most holy spouse, we confidently ask your patronage also. Through that charity which bound you to the Immaculate

Virgin Mother of God and through the fatherly love with which you embraced the child Jesus, we humbly beg you graciously to look upon the inheritance which Jesus Christ has purchased by his blood, and to aid us in our necessities with your power and strength.

Most watchful guardian of the Holy Family, defend the chosen children of Jesus Christ; most loving father, keep far from us every error and sinful influence. Our most mighty protector, be gracious to us and from heaven assist us in our struggle against the power of darkness. And, as once you rescued the child Jesus from danger, so now protect God's holy Church from the power of Satan and from all harm. Shield, too, each one of us by your constant protection, so that, supported by your example and your help, we may be able to live devoutly, to die holily, and to obtain eternal happiness in heaven. Amen.

Litany of St. Joseph

Lord, have mercy on us.
Christ, have mercy on us.
Lord, have mercy on us.
Christ, hear us.
Christ, graciously hear us.
God, the Father of heaven, have mercy on us.

God the Son, Redeemer of the world,*
God the Holy Spirit,
Holy Trinity, one God,
Holy Mary, pray for us.**
St. Joseph,
Renowned offspring of David,
Light of patriarchs,
Spouse of the Mother of God,
Chaste guardian of the Virgin,
Foster father of the Son of God,
Diligent protector of Christ,
Head of the Holy Family,
Joseph most just,
Joseph most chaste,
Joseph most prudent,
Joseph most strong,
Joseph most obedient,
Joseph most faithful,
Mirror of patience,
Lover of poverty,
Model of artisans,
Glory of home life,
Guardian of virgins,

---

* *have mercy on us.*
** *pray for us.*

Pillar of families,

Solace of the suffering,

Hope of the sick,

Patron of the dying,

Terror of demons,

Protector of Holy Church,

Lamb of God, you take away the sins of the world, spare us, O Lord.

Lamb of God, you take away the sins of the world, graciously hear us, O Lord.

Lamb of God, you take away the sins of the world, have mercy on us.

V. He made him lord of his household,

R. And ruler over all his possessions.

Let us pray. O God, in your providence you chose blessed Joseph to be the spouse of your most holy Mother. Grant, we beg you, that we may be worthy to have as our intercessor in heaven him whom we venerate as our protector on earth. You live and reign forever and ever. Amen.

To St. Joseph, for the Dying

St. Joseph, foster father of our Lord Jesus Christ, and true spouse of the Virgin Mary, pray for us and for the dying of this day.

Prayer of St. Clement Mary Hofbauer

St. Joseph, my loving father, I place myself forever under your protection. Look on me as your child and keep me from all sin. I take refuge in your arms, so that you may lead me in the path of virtue and assist me at the hour of my death.

Praises of St. Joseph

O holy Joseph, ever blessed be your soul, which was adorned with all the virtues and gifts of the Holy Spirit.
Glory be.

O holy Joseph, ever blessed be your mind, which was full of the most sublime knowledge of God and enlightened with revelations.
Glory be.

O holy Joseph, ever blessed be your will, which was aflame with love for Jesus and Mary and always perfectly abandoned to the divine will.
Glory be.

O holy Joseph, ever blessed be your eyes, to which it was granted to look continually upon Jesus and Mary.
Glory be.

O holy Joseph, ever blessed be your ears, which merited to hear the words of Jesus and Mary.

Glory be.

O St. Joseph, ever blessed be your tongue, which continually praised God and with profound humility and reverence conversed with Jesus and Mary.

Glory be.

O chaste St. Joseph, ever blessed be your most pure and loving heart, with which you ardently loved Jesus and Mary.

Glory be.

O holy Joseph, ever blessed be your thoughts, words and actions, each and all of which always tended to the service of Jesus and Mary.

Glory be.

O holy Joseph, ever blessed be all the moments of your life, which you spent in the service of Jesus and Mary.

Glory be.

O glorious St. Joseph, ever blessed be that moment in which you most peacefully died in the arms of Jesus and Mary.

Glory be.

O glorious St. Joseph, ever blessed be that moment in which you entered into the eternal joys of heaven.

Glory be.

O St. Joseph, ever blessed in eternity be the incomprehensible bliss of union with God, with Jesus and Mary that you enjoy together with all the saints of heaven.

Glory be.

Great protector! Be ever blessed by me and by all creatures, for all eternity, with all the blessings given you by the Most Holy Trinity, Mary and the whole Church.

Glory be.

O holy Joseph, blessed in soul and in body, in life and in death, on earth and in heaven, obtain also for me, a sinner, but nevertheless your true and faithful follower, a share in your blessings, the grace to imitate you ardently, the grace to love and faithfully serve Jesus, Mary and yourself, and especially the happiness of dying in your holy arms.

Glory be.

Consecration to St. Joseph

I come before you, O glorious St. Joseph, and sincerely venerate you as the chaste spouse of the Mother of God, as the head of the holiest family that ever existed, as the foster father of Jesus Christ, as the faithful preserver of the treasures of the Blessed Trinity. In you I venerate the choice of God the Father. He desired to share with you his power over his eternal, only-begotten Son, who wished to be dependent on you and to owe his subsistence to the labor of your hands. In you I venerate the choice of God the Holy Spirit, who wished to entrust to you his faithful spouse and to give you to her as her guardian and companion through life.

I honor you for the privilege of being permitted to carry Jesus Christ, the Son of God, in your arms, to hold him close to you, to embrace him lovingly. Who can comprehend the overwhelming treasures of light, wisdom and grace which you acquired during the time you lived in the company of Jesus and Mary!

Penetrated with reverence and love at the sight of your greatness and sanctity, I offer and consecrate to you my heart. After Jesus and Mary, you shall be its lord and master. Henceforth I shall consider you as my father and protector. Regard me as your child.

Let me experience the effects of the high esteem in which you are held by God, and your tender love toward me who have commended myself to your keeping.

Obtain for me a sincere and lasting conversion, with all the graces I need to fulfill the holy will of God. Obtain for me your spirit of interior recollection, your fidelity to grace, your intimate union with God, your profound humility, your patience in trials, your perfect devotion to the ways of divine Providence and especially your fervent love for the most sacred Person of Jesus Christ and for Mary, his immaculate Mother: the virtues which constitute your special, incomprehensible sanctity.

O great saint, take under your protection the devout persons who, after your example, endeavor to imitate Jesus and Mary by leading a hidden, secluded life.

Finally, O glorious saint, through the special grace of your holy death in the arms of Jesus and Mary, obtain for me a similar death, with perfect surrender to the will of God, and the assistance of Jesus and Mary. Amen.

Ven. Henry Maria Boudon

Salutations to St. Joseph

I salute you, Joseph, image of God the Father.

I salute you, Joseph, reputed father of God
the Son.

I salute you, Joseph, sanctuary of the Holy Spirit.

I salute you, Joseph, beloved of the Most Blessed
Trinity.

I salute you, Joseph, spiritual father of the faithful.

I salute you, Joseph, guardian of virginal souls.

I salute you, Joseph, model of patience and
gentleness.

I salute you, Joseph, mirror of humility and
obedience.

I salute you, Joseph, protector of the holy Church.

Blessed are the eyes which have seen what you
have seen.

Blessed are the ears which have heard what you
have heard.

Blessed are the hands which touched the Word
Incarnate.

Blessed are your arms which carried him who
carries all things.

Blessed are your arms in which the Son of God
quietly rested.

Blessed is your heart, which, on the heart of Jesus,
was inflamed with ardent love.

Blessed be the Eternal Father, who chose you
for so sublime a dignity.
Blessed be the Holy Spirit, who sanctified you
in so marvelous a manner.
Blessed be Mary, your spouse, who loved you as
her spouse and brother.
Blessed be the angel who guarded you on earth.
Blessed forever be all who venerate and love you.

M. Olier

Prayer of Confidence in St. Joseph

O St. Joseph, faithful foster father of Jesus Christ, I devoutly come before your sacred image and beg your aid and intercession in my present need. I know and firmly believe that to you all things are possible with God, and that Jesus, who on earth was subject to you, his foster father, can now in heaven refuse you no request. Your faithful servant, the seraphic St. Teresa, experienced this. She declared that she never made a request that you did not grant. She invites all to have recourse to you, assuring them that they will not come away unconsoled.

Encouraged by this promise, I fly to you, O holy Joseph, foster father of Jesus Christ and chaste spouse of Mary. I beg you by the tender love you bore to both, to bestow on me your love and mercy. Comfort me in my present trial and sorrow, and obtain, through the intercession of Jesus and Mary, my request from God the Father. Send but a single sigh up to the heart of your beloved Jesus. Lovingly present my request; then I shall certainly obtain it and be consoled in my distress. *(To obtain this favor I shall now say the Our Father and Hail Mary three times.)*

Ven. Martin Von Cochem

Memorare of St. Joseph

Remember, O most pure spouse of the Virgin Mary, St. Joseph, my beloved patron, that never has it been heard that anyone sought your aid without being comforted. Inspired by this confidence, I come to you and fervently commend myself to you. Despise not my petition, dear foster father of our Redeemer, but graciously accept it. Amen.

Daily Prayer for Protection

Hail, St. Joseph! I, your unworthy child, greet you! You are the faithful protector and intercessor of all who love and venerate you. You know that I have special confidence in you, and, after Jesus and Mary, place all my hope of salvation in you, for you are all-powerful with God and will never abandon your faithful servants. Therefore, I humbly call upon you and entrust myself, with all who are dear to me, and all my possessions, to your secure protection and powerful intercession. I beseech you, by the love of Jesus and Mary, do not abandon me during life, and assist me at the hour of my death. Amen.

Ven. Martin Von Cochem

Prayer for Guidance

O glorious St. Joseph, spouse of the Immaculate Virgin, obtain for me a pure, humble and charitable mind, and perfect abandonment to the divine will. Be my guide, my father and my model through life, that I may merit to die as you did in the arms of Jesus and Mary. Amen.

Prayer for a Lively Faith

St. Joseph, obtain for me a lively faith, the foundation of all sanctity, that faith without which no one can be pleasing to God. Obtain for me that faith which triumphs over all temptations of the world and conquers human respect, that faith which can be shaken by nothing, and is directed solely toward God. Cause me after your example to live by faith, to subject my heart and understanding to God, that at last I may behold in heaven what I now firmly believe on earth.

Prayer to Obtain a Conversion

O holy St. Joseph, who merited to be called just by the Holy Spirit, I urgently recommend to you the conversion of *(N.)*, whom Jesus redeemed at the price of his precious blood. You know how sad is the state and how unhappy the lives of those who have banished this loving Savior from their hearts, and how greatly they are exposed to the danger of losing him eternally. I beg you not to permit a person so dear to me to live far from God. Preserve him/her from all danger. Touch the heart of this prodigal, and lead him/her back to God. Do not abandon him/her until you have opened to him/her the gates of the heavenly city, where he/she will praise and bless you throughout eternity for the graces owed to your powerful intercession.

Prayer to St. Joseph, the Worker

Glorious St. Joseph, pattern of all who are devoted to work, obtain for me the grace to labor in the spirit of penance, to atone for my many sins; to work conscientiously, putting devotion to duty before my own inclinations; to work with thankfulness and joy, deeming it an honor to use and to develop, by my labor, the gifts I have received from God; to work with order, peace, moderation and patience, without ever shrinking from weariness and difficulties; to work above all with a pure intention and with detachment from self, having always before my eyes the hour of death and the account which I must then render of time poorly spent, of talents unused, of good undone, and of my empty pride in success, which is so fatal to the work of God. All for Jesus, all through Mary, all in imitation of you, O holy Joseph! This shall be my motto in life and in death. Amen.

St. Pius X

Parents' Prayer to the Holy Family

Jesus, only-begotten Son of the Eternal Father, beloved Son of the Blessed Virgin and foster child of St. Joseph, we fervently implore you, through Mary, your ever blessed Mother, and your adopted father, St. Joseph, to take our children under your special charge and enclose them in the love of your Sacred Heart. They are the children of your Father in heaven, and they were created after his own image. They are your possession, for you have purchased them with your precious blood. They are temples of the Holy Spirit, who sanctified them in baptism and implanted in their hearts the virtues of faith, hope and charity.

O most loving Jesus, rule and guide them, that

they may live according to our holy faith, that they may not waver in their confidence in you and may ever remain faithful in your love.

O Mary, blessed Mother of Jesus, grant to our children a place in your pure, maternal heart! Spread over them your protecting mantle when danger threatens their innocence. Keep them firm when they are about to stray from the path of virtue, and should they have the misfortune to fall, then raise them up again, and reconcile them with your divine Son.

And you, O holy foster father, St. Joseph, do not abandon our children! Protect them from the assaults of the devil, and deliver them from all dangers of soul and body. Jesus and Mary, parents of the holy child Jesus, intercede for us also, that we may bring up our children in the love and fear of God, and one day attain with them the beatific vision. Amen.

Covenant of Love
with Jesus, Mary and Joseph

Jesus, Mary and Joseph, I, a poor creature offer and consecrate to your most loving and gentle hearts my whole life, all my labors, trials and sufferings, that henceforth I may be enclosed in your love and belong to you entirely, with the intention to do and suffer everything for the love of you, and to renounce everything that might displease or separate me from you.

I consecrate to you my heart, that by its every beat I may offer you, in sincere love, all the homage that a devout heart is capable of rendering.

I consecrate to you my tongue, to offer you all the praise and gratitude that is due to you, and to atone for all the insults with which you have ever been offended.

I consecrate to you my eyes, that they may ever remain pure, and that I may one day be permitted to gaze upon you in heaven.

I consecrate to you my hands, that in spirit I may embrace you and in fervent love press you to my heart.

I consecrate to you my feet, that every step may be for you, and that through you I may advance in every virtue.

Jesus, Mary and Joseph, I will belong to you in life and in death. Amen.

Prayer to St. Joseph for Purity

St. Joseph, father and guardian of virgins, into whose faithful keeping were entrusted innocence itself, Jesus Christ, and Mary, the virgin of virgins, I pray and beseech you, through Jesus and Mary, those pledges so dear to you, to keep me from all uncleanness, and to grant that my mind may be untainted, my heart pure and my body chaste. Help me always to serve Jesus and Mary in perfect chastity. Amen.

A Morning Offering to St. Joseph

Receive me, St. Joseph, and the offering of every movement of body and soul, which I desire to present through you to my blessed Lord. Purify everything! Make all a perfect sacrifice! May every beat of my heart be a spiritual communion; every look and thought an act of love; every action a holy sacrifice; every word an arrow of divine love; every step an advance toward Jesus; every visit to our Lord as pleasing to God as the errands of angels; every thought of you, St. Joseph, an act to remind you that I am your child.

I recommend to you the situations in which I usually fail, particularly.... Accept each little devotion of the day, though imperfect, and offer it to Jesus, whose mercy will overlook all, since he regards not so much the gift as the love of the giver.

Offering to St. Joseph

Great St. Joseph, generous trustee and dispenser of heavenly riches, we ask you to receive us as your servants and your children. Next to the sacred hearts of Jesus and Mary, of which you are the faithful copy, we acknowledge that there is no heart more tender or compassionate than yours. We have nothing to fear, and we can hope for everything, since you are our benefactor, our teacher, our model, our father and our mediator. Obtain this favor for us, O powerful protector! We ask it of you by the love you have for Jesus and Mary. Into your hands we commit our souls and our bodies, but above all, the last moments of our lives. After having honored, imitated and served you on earth, may we eternally sing with you the mercies of Jesus and Mary. Amen.

O holy St. Joseph, we give thanks to God for the outstanding favors conferred on you, and we beg your intercession to help us imitate your virtues. Pray for us, O great saint, that we may be humble, patient and trustful like you, and by that love which you have for Jesus and Mary, and the love which they have for you, obtain for us the grace to live and die in their love. Amen.

Blessing of St. Joseph

May the poverty of my sweet and suffering little child be your riches; his sighs and tears, the consolation of your days; the love of his Infant Heart, all your earthly treasure; and the clear vision of his adorable and glorified humanity, your eternal joy and recompense. Amen.

O Joseph, foster father of Jesus, most pure spouse of the Virgin Mary, pray every day for us to the Son of God, that we, being defended by the power of his grace and striving for holiness in life, may be crowned by him at the hour of death.

Patron of a Happy Death

It is undeniable that St. Joseph is a special protector of his dying followers and all those in their last agony. This has been experienced by countless persons who practiced special devotion to St. Joseph during life. At the hour of death, a person may be subject to untold suffering and anguish. At that supreme moment the Christian may undergo a terrible trial, upon which depends eternal joy or endless woe. The fury of hell, the remembrance of past sins, the uncertainty of the future, the pains of death, the terror of the judgment—all these are sources of untold sufferings. What saint could defend us better than St. Joseph, whom the Christian world acknowledges as the protector and patron of the dying!

St. Joseph is a special patron of the dying for three reasons: 1) He is the foster father of the eternal judge, who can refuse him no request. 2) He is terrible to demons; the Church calls him the conqueror of hell. 3) His own death was most holy, for he died in the arms of Jesus and Mary. This is the principal reason why he is the patron of a happy death; the death of no other saint was so blissful, so glorious. Jesus and Mary together closed Joseph's eyes in death and shed tears at his departure. If Jesus wept over Lazarus, how he must have wept over St. Joseph!

Wonderful examples from the lives of many ordinary Christians could be cited to show how St. Joseph obtained for them a happy death because during life they had prayed to him for this grace. Let us remind him of his holy departure in the arms of Jesus and Mary, and daily ask him to assist us at the hour of our own death.

Prayers for a Happy Death

O blessed St. Joseph, who breathed forth your last breath in the holy presence of Jesus and Mary, when my death approaches, come, holy father, with Jesus and Mary, to aid me and obtain for me the only consolation which I ask at that hour—to die under your protection. Into your sacred hands, O Jesus, Mary and Joseph, I commend myself in life and at the point of death.

Jesus, Mary and Joseph, I give you my heart and my soul.

Jesus, Mary and Joseph, assist me in my last agony.

Jesus, Mary and Joseph, may I breathe forth my soul in peace with you.

Hail, Joseph, most holy virginal spouse of the Virgin Mother of God and foster father of Jesus! You were worthy of seeing, hearing, embracing and greeting the infant Incarnate Word, and you enjoyed the special privilege of pleasant conversations with Jesus and Mary. Because it was in their arms that your immaculate soul passed forth from your chaste body, be to me a powerful defender at the moment of death. As you surpassed everyone in sanctity on earth and in glory among the blessed, obtain for me a holy life and a peaceful death. Amen.

Prayer to Jesus, Mary and Joseph for a Happy Death

My dearest and most beloved Jesus, who sacrificed everything, even your life, for my soul, that it should not be lost, be to me a Savior in my last hour, and deliver my soul from the power of its enemies. I am a weak sinner; I have fallen into so many sins! How would I endure my final struggle and escape the last temptations of the enemy, if you, O my Jesus, were to desert me, and not put the evil one to flight?

By that abandonment which you endured for me on the cross, and by the agony of death you suffered for me, I earnestly beg you to strengthen my faith, support my hope, preserve and increase my love, and grant me the grace to surrender my spirit with perfect trust into the hands of your heavenly Father, that I may obtain a favorable and merciful judgment. Do not permit that your precious blood, your bitter passion and death, shall have been offered in vain for me!

O Mary, most tender Virgin, and Mother of Jesus, health of the sick, hope of the dying, see how much I need your help! Come to my assistance, O comforter of the afflicted. After God, you are my surest hope. I believe that I cannot be lost if I hold fast to you.

My loving Mother, faithfully I entrust myself to you and ask you to enclose me in your motherly heart. Remember me not only now, but especially in my last agony when I shall be abandoned by the world. Assist me when my strength fails and my tongue can no longer pronounce the holy name of Jesus and your own consoling name. Remember then my earnest pleading, and let me experience your tender care, that I may arrive happily at the end of my earthly pilgrimage.

St. Joseph, faithful foster father of Christ, you have been appointed by God as a special patron of the dying, and as such the Church venerates you. I therefore call upon you in my distress and commend myself to you in my departure from this world.

O St. Joseph, obtain for me the grace that I, too, may have the inexpressible happiness of dying assisted by Jesus and Mary. When my soul enters its last struggle, call upon your divine foster child and your most holy spouse, that the evil one may not approach, and that my soul may depart in peace. Amen.

Petition for Our Dying Moment

O glorious St. Joseph, whom I contemplate dying between Jesus and Mary, obtain for me, as well as for all those who are dear to me, the grace of leading a life like yours, so that, like you, we may die the death of the just, assisted in our last struggle by our divine Savior and his most holy Mother. O Joseph, holy patron of a good death, I take refuge in you, to implore you to aid me at the moment when the sovereign judge will call me to appear in his presence. When my eyes shall be ready to close to the light of this world, when my tongue shall be able to repeat the names of Jesus and Mary only with difficulty, come to me—come to present my soul to

God, who wished to be as a son to you, and obtain that the judgment he shall pronounce over me may make me a partaker of the glory you enjoy in heaven.

For the Dying

Eternal Father, by your love for St. Joseph, whom you chose to represent you on earth, have mercy on us and on the dying.

(Our Father, Hail Mary, Glory be)

Eternal divine Son, by your love for St. Joseph, who was your faithful guardian on earth, have mercy on us and on the dying.

(Our Father, Hail Mary, Glory be)

Eternal divine Spirit, by your love for St. Joseph, who so carefully watched over Mary, your beloved spouse, have mercy on us and on the dying.

(Our Father, Hail Mary, Glory be)

Litany for the Dying

(For private use)

Lord, have mercy on us.
Christ, have mercy on us.
Lord, have mercy on us.
Christ, hear us.
Christ, graciously hear us.
God, the Father of heaven, have mercy on us.

God the Son, Redeemer of the world,*

God the Holy Spirit,

Holy Trinity, one God,

St. Joseph, foster father of Christ, we beseech you,
hear us.

St. Joseph, patron of the dying,**

Obtain for them the forgiveness of their sins,

Obtain for them great patience,

Obtain for them perfect resignation,

Obtain for them a living and unshaken faith,

Obtain for them a firm confidence,

Obtain for them ardent charity,

Avert from them the attacks of the enemy,

Protect them from the temptations
that assail them,

Preserve them from despondency and despair,

Obtain for them the grace of Jesus Christ,

Assist them and do not abandon them,

Come to their aid in their weakness,

Assist them in their abandonment,

Obtain for them a happy death,

Obtain for them a merciful judgment,

Conduct their souls to the vision of Jesus,
there to obtain mercy for them,

---

* *have mercy on us.*
** *we beseech you, hear us.*

Aspirations

To be pronounced to a dying person

O God, be gracious to me; O God, have mercy on me; O God, forgive me my sins! O God the Father, have mercy on me; O Jesus, be gracious to me; O Holy Spirit, strengthen me!

O God the Father, do not reject me; O Jesus, do not abandon me; O God the Holy Spirit, do not forsake me!

O my God, into your hands I commend my spirit; O Jesus, Son of David, have mercy on me! O Jesus, Son of Mary, have mercy on me!

O Jesus, I believe in you; O Jesus, I hope in you; O Jesus, I love you!

O Jesus, I place all my trust in your bitter passion!

O Jesus, I hide myself in your sacred wounds!

O Jesus, I enclose myself in your Sacred Heart!

Holy Mary, Mother of God, assist me!

Holy Mary, protect me from the evil spirit!

Holy Mary, turn your eyes of mercy toward me!

O Mary, Mother of mercy, obtain grace for me from your dear Son!

O Mary, come to my aid in my anguish and need!

O Mary, enclose me in your virginal heart!

O Mary, commend me to your Son; present me to your Son; reconcile me with your Son!

St. Joseph, obtain for me grace and mercy!

St. Joseph, assist me in my struggle!

St. Joseph, to you I entrust my soul. Save it for me!

St. Joseph, remember me, and obtain mercy for me!

O holy guardian angel, do not abandon me, but combat for me and preserve me from the evil one!

My dear patron saint, pray for me!

Jesus, into your hands I commend my spirit!

Prayer for Those at the Point of Death

O St. Joseph, protector of those in agony, take pity on those who at this very moment are engaged in their last combat. Take pity on my own soul when the hour of death shall come for me. Do not abandon me; in granting your assistance, show that you are my good father, and grant that my divine Savior may receive me with mercy into that dwelling where the elect enjoy a life that shall never end!

Prayers to St. Jude

Patron of Impossible, Desperate Cases

St. Jude is mentioned only briefly in the New Testament, as one of the twelve apostles. He bears the surname "Thaddeus" (meaning amiable or loving), which distinguishes him from Judas Iscariot, the disciple who betrayed Jesus. Beyond that, very little is known about St. Jude. Ancient traditions recount that he preached the Gospel in Mesopotamia and Persia, and was eventually martyred.

It wasn't until the 20th century that devotion to St. Jude became popular. He is venerated as the patron of hopeless and desperate cases, and his intercession has obtained countless favors. Jude's feast-day is October 28.

Novenas

Any of the following prayers may be used for a novena, according to one's needs.

Prayer for a Special Favor

Glorious apostle St. Jude Thaddeus, true lover of Jesus and Mary, through the Sacred Heart of Jesus

I praise and thank God for all the graces he has bestowed upon you. With humility I ask you to look down upon me with compassion. Please hear my poor prayers; do not let my trust be disappointed; to you God has granted the privilege of giving help in the most desperate cases. Come to my aid, that I may praise the mercies of God! All my life I will be grateful to you and will be your faithful devotee until I can thank you in heaven. Amen.

Prayer for Spiritual Help

Glorious apostle, martyr and servant of Jesus, St. Jude Thaddeus, you spread the Gospel among the most distant nations, and won many people to faith in Jesus Christ by the power of his holy word. Grant, I beg you, that from this day I may renounce every sinful habit, that I may be preserved from all evil thoughts, that I may always obtain your assistance, particularly in danger and difficulty, and that I may reach the heavenly country, with you to adore the Most Holy Trinity, the Father, Son and Holy Spirit, forever and ever. Amen.

Prayer for Help in Trials

This and the following prayer may be said in times of great affliction, or when one seems to be deprived of all visible help, and for cases despaired of.

Most holy apostle St. Jude, faithful servant and friend of Jesus, the name of the traitor who delivered your beloved Master into the hands of his enemies has caused you to be forgotten by many. But the Church honors and invokes you universally as the patron of hopeless cases—of things despaired of. Pray for me in my present necessity. Make use, I implore you, of that particular privilege accorded you of bringing visible and speedy help where help is almost despaired of. Come to my assistance in this great need, that I may receive the consolations and help of heaven in all my necessities, tribulations and sufferings, particularly...*(here make your request),* and that I may bless God with you and all the elect throughout eternity.

I promise you, O blessed St. Jude, to be ever mindful of this great favor, and I will never cease to honor you as my special and powerful patron and to do all in my power to encourage devotion to you. Amen.

Prayer in Serious Trouble

St. Jude Thaddeus, relative of Jesus and Mary, glorious apostle and martyr, you are renowned for your virtues and miracles, and are a faithful and prompt intercessor for all who honor you and trust in you. Powerful patron and helper in times of serious trouble, I come to you and ask you with all my heart to come to my aid, for you have received from God the privilege of assisting with manifest help those who almost despair. Look down upon me; I have a heavy cross to carry. I feel discouraged and even almost hopeless. Divine Providence seems lost to my sight, and faith seems to falter in my heart. You cannot forsake me in this serious difficulty! I will not depart from you until you have heard me. Hasten to my aid. I will thank God for the graces bestowed upon you, and will propagate your honor in whatever way I can. Amen.

Prayer for a Sick Person

Almighty and Eternal God, the everlasting salvation of those who believe, hear us on behalf of your servant *N.*, for whom we implore the aid of your tender mercy, that being restored to bodily health, he/she may give thanks to you in your Church, through Christ our Lord. Amen.

Praise and Thanksgiving

It was revealed to St. Gertrude that it is a source of great joy to the saints when we praise and thank God for the graces and privileges he has bestowed upon them. Devotees of St. Jude may recite the following act of thanksgiving frequently.

Lord Jesus Christ, I praise, glorify and bless you for all the graces and privileges you have bestowed upon your chosen apostle and intimate friend, Jude Thaddeus. I implore you for the sake of his merits, grant me your grace, and through his intercession come to my aid in all my needs. Especially at the hour of my death strengthen me against the power of my enemies. Amen.

Litany in Honor of St. Jude

(For private use)

Lord, have mercy.

Christ, have mercy.

Lord, have mercy.

Christ, hear us.

Christ, graciously hear us.

God the Father of heaven, have mercy on us.

God the Son, Redeemer of the world,*

---

* *have mercy on us.*

God the Holy Spirit,

Holy Trinity, one God,

St. Jude, relative of Jesus and Mary, pray for us.

St. Jude, while on earth deemed worthy to see Jesus
and Mary, and to enjoy their company,**

St. Jude, raised to the dignity of an apostle,

St. Jude, honored in beholding the Divine Master
humble himself to wash your feet,

St. Jude, who at the Last Supper received the
Holy Eucharist from the hands of Jesus,

St. Jude, who after the profound grief which the
death of your beloved Master caused you,
had the consolation of seeing him risen from
the dead, and of assisting at his glorious
ascension,

St. Jude, filled with the Holy Spirit on the day
of Pentecost,

St. Jude, who preached the Gospel in Persia,

St. Jude, who converted many people to the Faith,

St. Jude, who performed wonderful miracles
in the power of the Holy Spirit,

St. Jude, who restored an idolatrous king to health
of both soul and body,

St. Jude, who imposed silence on demons and
confounded their oracles,

** *pray for us.*

St. Jude, who foretold to a weak prince an
  honorable peace with his powerful enemy,
St. Jude, who, disregarding the threats of
  unbelievers, courageously preached the
  doctrine of Christ,
St. Jude, who gloriously suffered martyrdom for the
  love of your Divine Master,
Blessed Apostle, with confidence we invoke you!
  (Say this 3 times.)
St. Jude, help of the hopeless, aid me in my distress!
  (Say this 3 times.)
That by your intercession, both priests and lay
  members of the Church may obtain an ardent
  zeal for the Faith of Jesus Christ, hear us, we
  pray you.
That you would defend our Sovereign Pontiff and
  obtain peace and unity for the Church,*
That all unbelievers may receive the good news
  and be led to the Faith,
That faith, hope and charity may increase in our
  hearts,
That we may be delivered from evil thoughts and
  from the snares of the devil,
That you would aid and protect all those who
  honor you,

---

* *hear us, we pray you.*

That you would preserve us from all sin and from
    all occasions of sin,

That you would defend us at the hour of death
    against the fury of the devil and of all evil
    spirits,

Pray for us, that before death we may expiate
    all our sins by sincere repentance and the
    worthy reception of the holy sacraments,

Pray for us, that we may appease the divine
    justice and obtain a favorable judgment,

Pray for us, that we may be admitted into the
    company of the blessed to rejoice in the
    presence of our God forever,

Lamb of God, you take away the sins of the world,
    spare us, O Lord.

Lamb of God, you take away the sins of the world,
    graciously hear us, O Lord.

Lamb of God, you take away the sins of the world,
    have mercy on us.

Prayers to St. Lucy[*]

St. Lucy was born in Syracuse, Sicily and was martyred about 304 during the persecution of Diocletian. St. Lucy is invoked as the protectress against eye trouble. In art and sculpture she is usually represented holding her eyes on a tray. One medieval artist, Francesco del Cossa, showed her holding a twig on which her eyes were the blossoms. The most popular legends say that the pagan tyrant of Syracuse, Paschasius, had Lucy's eyes put out when she resisted his advances. However, her eyes were miraculously restored.

She has been venerated from time immemorial, and is invoked in the Roman Canon of the Mass. Her feastday is December 13.

---

*These prayers to St. Lucy are reprinted with the kind permission of St. Anthony's Guild, Paterson, New Jersey.

Thirteen Days' Devotion in Honor of St. Lucy, Virgin and Martyr

First Day

St. Lucy, virgin and martyr, glory and honor of the city of Syracuse, I thank God for having given you such great virtues. As you knelt in prayer at St. Agatha's tomb to ask that your mother's health be restored, so I kneel before your image and pray for your protection. Victorious virgin, you are near to the throne of God; obtain for me the fullness of heavenly blessings during these thirteen days while I meditate on your glories. I fervently beseech you and feel certain that in his infinite goodness God will listen to your prayers. If nothing else, O virgin, obtain for me the strength to bear life's struggles and to understand that earthly sufferings will pass and through them I can merit great glory in heaven.

(Our Father, Hail Mary, Glory be)

Second Day

O virgin St. Lucy, you who though living in pagan times preserved your faith in the living and true God, help me through your intercession to keep that precious gift I received in Baptism. You see the many ways that secular society attacks that greatest gift, the Christian Faith.

Virgin and martyr of Jesus Christ, you who did not hesitate to offer your life in witness to the Faith, awaken in everyone's heart a love for God. Intercede with our Lord that those who through ignorance or prejudice are estranged from the true fold may repent and return to it, and thus believe in the only God, the only Shepherd, the only Church.

(Our Father, Hail Mary, Glory be)

Third Day

O virgin of Syracuse, who, inspired by God's love, had a heart full of charity for others, intercede for me that the beauty of Christ's law of love may shine forth in my heart. Many, forgetful of God, turn away from helping the needy, but freely spend money for their own pleasure and enjoyment. Obtain, O beloved virgin, that my heart may always be open to charity and closed to greed.

May the spirit of charity which made you see in the poor the image of the Savior, be in me so that by imitating you I may on the day of judgment merit to answer the call: "Come, blessed of my Father."

(Our Father, Hail Mary, Glory be)

Fourth Day

O virgin St. Lucy, whose life bore fruits of great holiness in the Church, help me to see that humility is the foundation of all virtue. You were brought up to enjoy the riches and honor of a noble family yet chose to renounce all that, to live in obscurity, forgotten by all. Teach me how useless it is to try to attain perfection without humility. For the increase of virtue and not for empty praise, you did not hesitate to humble yourself for the sake of the suffering poor. Make me see my own spiritual poverty and my neighbors' virtues. Inspire in me a love for all people so that I may be pleasing to God.

(Our Father, Hail Mary, Glory be)

Fifth Day

O St. Lucy, who, living apart from the world, was filled with love for the Lamb of God, who gave himself as our food, increase my love for the Holy Eucharist. Just as Christ sacramentally entered the hearts of earlier Christian martyrs before their heroic death, so you had the grace to receive the pure flesh of Jesus in Holy Communion. By the love you felt for our Lord in the Blessed Sacrament, obtain for me the grace to receive him at the hour of death. May the flame of love be enkindled in me so that all may know the charity burning within the heart of Jesus hidden in our holy tabernacles.

(Our Father, Hail Mary, Glory be)

Sixth Day

O virgin of strength, St. Lucy, you who, possessing true faith, were not intimidated by a tyrant's threats, obtain for me from God the gift of perseverance. To the very moment of your martyrdom, which was your life's crown, you suffered temptation and endured scorn, but nothing could make you leave the road to holiness. By reason of the perseverance that was your glory, I beseech you to assist me every moment of my life. If I have ever allowed the pull of temptation to lead me away from God, intercede for me, St. Lucy, that I may be steadfast in my good resolutions, so that by persevering in good works I may gain eternal salvation.

(Our Father, Hail Mary, Glory be)

Seventh Day

O virgin St. Lucy, model of all virtue, kneeling before your image I ask for the gift of mercy. While still young and knowing the saying of Holy Scripture, "Charm is deceitful, and beauty is vain, but a woman who fears the Lord is to be praised" (Prov 31:30), you sacrificed earthly love to consecrate your life to our Savior. By your love for Jesus, whom you knew to be living within you, I beseech you to obtain for me detachment from material things. Let me be blessed, through your intercession, with the seven gifts of the Holy Spirit, so that I may know that all is vanity and emptiness except to love and serve God.

(Our Father, Hail Mary, Glory be)

Eighth Day

O glorious virgin St. Lucy, who in an era of pagan immorality preserved the virtue of chastity, help me to esteem and practice that virtue also. Surrounded as I am by a thousand dangers, I might easily run the risk of falling into sin if I could not find protection and comfort in your powerful intercession. You know it is impossible to preserve purity without the grace of God. Ask that grace for me, so that I may resist temptation just as you refused the tyrant's advances. O chaste martyr, through your intercession, on the day of judgment may I present to God without any stain upon it, the stole of innocence I received in holy Baptism.

(Our Father, Hail Mary, Glory be)

Ninth Day

O blessed virgin Lucy, protectress of those suffering from diseases of the eye, preserve my gift of sight so that I may more easily praise our Lord. O victorious virgin, in contemplating the beauty of the sky, the serenity of the sea, the starlit nights, may my eyes see in creation the glory of God, who directs and rules over all. You who shine as a star—whose very name suggests the splendor of light—obtain for me that my eyes may be opened to the beauty of creation and closed to the ugliness of sin. If through great misfortune I should be tempted by the devil and fall into sin, through your intercession may God grant me the gift of wholehearted repentance of my sins.

(Our Father, Hail Mary, Glory be)

Tenth Day

O glorious martyr of Jesus, St. Lucy, who, although faced with great temptations, in the presence of the tyrant Paschasius gave proof of the beauty of your faith to the point of shedding your blood for it, obtain for me strength and courage to fight the battles of the Lord. It is true, O beloved martyr, that these times are different from yours, but in society today forces are at work to undermine faith. Weak as I am, I might easily fall prey to them. By your intercession obtain for me God's assistance. In the midst of the utter coldness which surrounds me, enkindle in my heart a flaming love for God, that I may overcome all adversities.

(Our Father, Hail Mary, Glory be)

Eleventh Day

O most beloved virgin, recalling your life I am filled with great hope for the triumph of Jesus Christ. St. Lucy, before your death at the hand of the tyrant, with prophetic vision you foretold the end of the persecution and the triumph of the Church. I would also be happy to hear your voice comforting me. You can see, O faithful martyr, that a battle is being waged in the world against our Lord Jesus Christ in which the forces of secularism are striving to drive him from society. May God prevent so great a calamity from happening while I join my prayers with those of the faithful all over the world, to hasten the victory of Jesus Christ, the honor of the Roman Pontiff, the peace of all Christians.

(Our Father, Hail Mary, Glory be)

Twelfth Day

O most pure virgin, in the designs of God you are venerated as protectress of those suffering from eye trouble. I ask you to help me always to preserve the light of my soul. In the midst of the surrounding darkness, intercede for me that I may keep the eyes of my soul always open to truth and closed to error. I implore you, O holy virgin, by virtue of the love you had for truth, not to take away from me your powerful help, which makes me know the beauty of faith, the goodness and infinite mercy of God. Through your intercession may the eyes of my mind never be dimmed by disordered passions, so that after having adored Jesus hidden on the altar I may in heaven openly contemplate him forever.

(Our Father, Hail Mary, Glory be)

Thirteenth Day

St. Lucy, at the end of these thirteen days of prayer, I thank you with all my heart for the graces you have obtained for me. Above all, I thank God for having let fall upon you a ray of his infinite goodness. In contemplating your glories, O victorious martyr, I feel strongly urged to love God, the author of all sanctity. I shall never cease to praise you as an example of strength, a glory of the faith, a light to my soul. And you holy virgin, who were represented as an exemplar of illuminating grace, obtain for me the enlightenment of my mind that I may know God and love him to the end of my life.

(Our Father, Hail Mary, Glory be)

Novena to St. Lucy

1. By your steadfast faith, O glorious St. Lucy, you firmly declared to the ruler that no one could take from you the Holy Spirit, who dwelt in your

heart as in his temple. Obtain for me from God that I may always live in a holy and salutary fear of losing his grace and that I may flee everything that might cause so grievous a loss.

(Our Father, Hail Mary, Glory be)

2. By the great love which your immaculate spouse Jesus Christ had for you, O glorious St. Lucy, when by an unheard-of miracle he rendered you immovable in spite of the attempts of your enemies to drag you into a place of shame and sin, I ask you to obtain for me the grace never to consent to the temptations of the world, the flesh and the devil, and to fight constantly against their assaults by the continuous mortification of all my senses.

(Our Father, Hail Mary, Glory be)

3. By that same ardent love you had for Jesus, O glorious St. Lucy, after consecrating yourself to him by an irrevocable vow, you refused profitable offers of marriage. After distributing all your goods to aid the poor, you sacrificed your life by the blade that pierced your neck. Obtain for me the grace to be filled with holy charity, that I may be ready to renounce worldly goods and to endure all evil rather than become, even in the least degree, unfaithful to Jesus.

(Our Father, Hail Mary, Glory be)

V. Pray for us, St. Lucy.

R. That we may be made worthy of the promises of Christ.

Let us pray. Graciously hear us, O God of our salvation, that even as we rejoice in the constant faith of blessed Lucy, your virgin and martyr, so may we grow in faith, hope and charity. Through Christ our Lord. Amen.

O blessed and beloved St. Lucy, I beseech you to ask the Lord Jesus to protect the light of my eyes that I may make good use of them for the well being of my soul.

Obtain for me the grace that my mind may never be troubled nor my imagination filled with dangerous images and that all I see that is sacred and religious may be healthy food for my spirit, so that I may daily grow in love for my Creator and Redeemer Jesus. Through your intercession I hope to see and love him forever in heaven. Amen.

V. Pray for us, St. Lucy.

R. That we may be made worthy of the promises of Christ.

Let us pray. O God, you were pleased to bless your virgin Lucy with the flame of faith and the crown of martyrdom; grant now through her intercession that we your servants, being freed from all blindness of mind and body, may be more deserving to raise our eyes to heavenly things. Through Christ our Lord.

O God, who gave the world the brightness of the glorious virgin and martyr Lucy—yours through her gift of virginity and wisdom—grant through her intercession that by loving you with a pure heart we may deserve to possess the wisdom of the saints. Through our Lord Jesus Christ, who lives and reigns with you in the unity of the Holy Spirit, God forever and ever. Amen.

St. Lucy, whose name signifies light, to you I come full of confidence, and I ask you to obtain for me a holy light that will make me careful not to walk in the path of sin, nor to remain surrounded by the darkness of error. I ask also, through your intercession, for the preservation of the light of my eyes and an abundance of grace that I may use my sight according to the divine will, without any spiritual harm. Grant, O St. Lucy, that, after venerating and thanking you for your powerful protection here on earth, I may finally share your joy in heaven in the eternal light of the Lamb of God, your beloved Bridegroom, our Lord Jesus Christ. Amen.

Prayers to St. Martin de Porres
(1579-1639)

Patron of African-Americans

Born in Lima, Peru, Martin was the son of a Spanish knight and an African slave girl. Even as a young boy his good-hearted nature made him outstanding for works of charity. Feeling called to the religious life, Martin entered the Dominicans and became a brother. He worked in the hospital and studied medicine so as to be of greater service to the patients. Martin was always concerned about the poor, and he often gave away large amounts of food to the people who came to the monastery gate. But no matter how much he gave away, the pantry never grew bare. Martin's kindness extended even to the animals; he would often be seen feeding the stray dogs or cats who wandered onto the property.

Martin is especially venerated as the patron of African-Americans. His feastday is November 3.

Novena to St. Martin de Porres

First Day

St. Martin's Humility

St. Martin imitated our Lord who was meek and humble of heart. There was no pride or vanity in Martin, who realized that God is our Creator and that we are his creatures. Martin understood that God loves us as children and only wants us to be happy. So he had the wisdom to surrender entirely to the holy will of God. Let us imitate St. Martin by humbly doing the will of God in all things.

Prayer: St. Martin, ask our Lord and his Blessed Mother to give us the grace of true humility that we may not become proud, but may be contented with the gifts that God gives us. Obtain for us the light of the Holy Spirit that we may understand, as you did, that pride is an obstacle to union with God, and that true happiness comes only from doing the will of God. Amen.

Recite one Our Father, ten Hail Marys, one Glory be to the Father.

St. Martin de Porres, pray for us.

Second Day

St. Martin's Love of God

St. Martin was entirely filled with the fire of God's love. He knew that God sent his Son into the world to suffer and die on the cross for our sins. This thought stirred Martin's heart with deep affection for so loving a Redeemer, and his whole life gave evidence of his sincere gratitude. May we, too, learn to love our Savior more and more and show our love by our good works.

Prayer: St. Martin, why are our hearts so cold and lacking in love for the Son of God, who became a little child for our salvation? Why are we so slow to love Jesus, who loved us so much that he gave his life for us? Ask God and Our Lady of Sorrows to make us realize that the only way to happiness is by loving and serving God with our whole heart and soul. Amen.

Recite one Our Father, ten Hail Marys, one Glory be to the Father.

St. Martin de Porres, pray for us.

Third Day

St. Martin's Love for the Poor

St. Martin was called "the Father of the Poor." He saw the poor, the sick, and the dying as children of God, and he helped them in a thousand practical ways. He studied medicine that he might know how to cure the sick. Every day he distributed alms to the poor. He built an orphanage for children. Let us imitate the charity of St. Martin, that God may bless us as he blessed him.

Prayer: St. Martin, teach us to be generous with the gifts that God has given us. Make us sympathetic toward those who are suffering and afflicted. Pray to our Redeemer and to Our Lady of Mercy that we may be compassionate toward others, and that we may always be kind and generous to our neighbors because they are the children of our heavenly Father. Amen.

Recite one Our Father, ten Hail Marys and one Glory be to the Father.

St. Martin de Porres, pray for us.

Fourth Day

St. Martin's Faith

St. Martin had a lively faith in all the teachings of the Catholic Church. He knew the Church was founded by Jesus Christ, the Son of God, who came to teach us the way to the Father. God rewarded Saint Martin's humble faith by enlightening his mind so that he could understand the mysteries of our holy religion. May God give us the grace always to believe the truths which he has revealed.

Prayer: O St. Martin, we need strong faith in God and his holy Church, especially in these days when religion is often considered unimportant. Bring all people to a knowledge and love of the true Church, that they may find the way of salvation and happiness. Ask Christ and Our Lady of Good Counsel to make us faithful disciples of Jesus Christ in life and in death. Amen.

Recite one Our Father, ten Hail Marys, and one Glory be to the Father.

St. Martin de Porres, pray for us.

Fifth Day

St. Martin's Confidence in God

St. Martin put all his trust in the goodness and promises of God. He hoped to obtain an eternal reward, through the grace of God and the merits of Jesus Christ. We know that St. Martin's trust in God was not in vain. We, too, are confident that God will forgive us our sins if we are truly sorry, and that he will give us everlasting life if we serve him faithfully, by obeying his commandments.

Prayer: St. Martin, help us to have a great confidence in almighty God. Make us understand that he is one friend who will never desert us. Keep us from foolishly presuming that we will be saved without doing our part, but keep us also from despair, which forgets the mercy of God. Ask Jesus and his Mother to increase in our hearts faith, hope and charity. Amen.

Recite one Our Father, ten Hail Marys and one Glory be to the Father.

St. Martin de Porres, pray for us.

Sixth Day

St. Martin's Devotion to Prayer

St. Martin kept his mind and heart always lifted up to the Creator of all things. His prayer came from the depths of his being, not just from his lips. He naturally turned to praise and thank God, and to ask him for help. St. Martin prayed with humility and perseverance, and God answered his prayers in miraculous ways. Martin will pray for us before the throne of God in heaven.

Prayer: St. Martin, help us to have great faith in Christ's promise: "Ask, and it will be given you; search, and you will find; knock, and the door will be opened for you" (Mt 7:7). Make us faithful in participating in Holy Mass and in devoting time to personal prayer every day, to obtain the blessings of God. Ask the Queen of the Most Holy Rosary to intercede for us too. Amen.

Recite one Our Father, ten Hail Marys and one Glory be to the Father.

St. Martin de Porres, pray for us.

Seventh Day

St. Martin's Spirit of Penance

St. Martin was a hard worker who dedicated all his energies to his ministry. He did not seek an easy, comfortable life. Even though he labored so hard, he also imposed on himself severe penances for his sins and the salvation of others. If so holy a man did penances, how much more should we, who have seriously offended God by our sins!

Prayer: St. Martin, from you we learn how to be dedicated and unselfish. You teach us to avoid idleness and self-seeking. Give us some of that spirit of penance which you had, so that we may be constant in the struggle with temptation. Ask Jesus crucified and Mary, the Queen of Martyrs, to give us the grace to fight the good fight. Amen.

Recite one Our Father, ten Hail Marys and one Glory be to the Father.

St. Martin de Porres, pray for us.

Eighth Day

St. Martin's Reward

St. Martin died a holy and peaceful death. He had spent his life in doing good as a humble brother of the Dominican Order. But whoever humbles himself shall be exalted. Soon his heroic life became known all over the world, and on May 6, 1962, Pope John XXIII solemnly proclaimed him St. Martin de Porres. Let us rejoice that we have such a powerful intercessor among the saints of God!

Prayer: St. Martin, you have been raised up by God to show us the way to our true home. You have given us the good example and the encouragement that we need. We now realize from your life that all we have to do to win the reward of glory is to love and serve the best of Masters. May we ever be humble that we, too, may be exalted unto everlasting life. Amen.

Recite one Our Father, ten Hail Marys and one Glory be to the Father.

St. Martin de Porres, pray for us.

Ninth Day

St. Martin's Miracles

St. Martin performed many miracles during his life and after his holy death. We can go to him with confidence for he will obtain our petitions if they are for our true welfare. His great heart loves to help us in every way. We have only to tell him our troubles and to ask him to help us. If we do our part, we can be sure that our friend, St. Martin, will do his part.

Prayer: Lord Jesus Christ, who inflamed the heart of St. Martin with an ardent love of the poor and who taught him the wisdom of always surrendering to God's holy will, grant that, like him, we may be ever truly humble of heart and full of Christ-like charity for suffering humanity. Amen.

Recite one Our Father, ten Hail Marys and one Glory be to the Father.

St. Martin de Porres, pray for us.

Prayer to St. Martin de Porres

Most humble Martin of Porres, your burning charity embraced not only the poor and needy but even the animals of the field. For your splendid example of charity, we honor you and invoke your help.

From your place in heaven, hear the requests of your needy brethren, so that, by imitating your virtues we may live contentedly in that state in which God has placed us. And carrying our cross with strength and courage, may we follow in the footsteps of our blessed Redeemer and his most sorrowful Mother, so that at last we may reach the kingdom of heaven through the merits of our Lord Jesus Christ. Amen.

Prayers to St. Patrick
(389-461)

Patron of Ireland

Born in Britain around 389, Patrick was captured by pirates when he was a teenager and brought to Ireland as a slave. After about six years, he escaped and returned to Britain. After ordination to the priesthood, he returned to Ireland and spent the rest of his life there evangelizing the people. His work met with great success and the Catholic Faith has flourished in Ireland ever since.

Patrick could never have foreseen the impact which his life and work would have on the people of Ireland and through them, the world. "In the history of evangelization, the destiny of an entire people...was radically affected for time and eternity because of the fidelity with which St. Patrick embraced and proclaimed the Word of God" (Pope John Paul II).

Patrick died around 461. His feastday is March 17.

To St. Patrick

I salute you, great Saint Patrick, apostle of Ireland, glory of Christianity. I salute you, great saint, full of wisdom and divine love. I rejoice at the favors our Lord has so freely bestowed on you.

Grant that I may imitate your perfect detachment from creatures, your confidence in God, your abandonment to the divine will, your humility, obedience and charity, your generosity in the practice of virtue, and your great apostolic zeal. And having had the happiness of walking in your footsteps here below, may I one day enjoy with you the bliss of heaven.

The Lorica or Breastplate of St. Patrick

By Rev. Martin P. Harney, S.J.

The Lorica is an ancient Gaelic prayer which has been attributed to St. Patrick. It is an invocation of the Holy Trinity, and was usually recited in the morning. In the early Irish Church, loricas were numerous; some were written in Gaelic and some in Latin. Lorica, a Latin word, originally signified a piece of protective armor, a breastplate. This particular lorica has often been called the *Breastplate of St. Patrick.* Lorica-prayers were recited to obtain divine protection against evils, physical or spiritual, especially against the powers of darkness. The loricas replaced heathen incantations when the Irish embraced Christianity.

I bind to myself today
> The strong power of an invocation of the Trinity,
> The faith of the Trinity in Unity,
> The Creator of the universe.

I bind to myself today
> The might of the incarnation of Christ with that of his baptism,
> The might of his crucifixion with that of his burial,
> The might of his resurrection with that of his ascension,
> The might of his coming on the judgment day.

I bind to myself today
> The power in the love of the seraphim,
> In the obedience of the angels,
> In the ministration of the archangels,
> In the hope of resurrection unto reward,
> In the prayers of the patriarchs,
> In the predictions of the prophets,
> In the preaching of the apostles,
> In the faith of the confessors,
> In the purity of the holy virgins,
> In the deeds of righteous men.

I bind to myself today
    The power of heaven,
    The brightness of the sun,
    The whiteness of snow,
    The splendor of fire,
    The speed of lightning,
    The swiftness of wind,
    The depth of the sea,
    The stability of the earth,
    The firmness of rocks.

I bind to myself today
    God's power to pilot me,
    God's might to uphold me,
    God's wisdom to teach me,
    God's eye to watch over me,
    God's ear to hear me,
    God's word to give me speech,
    God's hand to guide me,
    God's way to lie before me,
    God's shield to shelter me,
    God's host to secure me.
      Against the snares of demons,
      Against the seductions of vices,
      Against the lusts of nature,
      Against everyone who meditates injury to me,
      Whether far or near,
      Whether few or with many.

I invoke today all these virtues
> Against every hostile merciless power which
>> may assail my body and my soul,
> Against the incantations of false prophets,
> Against the black laws of heathenism,
> Against the false laws of heresy,
> Against the deceits of idolatry,
> Against the spells of magicians and druids,
> Against every knowledge that blinds the human
>> soul.

Christ protect me today
> Against poison, against burning,
> Against drowning, against wounding,
> That I may receive abundant reward.
> Christ with me, Christ before me,
> Christ behind me, Christ within me,
> Christ under me, Christ above me,
> Christ at my right, Christ at my left,
> Christ in lying down, Christ in sitting,

Christ in rising up.
> Christ in the heart of everyone who
>> thinks of me,
> Christ in the mouth of everyone who speaks
>> to me,
> Christ in every eye that sees me,
> Christ in every ear that hears me.

I bind to myself today
    The strong power of an invocation of the Trinity,
    The faith of the Trinity in Unity,
    The Creator of the universe.
    Salvation is of the Lord,
    Salvation is of the Lord,
    Salvation is of Christ;
    May your salvation, O Lord, be with us forever.

St. Patrick

    Saintly preacher, gentle priest,
    Fearless man of God,
    Give us, we pray, the strength to walk
    The pathways you have trod.
    Give us the strength to do the right
    In spite of sword or spear,
    The courage that makes heroes
    Who know not craven fear.
    You braved the might of princes,
    You knew that they would yield,
    God's grace your only weapon,
    God's love your only shield.
    Teach us your tact and gentleness,
    Your love for truth and right,
    Teach us to rule as you once ruled,
    With kindly word, not might.

Teach us your art of preaching
By example more than word,
Teach us your own unselfishness
In the service of the Lord.

Rev. T. Foy

Prayers to St. Paul

Patron of Evangelizers and of Journalists

St. Paul was so much an evangelizer that he is often referred to as "the Apostle." Born in Tarsus, Paul was a zealous Pharisee who as a young man sought to destroy the Christians. Miraculously converted on his way to Damascus, Paul then turned all his fiery energies into preaching the Gospel of Jesus Christ. For over thirty years he traveled throughout the Roman Empire, preaching to both Jews and Gentiles and establishing Christian communities. He endured scourging, stoning and shipwreck. Nothing could stop him. When he was stoned at Lystra, dragged outside the city and left for dead, he stood up and went out to preach again the next day (cf. Acts 14:19-20).

Paul often wrote to the churches which he had formed. His letters give us a picture of the early Christian communities and contain apostolic teaching which forms the basis of our faith. The *Acts of the Apostles* is an important source of information for the details of Paul's life.

Paul was martyred around 67 AD during Nero's persecution. A shrine in Rome (the Three Fountains) commemorates the spot where he is believed to have been beheaded. June 29 is the feast of Saints Peter and Paul, and January 25 is the feast of Paul's conversion.

Powerful Novena to St. Paul to Obtain Favors

First Day

St. Paul valiantly proclaimed his faith.

"The one who is righteous will live by faith" (Rom 1:17). St. Paul's faith was profound from the start. On his way to Damascus, sternly determined to find and destroy all Christians, he was halted by a blinding light, and Jesus our Lord spoke: "Saul, Saul, why do you persecute me?" Paul asked: "Who are you, Lord?"

"I am Jesus, whom you are persecuting" (Acts 9:4-5).

St. Paul believed and was baptized. After his conversion, the Apostle grew steadily stronger in his faith in God and preached it with fervor and irresistible zeal.

St. Paul's faith was always firm, and for it he made great demands upon himself. In his own words we know that he was "...on frequent journeys, in danger from rivers, danger from bandits, danger from my own people, danger from Gentiles, danger in the city, danger in the wilderness, danger at sea, danger from false brothers and sisters" (2 Cor 11:26). In spite of all this, he never failed, he never stopped, not even before the executioner.

Let us ask St. Paul for an increase of faith, so that we may face the trials of life as he did.

Consideration: How do I react when our Lord permits me to suffer something? Do I turn to him in complete trust and confidence for strength to bear it? Suffering serves to bring persons of strong faith closer to God.

Prayer: O St. Paul the Apostle, preacher of truth, Doctor of the Gentiles, pray to God for us, and grant the grace we ask.

(Our Father, Hail Mary, Glory be)

St. Paul the Apostle, our patron, pray for us and for the apostolate of the media of social communication.

Second Day

"I can do all things through him who strengthens me" (Phil 4:13).

Hope is that virtue by which we trust in God and the necessary graces for our eternal salvation. St. Paul gave an outstanding example of Christian hope.

Amid all obstacles, St. Paul rejoiced greatly: "I

can do all things through him who strengthens me" (Phil 4:13). He teaches us how to avoid the dangers of despair and presumption, and he warns us, in our afflictions, never to lose hope, for little sufferings assure us of great glory in heaven. Being sinners, full of weakness and faults, we should never dare a presumption of any kind; rather, we should fear our frailty and inconstancy.

Consideration: Does hope spring abundantly in my heart? Let me remember that Jesus in the Gospel says: "If in my name you ask me for anything, I will do it" (Jn 14:14).

Prayer: O St. Paul the Apostle, preacher of truth, Doctor of the Gentiles, pray to God for us, and grant the grace we ask.

(Our Father, Hail Mary, Glory be)

St. Paul the Apostle, our patron, pray for us and for the apostolate of the media of social communication.

Third Day

"And now faith, hope, and love abide, these three; and the greatest of these is love" (1 Cor 13:13).

It is impossible to describe the immense charity of the Apostle. In his ardent desire and love for Jesus, he exclaimed: "It is no longer I who live, but it is Christ who lives in me" (Gal 2:20). He also said: "Who will separate us from the love of Christ? Will hardship, or distress, or persecution, or famine, or nakedness, or peril, or sword?... For I am convinced that neither death, nor life, nor angels, nor rulers, nor things present, nor things to come, nor powers, nor height, nor depth, nor anything else in all creation, will be able to separate us from the love of God in Christ Jesus our Lord" (Rom 8:35-39).

Such was St. Paul's love for God, and because of that love he merited to be caught up to the third heaven and speak to our Lord Jesus Christ.

The Apostle laid the greatest stress on the necessity of charity. He deemed this virtue to be so necessary, that he wrote to the Corinthians: "If I speak in the tongues of mortals and of angels, but do not have love, I am a noisy gong or a clanging cymbal. And if I have prophetic powers, and understand all mysteries and all knowledge, and if I have all faith, so as to remove mountains, but do not have love, I am nothing. If I give away all my possessions, and if I hand over my body so that I may boast, but do not have love, I gain nothing" (1 Cor 13:1-3).

The heart of the Apostle was so inflamed and transformed by the love of Jesus Christ, that St. John Chrysostom did not hesitate to affirm that the heart of the Apostle St. Paul was the heart of Christ.

Consideration: Keeping the commandments, receiving the sacraments and being faithful to the precepts of the Church increase our love of God. Am I faithful to my obligations?

Prayer: O St. Paul the Apostle, preacher of truth, Doctor of the Gentiles, pray to God for us, and grant the grace we ask.

(Our Father, Hail Mary, Glory be)

St. Paul the Apostle, our patron, pray for us and for the apostolate of the media of social communication.

Fourth Day

"I am being poured out as a libation over the sacrifice and the offering of your faith" (Phil 2:17).

The Apostle distinguished himself not only in the love of God, but also in the love of neighbor. He wrote to the Thessalonians: "So deeply do we care for you that we are determined to share with you not only the gospel of God but also our ownselves" (1 Thes 2:8).

Elsewhere he remarks that he helped all in need, that he would give himself to all the brethren and save them all. St. Paul worked tirelessly and covered most of the Roman world. He was always hated, threatened and persecuted by relentless enemies, but nothing could stop him; his love was boundless. He tells us to love one another, patiently bearing the shortcomings of others. He told the Romans: "Let love be genuine; hate what is evil, hold fast to what is good; love one another with mutual affection; outdo one another in showing honor" (Rom 12:9-10).

St. Paul also enumerated the characteristics of charity: "Love is patient; love is kind; love is not envious or boastful or arrogant or rude. It does not insist on its own way; it is not irritable or resentful; it does not rejoice in wrongdoing, but rejoices in the truth. It bears all things, believes all things, hopes all things, endures all things" (1 Cor 13:4-7).

Consideration: Lack of charity pierces the heart of Jesus deeply. Do I love my neighbor? How do I show our love? Am I always ready to help others and to defend their reputation?

Prayer: O St. Paul the Apostle, preacher of truth, Doctor of the Gentiles, pray to God for us, and grant the grace we ask.

(Our Father, Hail Mary, Glory be)

St. Paul the Apostle, our patron, pray for us and for the apostolate of the media of social communication.

Fifth Day

St. Paul considered himself the least of all.

God resists the proud and gives grace to the humble. They are blessed by our Lord and loved by all. St. Paul is a model of humility. Speaking of himself, he says: "I will boast all the more gladly of my weaknesses, so that the power of Christ may dwell in me. Therefore I am content with weaknesses, insults, hardships, persecutions and calamities for the sake of Christ; for whenever I am weak, then I am strong" (2 Cor 12:9-10).

Not only in his writings, but also in his life, the humility of the Apostle is evident. Among his own associates he appeared modest and unassuming, for even when commanding or exhorting them to do good for the salvation of others, his attitude was full of humility.

St. Paul humbly admitted, "I am the least of the apostles, unfit to be called an apostle, because I persecuted the church of God" (1 Cor 15:9).

Inspiring humility! He had labored and preached among many peoples, performing miracles and winning converts, yet, he calls himself the least of all. What an example for us! St. Paul considered himself a poor sinner, and we, quite often, forget our failings and our sins and seek praise and honor. At times, we take much pleasure in the little good we do, and boast about it.

Let us imitate St. Paul and heed his warnings: "What do you have that you did not receive? And if you received it, why do you boast as if it were not a gift?" (1 Cor 4:7).

Consideration: How do I practice humility? Do I, perhaps, feel in my heart a desire to show off and be praised? Remembering that the first condition to gain grace from God is humility will help me reject these desires.

Prayer: O St. Paul the Apostle, preacher of truth, Doctor of the Gentiles, pray to God for us, and grant the grace we ask.

(Our Father, Hail Mary, Glory be)

St. Paul the Apostle, our patron, pray for us and for the apostolate of the media of social communication.

Sixth Day

He suffered hunger and thirst.

An excessive desire for riches can put us in danger of eternal ruin, for whoever is extremely attached to riches and other things of this world cannot love and comprehend the things of God. St. Paul persistently warns us to be content with our food and clothing, for we can take nothing with us when we die.

The virtue of poverty shone throughout the Apostle's life. He loved to be poor. In his apostolic journeys he often went without provisions, with only the bare necessities. His food, often received from charitable hands, was very scanty; in many places he suffered hunger and thirst. St. Paul had poor health, yet he traveled many long days under the burning sun, or in the rain, or braving the cold weather. And where did he rest?—on the floor, and often on the bare ground. What a contrast between the life of the Apostle and ours. Before his example, our efforts pale.

Let us ask St. Paul the grace of contentment. If we are well off, let us do some good work, never forgetting our duty to help the Catholic communications apostolate, which is, in our present day, a powerful means of light and salvation.

Consideration: Am I wealthy? Then let me keep my heart free from undue attachment to riches, and be generous in giving to the needy, if I wish to avoid the terrible sentence of our Lord: "It is easier for a camel to go through the eye of a needle than for someone who is rich to enter the kingdom of God" (Mt 19:24). Are my affairs prospering? Then let me practice charity, avoid wasteful spending, and help the Lord to provide for the needy. Am I poor? Let me bear my lot with patience even as I strive to improve it, for in this manner I shall be like our Lord Jesus Christ and St. Paul.

Prayer: O St. Paul the Apostle, preacher of truth, Doctor of the Gentiles, pray to God for us, and grant the grace we ask.

(Our Father, Hail Mary, Glory be)

St. Paul the Apostle, our patron, pray for us and for the apostolate of the media of social communication.

Seventh Day

"I am your father..."

Openly St. Paul proclaims that he is our father, having begotten us in the Gospel of Christ (cf. 1 Cor 4:15). He kept all people in his heart and repeated: "Who is weak, and I am not weak? Who is made to stumble, and I am not indignant?" (2 Cor 11:29).

St. Paul is truly a conqueror and great lover of souls! We are much indebted to him. Let us show our gratitude and pray to imitate him; let us read his life and letters, and spread devotion to him. Let us become better acquainted with his kind and affectionate spirit. No, he is not the severe and grim saint he often appears to be in certain pictures.

We know from his own words that he loves us as a mother loves her children. Let us then stay near to him; he will set us afire with the love of our Savior, and will guard us from all dangers. No one should be afraid to love St. Paul. Our Lord loved St. Paul so much that he made him a vessel of election. St. Paul loves us so much that he said, "For I could wish that I myself were accursed and cut off from Christ for the sake of my own people, my kindred according to the flesh" (Rom 9:3).

While in prison, like a criminal and suffering from anguish and hunger, he remembered that Timothy was suffering from a stomach ailment, and advised him to take certain medicines. The great love of St. Paul! Let us pray to him, and remain under his protection.

Consideration: Let me feel sure that St. Paul loves me and has great powers of intercession. Do I want to enjoy the protection of St. Paul? Pray and confide in him; keep his picture in the home; read his life.

Prayer: O St. Paul the Apostle, preacher of truth, Doctor of the Gentiles, pray to God for us, and grant the grace we ask.

(Our Father, Hail Mary, Glory be)

St. Paul the Apostle, our patron, pray for us and for the apostolate of the media of social communication.

Eighth Day

His zeal had no limits.

St. Paul's zeal was as great as his love. His burning heart longed to preach the Gospel everywhere. He wanted to reach all peoples either with his word or with his writings. His letters have come down through the centuries to us and still do good.

St. Paul's spirit was inflamed with love for Jesus Christ. The Holy Spirit made him say that he would spend himself to save all, for the grace of God was in him.

His labors in the vineyard of the Church were always fruitful with miracles and conversions. Even from prison he wrote: "I suffer hardship, even to the point of being chained like a criminal. But the word of God is not chained" (2 Tim 2:9). Even in prison he preached the Gospel. The jailer at Philippi was converted; at Malta, the Proconsul; at Rome, senators and Hebrews were converted. When the Apostle was taken out of the Mamertine prison to be flogged and executed, three soldiers were converted, and three days after the martyrdom of St. Paul, they too died as martyrs for the Faith.

How small we feel before the Apostle! Truly, many people failed St. Paul, but St. Paul never failed anyone.

Consideration: Am I full of zeal for the salvation of myself and others? Let me ask myself often: What would St. Paul do if he were in my place?

Prayer: O St. Paul the Apostle, preacher of truth, Doctor of the Gentiles, pray to God for us, and grant the grace we ask.

(Our Father, Hail Mary, Glory be)

St. Paul the Apostle, our patron, pray for us and for the apostolate of the media of social communication.

Ninth Day

St. Paul was obedient until death.

The life of St. Paul is an example of obedience to the will of God which was manifested in many ways to him. God commanded him to preach the Gospel to all the world, and he obeyed. St. Peter advised him to cease preaching in Tarsus, and Paul obeyed; he was told to set out on apostolic journeys, and Paul obeyed. He did not hesitate an instant in doing the will of God, even though his goal and intentions were often different and he knew he would meet persecution and sufferings.

Let us imitate St. Paul in his prompt and constant obedience, and say with him: "Lord, what do you want me to do?"

The Apostle tells us to obey promptly: "Obey your earthly masters in everything, not only while being watched and in order to please them, but wholeheartedly, fearing the Lord" (Col 3:22). Moreover, St. Paul tells us to obey the law of God and to persevere in our faith: "Take up the whole armor of God, so that you may be able to withstand on that evil day, and having done everything, to stand firm" (Eph 6:13).

Let us practice the Apostle's teachings, and strive to abandon ourselves to God's loving care.

Consideration: Am I willing to surrender myself to God? Being abandoned to God's holy will is a sure path to holiness and peace of heart, for God wants only the best for me.

Prayer: O St. Paul the Apostle, preacher of truth, Doctor of the Gentiles, pray to God for us, and grant the grace we ask.

(Our Father, Hail Mary, Glory be)

St. Paul the Apostle, our patron, pray for us and for the apostolate of the media of social communication.

Chaplet to St. Paul

I bless you, Jesus, for the great mercy granted to St. Paul in changing him from a bold persecutor to an ardent Apostle of the Church. And you, great saint, obtain for me a heart docile to grace, conversion from my principal defect and total configuration with Jesus Christ.

St. Paul, the Apostle, pray for us.

2. I bless you, Jesus, for having elected the Apostle Paul as a model and preacher of holy virginity. And you, St. Paul, my dear father, guard my mind, my heart and my senses, in order that I may know, love and serve only Jesus, and employ all my energies for his glory.

St. Paul, the Apostle, pray for us.

3. I bless you, Jesus, for having given through St. Paul examples and teachings of perfect obedience. And you, great saint, obtain for me a humble docility to all my superiors, for I am sure that in obedience I shall be victorious over my enemies.

St. Paul, the Apostle, pray for us.

4. I bless you, Jesus, for having taught me, by the deeds and by the words of St. Paul, the true spirit of poverty. And you, great saint, obtain for me the evangelical spirit of poverty, so that after having imitated you in life, I may be your companion in heavenly glory.

St. Paul, the Apostle, pray for us.

5. I bless you, Jesus, for having given to St. Paul a heart so full of love for God and for the Church, and for having saved so many souls through his zeal. And you, our friend, obtain for me an ardent desire to carry out the apostolate of the media of social communication, of prayer, of example, of activity and of word, so that I may merit the reward promised to good apostles.

St. Paul, the Apostle, pray for us.

Short Novena to St. Paul

Prayers during the Novena

For nine days, say the following prayers: *Our Father, Hail Mary, Glory be.*

Antiphon: O St. Paul, the Apostle, preacher of truth and Doctor of the Gentiles, intercede for us to God, who chose you.

V. You are a vessel of election, St. Paul the Apostle.

R. Preacher of truth to the whole world.

Let us pray. Lord, our God, who chose the Apostle Paul to preach your Gospel, grant that the whole world may be enlightened by the faith which he announced to kings and nations, so that your Church may be built up always as mother and teacher of peoples. Through Christ our Lord. Amen.

To St. Paul the Apostle

O holy Apostle who, with your teachings and with your charity, taught the entire world, look kindly upon us, your children and disciples.

We expect everything from your prayers to the Divine Master and to Mary, Queen of the Apostles. Grant, O Doctor of the Gentiles, that we may live by faith, save ourselves by hope, and that charity alone reign in us. Obtain for us, O vessel of election, willing correspondence to divine grace, so that it may always remain fruitful in us. Grant that we may ever better know you, love you, and imitate you, that we may be living members of the Church, the Mystical Body of Jesus Christ. Raise up many and holy apostles. May the warm breath of true charity permeate the entire world. Grant that all may know and glorify God and the Divine Master, Way and Truth and Life.

Lord Jesus, you know we have no faith in our own powers; in your mercy grant that we may be defended against all adversity, through the powerful intercession of St. Paul, our teacher and father.

Prayer to St. Paul for Patience

O glorious St. Paul, from a persecutor of Christianity, you became a very ardent and zealous apostle, and suffered imprisonment, scourging, stoning and shipwreck, and endured persecutions of every kind, in order to make the Savior Jesus Christ known to the farthest bounds of the world. In the end you shed your blood to the last drop. Obtain for us the grace to accept the infirmities, afflictions and misfortunes of the present life as favors of the divine mercy, so that the vicissitudes of this our exile may not make us grow cold in the service of God, but may make us ever more faithful and more fervent. Amen.

Prayer to St. Paul for the Apostolate of Social Communications

St. Paul, most glorious Apostle of the Gentiles, with so much zeal you spent yourself to destroy in Ephesus those writings which you knew would have done harm to the minds of the faithful. Now, too, look upon us kindly.

You see how an unbelieving media, without hindrance, sows seeds of errors opposed to faith and good morals. Enlighten, we beg you, O holy Apostle, the minds of many writers, so that they may cease harming people through their teachings opposed to the Gospel. Move their hearts to turn away from the evil that they do to people, especially innocent children. Obtain for us the grace to always listen to the voice of the Supreme Pontiff. May we seek to read, and as much as we are able, to distribute those books, cassettes, videos and other media whose salutary contents will help all to promote the greater glory of God, the progress of his Church, and the salvation of all people. Amen.

For Our Nation

St. Paul, teacher of the Gentiles, watch over, with a loving smile, this nation and her people. Your heart expanded so as to welcome and enfold all peoples in the loving embrace of peace.

Now, from heaven, may the charity of Christ urge you to enlighten everyone with the light of the Gospel, and to establish the kingdom of love.

Inspire vocations, comfort the evangelical laborers, render all hearts docile to the Divine Master. May this nation ever more find in Christ the Way and the Truth and the Life. May its light shine before the world, and may it always seek the kingdom of God and his justice.

Holy Apostle, enlighten, comfort and bless us all. Amen.

Litany in Honor of St. Paul

(For private use)

Charity of the Father, save us.

Grace of our Lord Jesus Christ, vivify us.

Communication of the Holy Spirit, sanctify us.

Blessed Paul, pray for us.

You who obtained the mercy of God,*

You in whom the Son of God was revealed,

You who were a vessel of election for Christ,

You who were made preacher, apostle and
Doctor of the Gentiles,

You whose apostolate was confirmed by marvels
and wonders,

You who were a most faithful minister of
the Church,

You who gave the nations the Gospel of Christ
and your very life,

You who carried the faithful in your heart and
in your chains,

You who were crucified with Christ,

You in whom Christ lived and spoke,

You whom nothing could separate from the love
of Christ,

You who underwent imprisonment and toil,

---

* pray for us.

You who suffered wounds and dangers,

You who were taken into heaven while still living on earth,

You who glorified your ministry,

You who awaited the crown after completing your mission,

Lamb of God, who converted the persecutor Paul, spare us.

Lamb of God, who crowned the Apostle Paul, graciously hear us.

Lamb of God, who glorified the martyr Paul, have mercy on us.

V. You are a vessel of election, St. Paul the Apostle.

R. Preacher of truth throughout the world.

Let us pray. O God, you have instructed many nations through the preaching of the blessed Apostle Paul. May the power of his intercession with you help us who venerate his memory this day. Amen.

Prayers to St. Peregrine
(1260-1347)

Patron of Cancer Patients

As a youth in Forli, Peregrine took an active part in the anti-papalist politics of his town. Fr. Philip Benizi was sent to Forli by the Pope to act as a mediator, but he was insulted and mistreated by the townspeople. A group of young troublemakers, led by Peregrine, attacked Fr. Philip and drove him from the town. Peregrine himself struck the saintly priest on his face. Fr. Benizi's only reply was to offer the other cheek.

Peregrine could not forget the look in the holy priest's eyes—a look of compassion, love and pardon. Peregrine's whole life changed and took on a new meaning. He begged Fr. Philip's forgiveness, left aside his former way of life, and dedicated himself to prayer and solitude.

During this time he developed a trusting and childlike confidence in the Blessed Mother. On one occasion Mary spoke to him and urged him to join "her servants"—the Servites. Fr. Philip Benizi received Peregrine into the Order.

After Peregrine had been ordained a priest, he asked to return to Forli to work among his own people. His favorite places were the hospitals, the prisons and the homes of the poor. He spent his days and nights visiting the sick and the dying, and comforting them by his presence, his words and his actions.

A life of poverty and penance eventually left its mark on the aging Fr. Peregrine. A painful cancerous sore developed on his leg. Yet he bore this suffering without complaint. To save his life, however, the doctors decided to amputate. Surgery was a great risk in those days. Peregrine was afraid and spent the night before the operation in prayer. Suddenly the figure on the crucifix above him began to move! Jesus came down and touched the painful sore, then disappeared. Fr. Peregrine thought it had been a dream—but he was cured! The doctors themselves testified that they could no longer detect any trace of the cancerous sore. For this reason St. Peregrine has been chosen as the patron of all who suffer from any type of cancer.

The suffering that St. Peregrine bore in his lifetime became his crown of glory. His reward was the heaven that each of us longs to someday enjoy. What we suffer in this life can never be compared to the glory, as yet unrevealed, which is waiting for us (cf. Rom 8:18).

Novena to St. Peregrine

O glorious wonder worker, St. Peregrine, you answered God's call with a ready spirit, forsaking the comforts of a life of ease and the empty honors of the world, to dedicate yourself to God in the Order of his most Holy Mother, the Servites. You labored courageously for the salvation of souls, meriting the title of "Apostle of Emilia." In union with Jesus Crucified, you patiently endured the most painful sufferings and so merited to be healed miraculously from an incurable wound in your leg with a touch of his divine hand. Obtain for me, I pray, the grace to answer every call from God. Enkindle in my heart a consuming zeal for the salvation of all people. Deliver me from the infirmities that so often afflict my weak body, and obtain for me the grace of perfect abandonment to the sufferings which our merciful God allows me to endure. So may I, imitating your virtues and tenderly loving our crucified Lord and his sorrowful Mother, merit eternal glory in paradise. Amen.

(Our Father, Hail Mary, Glory be)

Prayer to St. Peregrine

O God, you gave St. Peregrine an angel for his companion, the Mother of God for his teacher, and

Jesus for the physician of his infirmity. Grant, I beg you, through his merits, that on earth I may intensely love my holy angel, the Blessed Virgin, and my Savior, and in heaven bless them forever. Grant that I may receive the favor I now ask.... Through Christ our Lord. Amen.

(Our Father, Hail Mary, Glory be)

St. Peregrine, pray for us.

Litany in Honor of St. Peregrine

(For private use)

Lord, have mercy on us.

Christ, have mercy on us.

Lord, have mercy on us.

Christ, hear us.

Christ, graciously hear us.

God, the Father of heaven, have mercy on us.

God, the Son, Redeemer of the world,*

God, the Holy Spirit,

Holy Trinity, one God,

Holy Mary, Mother of God, pray for us.

Mother of Sorrows,**

Health of the sick,

---

* *have mercy on us.*
** *pray for us.*

Comforter of the afflicted,

Help of Christians,

St. Peregrine,

Converted by the prayers of St. Philip,

Afflicted with a cancerous growth,

Completely cured by the outstretched hand
of Jesus crucified,

Who performed many miracles in your lifetime,

Who multiplied food and drink,

Who cured the sick by the power of the
Name of Jesus,

Who converted hardened sinners by prayer
and fasting,

Who receive every favor you ask of God,

Most confident in prayer,

Most austere in penance,

Most patient in suffering,

Most humble in the holy priesthood,

Most zealous for souls,

Most kind toward the afflicted,

Most devoted to the passion of Jesus and the
sorrows of Mary,

Victim with Jesus and Mary for the salvation
of souls,

Wonder worker for the sick and diseased,

Hope of incurable cases,

Universal patron of all who suffer from cancer,

Beloved patron of Spain,

Glory of the Order of the Servants of Mary,

Lamb of God, you take away the sins of the world,
    spare us, O Lord.

Lamb of God, you take away the sins of the world,
    graciously hear us, O Lord.

Lamb of God, you take away the sins of the world,
    have mercy on us.

V. Pray for us, O glorious St. Peregrine,

R. That we may be made worthy of the promises of Christ.

Let us pray. O God, be gracious and hear the prayers which we present to you in honor of St. Peregrine, your beloved servant. May we who do not rely on our own merits receive help in our needs through the intercession of him whose life was so pleasing to you. Through Christ, our Lord. Amen.

Prayers to St. Rita
(1381-1457)

Patroness of Impossible Cases

A native of Cascia, Italy, Rita wanted to enter the cloister but was forced into an arranged marriage instead. Her husband Ferdinand was violent and abusive and caused Rita much suffering. She had two sons who followed their father's example. Through her prayers and Christian witness, Rita's husband eventually had a change of heart. Unfortunately, he was murdered soon after. About a year later both sons died after an illness. They too had converted and died as good Christians.

Having no more family, Rita then entered an Augustinian monastery and spent forty-four years in prayer and penance. She was especially devoted to meditation on the passion of Christ. After a life of great holiness, she died in 1457 at the age of seventy-six. After her death many favors were reported through her intercession and devotion to her soon spread throughout Italy. Pope Leo XIII canonized her in 1900. Like St. Jude, St. Rita is the patroness of impossible and desperate cases. As a wife, mother and religious sister, she is a model for people of diverse backgrounds. As a victim of domestic violence, Rita can also be invoked as the patroness of women who are caught in similar situations. She invites us to place our confidence in her protection and to invoke her in time of necessity. Rita's feast-day is May 22.

Novena in Honor of St. Rita

The following prayers are all to be said each day of the novena.

I. Glorious St. Rita, I rejoice with you that God has chosen you as one of his dearest saints. Obtain for me the grace to correspond with the designs of divine Providence, so that I may reach the goal of eternal salvation. Obtain for me the grace.... *(Here mention the special favor you request.)*

(Our Father, Hail Mary, Glory be)

II. Glorious St. Rita, I rejoice with you for the fortitude and fidelity with which you glorified God in the married state, performing every duty so faithfully as to deserve abundant merits before God. Obtain for me also the grace to fulfill properly the obligations of my state in life, and particularly the favor I now ask....

(Our Father, Hail Mary, Glory be)

III. Glorious St. Rita, I rejoice with you for the Christian witness you gave to your husband, which helped bring him to a conversion of life. I admire the fortitude and detachment you possessed—even when deprived of your own children. Obtain for me the grace of loving God, which will give me patience and strength in adversity, and particularly the favor I now ask....

(Our Father, Hail Mary, Glory be)

IV. Glorious St. Rita, you burned with the desire of consecrating your life to God in the cloister. Meeting grave obstacles, you had recourse to God with faith. He sent you St. John the Baptist, St. Augustine and St. Nicholas of Tolentino, who in turn, to your great happiness, introduced you miraculously into the convent. Be my intercessor with God, as those saints were for you, so that by fulfilling the duties of my state in life, I may merit eternal salvation, and particularly the favor I now request....

(Our Father, Hail Mary, Glory be)

V. Glorious St. Rita, if your fervor and virtue were so great in your service of God in the world, how much they must have increased in religion. In a short time, you attained the most sublime heights of perfection and sanctity. The affections and desires of your heart were for heaven. How different I am, so careless and neglectful concerning my eternal salvation. Renew in me the spirit of Christ with his holy virtues and obtain for me the favor I now ask....

(Our Father, Hail Mary, Glory be)

VI. Glorious St. Rita, convinced that the religious state is a life of sacrifice, you undertook to study day and night the life of Jesus crucified, in order to become like him in his humiliations and sufferings. Jesus wished to give you a proof of his love by piercing your forehead with a sacred thorn so that, having become a living image of the crucifix, you soared to the heights of celestial happiness, there to live within the sacred wounds of Jesus. How I rejoice for the wonderful crown of glory that God placed on your brow. Obtain for me the grace that the crucifix may be the book in which I can find my knowledge and happiness, and the particular favor I now ask....

(Our Father, Hail Mary, Glory)

VII. Glorious St. Rita, I rejoice with you for your holy life, rewarded with a saintly death at which Jesus and Mary assisted. They introduced you into the eternal bliss, and raised you to a most sublime glory by the wonderful miracles which took place after your death, helping your devoted servants even in the most desperate cases. I rejoice with holy exultation for such glory and so many merits, and I beg you to obtain for me the grace to lead a pure and holy life, and thus merit eternal glory in heaven.

(Our Father, Hail Mary, Glory be)

A Triduum to St. Rita to Ask the Grace of a Cure

First Day

O glorious St. Rita, through the heroic virtues you practiced in your lifetime, and especially through the merits of that remarkable charity you manifested in aiding the ill with vigilance, affection and patience, being mindful of all the pains you chose to suffer, I ask you to help this afflicted one to be restored to health of soul and body if this is in accord with the divine will. O St. Rita, I pray that you will obtain this favor for me.

(Our Father, Hail Mary, Glory be, three times)

Second Day

O glorious St. Rita, through the merits you gained in religious life and especially for the great privilege with which our crucified Redeemer wished to distinguish you, allowing you to share his sufferings by permitting a thorn to pierce your forehead, in the name of all the sufferings, mortifications and privations you endured for fifteen years for love of him, I ask you to come to the aid of this sick person, who with full confidence, turns to you. Obtain from our Savior, through your powerful intercession, the re-storation of good health and especially perseverance in the service of God during this earthly pilgrimage.

(Our Father, Hail Mary, Glory be, three times)

Third Day

O glorious St. Rita, by all the merits of your holy life, and in particular by that untiring patience and heroic resignation you practiced during the last years of your sickness, and much more by the ardent desire you manifested of draining the last drops of the Savior's bitter chalice through your numerous merits, I pray you to console and lighten the pains of this sick person. I place all my confidence in your powerful intercession, in order to obtain health of body, which I ask with all my heart, that God may be more and more glorified in his saints and in you, now and forever. Amen.

(Our Father, Hail Mary, Glory be, three times)

V. You have signed, O Lord, your servant Rita.

R. With the sign of your love and passion.

V. Pray for us, St. Rita.

R. That we may be made worthy of the promises of Christ.

Prayer to St. Rita

St. Rita, valiant woman, model of Christian and religious life, blessed advocate, whom Providence has given us to win for himself our earthly hearts, example of earnest and childlike prayer, I come before you with full confidence in your powerful intercession before our crucified Lord and his blessed Mother, whom you never petitioned in vain. I earnestly implore you to obtain for me the grace to be abandoned to the will of God, to share in your love for him, and to imitate the virtues of which you gave so perfect an example. Listen to my prayer, blessed Rita; show that you are truly the patroness of desperate cases by obtaining the favor that I ask. In return I will sing your praises and strive to imitate your virtues. St. Rita, advocate of the impossible, pray for me. St. Rita, patroness of desperate cases, pray for me. St. Rita, help me.

O glorious St. Rita, you who so wonderfully participated in the passion of Christ, obtain for me the grace to suffer with patience the pains of this life, and protect me in all my needs.

Daily Prayer to St. Rita

O glorious St. Rita, special intercessor before the throne of God, look upon me, a poor sinner, and obtain for me the special grace to be like you, an ardent admirer, a sincere lover, and a true follower of the Master, Jesus Christ. Obtain for me the grace to know my past sinfulness and to make amends for my ingratitude to God. I ask for a measure of that special grace which God bestowed on you, a love for the sacred passion of Jesus Christ. Make me realize the share I had in causing the awful agony that Christ endured for my sake and for countless other sinners. At the same time, obtain for me a sincere and heart-felt contrition for all my sins. Obtain for me a true courage so that the sight of my sins may not discourage me, but rather, because they have been so freely pardoned, may give me the consolation and fortitude I so greatly need to keep my good resolves to lead a better life.

Your example, St. Rita, inspires me with the resolve to correspond with the many graces that I shall receive this day and to be a more ardent follower of the Lord. I promise that I shall not do anything willfully to offend him today, but rather shall make a serious effort to live as though he were at my side, and so living, be in a state to receive at his hands many other graces and especially the favor I now ask. *(Here mention your request.)*

O great St. Rita, advocate of those in need, pray for me; intercede for me; obtain for me the graces I need, and especially the favor that I may, like you, thank God for all his benefits, and like you, praise him for the little trials which he may allow me to experience. I earnestly implore your compassion and commend myself and all those in whom I have any special interest: my family, relatives, friends, benefactors, neighbors and even my enemies, to your powerful intercession.

God has seen fit to raise you as an example to people in every walk of life. As a wife and mother you are an example to all Christian married women. As a religious you are an example for those in the consecrated life, for you possessed in an eminent degree all the virtues which adorn the faithful religious. You were modest, humble, obedient and a great lover of poverty. At death you were awaited by your Spouse who invited you to heaven.

If, in the past, I have been more or less unmindful of what God has done for me, I desire from now on to seek his holy will in all things. Intercede for me, O good St. Rita, that through your prayers he may grant to me the graces of soul and body that I need so much. Obtain for me the grace to resist the assaults of the devil, the temptations of the flesh, and the allurements of the world that lead to sin. Obtain for me, not only a horror and detestation for sin but also the time to repent for my past offenses. Ask for me especially the grace of a good death, so that living and dying in the grace of God, I may one day be united with you and all the other saints in heaven to praise the God of goodness and mercy. Amen.

Prayer to St. Rita to Obtain a Special Favor

O holy servant of God, St. Rita, whose intercessory powers have been manifested by the many favors you have obtained for your followers, as well as by the miracles that you have worked, I invoke you as the great friend of God that I firmly believe you to be, and as the true lover of the passion of Christ that your life shows you to have been. Pray for me, and by your prayers help me to obtain from God the favor I now ask. *(Here mention your request.)* As a lover of Christ Jesus, you were also a lover and follower of his Immaculate Mother. Pray to her also for me. Her Son will deny her nothing, and a word from you will influence her in my behalf. Pray to her, then, for me, and through her all-powerful intercession, obtain for me the grace I now ask. *(Again mention your request.)*

Obtain for me first and above all things, the cure of my soul, that like you I may know God and most faithfully love and serve him. O great St. Rita, obtain for me, also, the grace that like you, I may be faithful to the duties of my state in life. Obtain for me the grace to have the passion of Christ ever before me, so that I may truly repent of my sins. Like you may I one day merit the reward of eternal joy where together in heaven with you and countless saints and angels I may thank and adore the ever Blessed Trinity forever and ever. Amen.

To St. Rita

O holy protectress of those who are in greatest need, O you who shine as a star of hope in the midst of darkness, blessed St. Rita, bright mirror of God's grace, in patience and fortitude you are a model of all the states in life. I unite my will with the will of God through the merits of my Savior, Jesus Christ, and in particular through his patient wearing of the crown of thorns which with tender devotion you daily contemplated. Through the merits of the holy Virgin Mary and your own graces and virtues, I ask you to obtain my earnest petition, provided it be for the greater glory of God and my own sanctification. *(Here mention your request.)* Guide and purify my intention, O holy protectress and advocate, so that I may obtain the pardon of all my sins and the grace to persevere daily as you did in walking with courage, generosity and fidelity down the path of life. Amen.

St. Rita, advocate of the impossible, pray for us.
St. Rita, advocate of the helpless, pray for us.
(Our Father, Hail Mary, Glory be, three times)

Prayers to
St. Theresa of the Child Jesus

Patroness of Catholic Missions

Theresa was born in Lisieux, France in 1873. At the age of fifteen she entered the Carmelite Order. During the nine years of her religious life, she lived as a humble, obedient and charitable sister. She did nothing which could be called extraordinary. Her sanctity consisted in doing well all her daily duties and practices of prayer for the love of God and for the conversion of sinners. St. Theresa died in 1897 at the age of twenty-four and was canonized in 1925. Because she offered all her penances and sufferings for missionaries, she is the patroness of all Catholic missions. Her autobiography, *The Story of a Soul,* is a masterpiece of spiritual literature. Her feastday is October 1.

Novenas to St. Theresa

Any of the following prayers may be used for a novena, according to one's needs.

Prayer to Obtain Graces

St. Theresa, beautiful flower that bloomed in the garden of Carmel, I thank you for the love of God and of your fellow human beings which led you to embrace a life of unceasing prayer and penance. I know the graces you have obtained for me and for the world. In consequence, I know how deep a debt of gratitude I owe you. But, I beseech you, now that you are safe with God and are a blessed saint in the heavenly court, do not forget those for whom you offered your life, with its prayers and penance, while on earth. Watch over me in my needs. Beg grace for me from the merciful hand of God. The sinful world still needs your prayers and your intercession, and God will grant your requests because of the life of love and penance which you so freely gave him as a nun. Take all sinners under your protection and beg for them the grace of repentance. Watch over me that I may grow in holiness. Protect, too, I pray, those whom I love and for whom I am making this novena. Obtain for me the special favors I am asking during this novena. *(Three Hail Marys)*

Prayer for Purity of Intention

St. Theresa, model of the hidden life, I thank you for showing us that great deeds, miracles and ecstasies are not necessary for sanctity. I thank you for choosing to walk in your little way, which is possible for everyone to follow. My life is often monotonous, tedious and filled with commonplace duties. But I know now that I can take these everyday tasks and with them build a beautiful life worthy of God's favor. I therefore offer to God each day of my life, with all the simple duties it may contain. I do not ask for extraordinary work to do or great deeds to perform; I only ask that I may do the work God has given me to do, be it ever so simple and unromantic, in the spirit in which you went about the quiet life of the convent. Ask, O Little Flower, that God may accept these simple days and bless them with his approval. Obtain for me that I might do ordinary things in an extraordinarily perfect manner, and that I may do whatever God asks of me solely because I love him and because I am doing it for him. Bless those whom I love or for whom I am offering this novena with the grace to spend their days for the love of God and in his honor. Obtain for me the special favors I am asking during this time of prayer. *(Three Hail Marys)*

Prayer to Avoid Sin

Flower of childlike innocence and purity, St. Theresa, help me I beg, by your powerful intercession with Jesus and Mary, to imitate your cleanness of heart and your great hatred for sin. Help me avoid the occasions of sin; give me the fortitude to give up sinful pursuits; teach me to sacrifice anything, even life itself, rather than offend God. Watch over my entertainment, friendships, reading, work and play, all the busy and the leisure moments of my life, so that nothing sinful may enter my mind or heart. Extend your powerful protection also to all those who are dear to me, to all for whom I wish to pray, to all Catholics everywhere and to every person, all of whom are made in the image of God and called to the possession of eternal life.

Ask for me also, I pray, the favors which I wish to obtain through this holy novena. Amen. *(Three Hail Marys)*

Prayer for Love of God

Flower of fervor and love, St. Theresa of the Child Jesus and the Holy Face, I ask you to have pity on me and by your intercession enkindle in my heart a pure love of God like to your own. Help me to realize how good God is in himself and how worthy of all love. Lift my mind above earthly things to contemplate the beauty of Jesus, the gentleness of his Sacred Heart, his immense love which makes him grieve that people love him so little in return. Remind me often to offer to him an act of the pure love of God, saying with all my heart, "My God, I love you above all things for your own sake, because you are infinitely worthy of all my love; and I am sorry for all my sins for the love of you." Make this love the inspiration of my slightest action, the ruling motive of my life, and help me, in imitation of your example, to teach this love to the entire world. Amen.

Prayer for the Needs of the Church

St. Theresa, the Little Flower of Jesus, you desired upon earth to live for Jesus alone, to suffer for his sake, to make him better known and loved by all. Now that you rejoice in the everlasting vision of that Holy Face, continue to send upon the world a shower of roses, the sweetness of whose perfume will draw all persons from the passing things of time to the joys that never end.

Obtain for the Pope the favors which he so greatly needs; for bishops, all things necessary to enable them to be true shepherds of the flocks committed to their care; for priests, a right understanding of their vocation and a burning zeal for souls; for religious, the true spirit of their holy state; for lay people, the gift of loyalty to Christ and his holy Church; for fallen-away Catholics, the grace to return to the fold; for non-Catholics, the light of the fullness of the true Faith; for the foreign missions, zealous workers in those distant vineyards of the Master.

(Hail Mary and Glory to the Father)

Prayer for Missionaries

St. Theresa of the Child Jesus, you who have been rightly proclaimed the patroness of Catholic missions throughout the world, remember the burning desire which you manifested here on earth to plant the cross of Christ on every shore and to preach the Gospel even until the end of the world. I ask you, according to your promise, to assist all priests, missionaries and the whole Church of God.

Prayer for Our Homes

Blessed Little Flower of Jesus, the roots of your sanctity and purity were fixed deep in the soil of a holy and loving home. By the memory of the tender care of your parents and the loving solicitude of your sisters, obtain, I beseech you, for my family and for those of the entire world the blessings of a truly holy home life, full of simple and sincere piety, devoted family love, and good example. Fill parents with the spirit of devotion and self-sacrifice and children with obedient love so that all homes may be like the home of Nazareth and all lives like the lives of Jesus, Mary and Joseph. Bless all homes; fill them abundantly with wholesome reading and audio-visual material and protect them from all evil influences of speech or of example.

Prayer of Thanksgiving

Eternal Father, I offer you the precious blood of Jesus in thanksgiving for all the graces you have bestowed upon St. Theresa. I thank you for ever preserving the baptismal innocence of her pure soul and for calling her at a young age to the cloister of Carmel; I thank you for the grace with which you flooded her soul with heavenly light and inflamed her heart with burning love of you; I thank you for the grace with which you made her humble and gentle, kind and patient and ever abandoned to your holy will; I thank you for the grace with which you made her victorious in the severe temptations against faith that beset her during the last years of her life and caused her unspeakable interior suffering. I offer the precious blood of Jesus a thousand times to you, O heavenly Father, for these and all the graces that made St. Theresa of the Child Jesus so beautiful in your sight and so lovable to our hearts. Grant me the grace to imitate her whom I love, to be pure, humble and abandoned to your holy will, to be your devoted child, heavenly Father, and a worthy brother (or sister) of St. Theresa of the Child Jesus.

Novena Prayer to the Little Flower

Eternal Father in heaven, where you crown the merits of those who in this life serve you faithfully, for the sake of the most pure love which St. Theresa of the Child Jesus had for you, so as all but to bind you to give her whatever she desires, seeing that while on earth she always did your will, hear the petitions which she offers to you on my behalf, and hear, too, my prayers by granting me the grace I ask.

(Our Father, Hail Mary, Glory be)

Eternal Son of God, you who have promised to reward the least service rendered to you in the person of our neighbor, look with love on your spouse, St. Theresa of the Child Jesus, who with such great zeal had ever at heart the salvation of souls; for the sake of all she has done and suffered, grant her wish of "spending her time in heaven doing good upon earth" and grant me the grace I plead for so earnestly from you.

(Our Father, Hail Mary, Glory be)

O eternal Holy Spirit, who made perfect with so many graces St. Theresa of the Child Jesus, I ask you for the sake of the fidelity she showed in ever corresponding with your graces, to listen to the prayers she offers to you on my behalf, and having before you her promise of "letting fall from heaven a shower of roses," mercifully grant me the grace of which I stand in such great need.

(Our Father, Hail Mary, Glory be)

Another Prayer to St. Theresa

St. Theresa of the Child Jesus, who during your short life on earth became a mirror of angelic purity, of love strong as death, and of wholehearted abandonment to God, now that you rejoice in the reward of your virtues, cast a glance of compassion on me as I leave all things in your hands. Make my troubles your own; speak a word for me to our Lady Immaculate, whose flower of special love you were—to that Queen of Heaven "who smiled on you at the dawn of life." Beg her as Queen of the Sacred Heart of Jesus to obtain for me, by her powerful intercession, the grace I desire so ardently at this moment, and that she join with it a blessing that may strengthen me during life, defend me at the hour of death, and lead me to a happy eternity.

(Hail, Holy Queen)

Litany of St. Theresa

(For private use)

Lord, have mercy on us.

Christ, have mercy on us.

Lord, have mercy on us.

Christ, hear us.

Christ, graciously hear us.

God, the Father of heaven, have mercy on us.

God, the Son, Redeemer of the world,
    have mercy on us.

God, the Holy Spirit, have mercy on us.

Holy Mary, Mother of God, pray for us.

St. Theresa of the Child Jesus,*

St. Theresa of the Holy Face,

St. Theresa, child of Mary,

St. Theresa, devoted to Joseph,

St. Theresa, angel of innocence,

St. Theresa, model child,

St. Theresa, pattern of religious,

St. Theresa, flower of Carmel,

St. Theresa, converter of hardened hearts,

St. Theresa, healer of the diseased,

St. Theresa, filled with love for the
    Blessed Sacrament,

---

* *pray for us.*

St. Theresa, filled with angelic fervor,

St. Theresa, filled with an apostle's zeal,

St. Theresa, filled with loyalty to the Holy Father,

St. Theresa, filled with a great love for the Church,

St. Theresa, filled with extraordinary love for
God and neighbor,

St. Theresa, wounded with a heavenly flame,

St. Theresa, victim of divine love,

St. Theresa, patient in sufferings,

St. Theresa, eager for humiliations,

St. Theresa, consumed with love,

St. Theresa, rapt in ecstasy,

Who desired always to be as a little child,

Who taught the way of spiritual childhood,

Who gave a perfect example of trust in God,

Whom Jesus filled with a desire for suffering,

Who found perfection in the little things,

Who refused God nothing,

Who understood the value of suffering
in this life,

Who offered her life to God for priests and
missionaries,

Who gained countless persons for Christ,

Who promised to send, after death, a shower
of roses,

Who foretold, "I will spend my heaven doing good
upon earth,"

Lamb of God, you take away the sins of the world,
spare us, O Lord.

Lamb of God, you take away the sins of the world,
graciously hear us, O Lord.

Lamb of God, you take away the sins of the world,
have mercy on us.

V. Pray for us, St. Theresa.

R. That we may be made worthy of the promises
of Christ.

Let us pray. O Lord, who has said, "Truly I tell
you, unless you change and become like children,
you will never enter the kingdom of heaven" (Mt
18:3), grant us, we beseech you, so to follow in
humility and simplicity of heart the footsteps of St.
Theresa, the virgin, that we may obtain everlasting
rewards. Who lives and reigns forever. Amen.

Chaplet to the Little Flower

This chaplet consists of twenty-four beads, commemorating the twenty-four years of St. Theresa's
life, and one additional bead. On that bead, the following prayer is said, "St. Theresa of the Infant
Jesus, patroness of the missions, pray for us." On the
other twenty-four beads the *Glory Be* is said to honor
the Holy Trinity in thanksgiving for having given us
this saint who lived in this world only twenty-four
years.

St. Thomas Aquinas
(1224/25-1274)

Patron of Students

Thomas was born to a noble family in Roccasecca, which is near Naples, Italy. As a young man he met some friars from the newly-established Dominican Order, and was drawn to their way of life. His family strongly opposed his entering the Dominicans and actually kept Thomas under a form of "house arrest" for about a year. But he persisted and finally managed to escape and follow his dream.

The Dominicans noticed Thomas' intellectual abilities and sent him to study under St. Albert the Great, first at Paris, then at Cologne. Becoming a master of theology, Thomas then began to teach at the University of Paris. His brilliance made him outstanding, and he quickly became noted as an astute philosopher and theologian.

In the 13th century, the writings of Aristotle were rediscovered and introduced to the West. Thomas studied the thought of the great Greek philosopher and wrote twelve commentaries on his works. This formed the basis for ground-breaking work in philosophy. Besides his philosophical writings, Thomas wrote many theological works such as the *Summa Theologica,* and commentaries on Scripture.

Thomas was also outstanding for his virtues, especially his humility and simplicity. Despite his intellectual accomplishments, he was first of all a friar and sought to live the Gospel faithfully. He was noted for showing great charity even in the midst of the heated debates that took place at the university.

Thomas was canonized in 1323. In 1567 Pope Pius V proclaimed him a Doctor of the Church. His feastday is January 28.

Novena to St. Thomas Aquinas

First Day

St. Thomas, called by God

"Whoever loves father or mother more than me is not worthy of me; and whoever loves son or daughter more than me is not worthy of me" (Mt 10:37).

St. Thomas, as a young man you became convinced that God was calling you to religious life. Although your family was opposed to it, you were determined to follow God's call. Even when your brothers kidnapped you and forced you to remain a prisoner in your own house, you did not give up but waited patiently for God's hour.

St. Thomas, pray for all young people who are considering their vocation in life. Help them to be open to the call of God. Inspire them to make choices motivated by love for God and an unselfish love for other people. Whatever their state in life, help them to see their chosen path as a call to service. May all married couples, single persons, priests and religious build up the Church through lives of unselfish devotion and love.

Novena prayer

St. Thomas Aquinas, patron of students and Catholic schools, I thank God for the gifts of light and knowledge God bestowed on you, which you used to build up the Church in love. I thank God, too, for the wealth and richness of theological teaching you left in your writings. Not only were you a great teacher, you lived a life of virtue and you made holiness the desire of your heart. If I cannot imitate you in the brilliance of your academic pursuits, I can follow you in the humility and charity which marked your life. As St. Paul said, charity is the greatest gift, and it is open to all. Pray for me that I might grow in holiness and charity. Pray also for Catholic schools, and for all students. In particular, please obtain the favor I ask during this novena...*(here mention your request).* Amen.

Second Day

St. Thomas, lover of purity

"For God did not call us to impurity but in holiness" (1 Thes 4:7).

St. Thomas, you had a great esteem for the virtue of purity. When your family tried to deter you from entering the Dominicans by sending a woman to lead you into sin, you resisted the temptation and determined to consecrate your chastity to God forever.

Today we are immersed in a culture that degrades the gift of human sexuality. Human persons are viewed as objects of pleasure and their human dignity is devalued. As a consequence, society tolerates abortion, disregarding human life at the very outset. Children suffer abuse and families are damaged by infidelity.

Pray that our society may once again value the virtue of chastity. Pray that those in the media will work to promote a Christian view of marriage and family life. May the plague of pornography in all its forms be eliminated. May Christian moral standards act as a leaven in society and bring about a greater respect for human life.

(Recite the novena prayer.)

Third Day

St. Thomas, example of humility

"All who exalt themselves will be humbled, and all who humble themselves will be exalted" (Mt 23:12).

St. Thomas, when you were a young student some of your classmen called you the "dumb ox." Although you were more intelligent than all of them, you bore their insults patiently without retaliating. You were endowed with a keen mind but recognized that God is the source of all gifts. You humbly acknowledged your dependence on God, and begged him to enlighten you so that you could act only for his glory.

St. Thomas, pray for me that I too learn to act out of humility and never from the empty desire for esteem in the sight of others. Help me to seek only God's glory and to act with a right intention. May I seek to humble myself now, so that in heaven I will shine like the stars for all eternity.

(Recite the novena prayer.)

Fourth Day

St. Thomas, devoted to truth

"But speaking the truth in love, we must grow up in every way into him who is the head, into Christ" (Eph 4:15).

St. Thomas, you devoted your life to seeking the truth and explaining it to others. You dedicated your mind to God, and used it to probe God's word more deeply. Your gifts as a theologian and philosopher make you stand out as one of the greatest Doctors of the Church. In your discussions, you made truth your primary aim, while treating respectfully anyone who differed with you.

Obtain for me too a great love of truth. Help me to ponder God's word so as to draw from it the light I need to nourish myself spiritually. Keep me firmly rooted in the truth, and never let me be swayed by false teachings. I pray also for those who are lost in darkness; please bring them into the light of truth.

(Recite the novena prayer.)

Fifth Day

St. Thomas, afire with love for the Blessed Sacrament

"So Jesus said to them, 'Very truly, I tell you, unless you eat the flesh of the Son of Man and drink his blood, you have no life in you'" (Jn 6:53).

St. Thomas, you had a great love for Jesus in the Holy Eucharist and spent many hours in adoration before the Blessed Sacrament. You once said that you learned more from prayer before the tabernacle than from many hours of study. The Church owes you a debt of gratitude for the beautiful Eucharistic hymns you wrote at the request of Pope Urban IV, for the newly-established feast of Corpus Christi.

Pray that I too might be inflamed with an ardent love for the Holy Eucharist. Help me to always esteem and reverence this wonderful sacrament. Pray for me that I might always participate devoutly in Mass, receive Holy Communion with great fervor, and often visit Jesus in the tabernacle. Through contact with the Eucharistic Lord, may my heart overflow with love for God and for my neighbor.

(Recite the novena prayer.)

Sixth Day

St. Thomas, filled with charity

"Love is patient; love is kind; love is not envious or boastful or arrogant or rude. It does not insist on its own way; it is not irritable or resentful; it does not rejoice in wrongdoing, but rejoices in the truth" (1 Cor 13:4-6).

St. Thomas, you were noted during your life for

the charity you showed to others. During debates at the university, you did not ridicule those who argued with you but treated them with respect and love. You showed consideration for the needs of other people.

Help me also to be more deeply rooted in love of God and neighbor, keeping in mind Jesus' words, "By this everyone will know that you are my disciples, if you have love for one another" (Jn 13:35). Help me to practice this same charity in a concrete way that does not stop at words, but is shown with sacrifice. May it begin first of all in my family, and then radiate to everyone I meet.

(Recite the novena prayer.)

Seventh Day

St. Thomas, defender of the Church

"...the church of the living God, the pillar and bulwark of the truth" (1 Tim 3:15).

St. Thomas, from your youth you learned to love the Church, your spiritual home. In your teaching, you sought to explain and defend the doctrine of the Church, making it known through your writings. You understood that true wisdom means to let oneself be instructed by the Church, for Jesus guaranteed that the Holy Spirit would always be with the Church, to lead it into all truth. At the end of your life you said, "I have taught and written much... according to my faith in Christ and in the holy Roman Church, to whose judgment I submit all my teaching."

Intercede for the Church today, that it might grow stronger and more spiritually fruitful in the world. Raise up holy priests, religious and laity, that they may all be the salt of the earth and the light of the world. Bless the Pope in his efforts to guide the Church, witnessing to the power of the Gospel to renew the face of the earth. May all theologians work to explore the richness of Catholic teaching so as to show forth its truth and benefit the faithful. Pray for missionaries as they work to spread the Gospel. May the whole Church be renewed by the power of the Spirit to more effectively witness to Christ in the world today.

(Recite the novena prayer.)

Eighth Day

St. Thomas, teacher of prayer

"Devote yourselves to prayer, keeping alert in it with thanksgiving" (Col 4:2).

St. Thomas, you knew that prayer is the source of wisdom and you spent long hours in conversation with God. Prayer became your very life. Whenever you pondered over a problem in theology, you turned to prayer to seek God's enlightenment.

Now in heaven you see God face to face. Pray for me, too, that I might become a person of profound prayer. Obtain for me the grace that I might always pray with humility, confidence and perseverance. Help me to grow more and more in the spirit of prayer, so that my whole life may become a prayer. May I always seek the face of the living God.

(Recite the novena prayer.)

Ninth Day

St. Thomas, patron of students

"For in every way you have been enriched in him, in speech and knowledge of every kind" (1 Cor 1:5).

St. Thomas, God called you to spend most of your life in academic pursuits, first as a student, and then as a professor of theology. In your work as a teacher, you desired to help your students apply what they learned to their lives, in order to grow in holiness. You realized that knowledge is meant to draw people closer to God. In your teaching you sought to communicate the truth, desiring to help your students become better Christians.

Pray for all students. Pray for those who may have difficulty in their studies, as well as for those who can study with ease. Pray that they may all be open to the truth, and always seek to better understand it. May they seek to grow in knowledge so as to know God better and to be able to serve their brothers and sisters as the Lord desires. St. Thomas, pray especially for theologians, that in their studies and research they may come to a deeper knowledge of revealed doctrine in keeping with the mind of the Church. May their lives reflect the holiness of the word of God which they seek to more fully understand.

(Recite the novena prayer.)

Novena by Marianne Lorraine Trouvé, FSP

Prayers for the Souls in Purgatory

The Catechism of the Catholic Church states: "All who die in God's grace and friendship, but still imperfectly purified, are indeed assured of their eternal salvation; but after death they undergo purification, so as to achieve the holiness necessary to enter the joy of heaven" (n. 1030).

The communion of saints is the basis for suffrages offered for those in purgatory. Prayers and good works can atone for sin. In God's providence, we can offer them not only for ourselves, but for the holy souls in purgatory. Because we are united in Christ, we can help those who need us, and the souls in purgatory greatly need our aid.

Another way to help them is to gain indulgences for the deceased. Every good action which we do while we are living in God's grace has a special value to make up for the effects of sin. An indulgence simply means that the Church, through the merits of Christ, adds to that value so that our action will make up for sin to an even greater degree. Only certain prayers and good works have indulgences attached to them. Some examples are: to make a visit to the Blessed Sacrament, to pray the rosary, and to give religious instruction. There are many others, and if we have a general intention to gain indulgences we can ask God to apply them to the holy souls.

The following prayers can be used to pray for the souls in purgatory.

Prayers for the Holy Souls

1. Lord, my Creator and Redeemer, I believe that in your justice, you established purgatory for those souls who pass into eternity before having totally paid their debts of sin or punishment. I also believe that in your mercy you accept suffrages, particularly the holy sacrifice of the Mass, for their relief and liberation. Stir up my faith and infuse in my heart sentiments of pity toward these dear suffering brothers and sisters.

Eternal rest grant unto them, O Lord, and let perpetual light shine upon them. May they rest in peace. Amen.

2. Lord Jesus Christ, king of glory, through the intercession of Mary and all the saints, free the souls of the faithful departed from the punishments of purgatory. And through the intercession of St. Michael, standard-bearer of the heavenly army, guide them to the holy light promised to Abraham and to his descendants. I offer you, Lord, sacrifices

and prayers of praise. Accept them for these souls and admit them to eternal joy.

Eternal rest...

3. Jesus, good Master, I plead with you on behalf of the souls toward whom I have a greater debt of gratitude, justice, charity and family bonds: parents, brothers and sisters, other relatives and friends. I recommend to you those who had greater responsibilities on earth, especially religious and civil authorities. I plead with you also for forgotten souls, and for those who were more devoted to you, the Divine Master, to Mary, Queen of the Apostles, and to St. Paul the Apostle. Lord, admit them soon into eternal happiness.

Eternal rest...

4. Jesus, Divine Master, I thank you for having come down from heaven to free us from so many evils by your teaching, holiness and death. I plead with you on behalf of the souls who are in purgatory because of the press, motion pictures, radio and television. I have confidence that these souls, once freed from their sufferings and admitted into eternal joy, will supplicate you on behalf of the modern world, so that the many means you have granted us for elevating this earthly life may also be used as means of apostolate and life everlasting.

Eternal rest...

5. Merciful Jesus, by your sorrowful passion and by that love which you have for me, I beg you to cancel the punishments which I deserve in this life or in the next because of my many sins. Grant me, Lord, a spirit of penance, purity of conscience, hatred for every deliberate venial sin, and the dispositions necessary to gain indulgences. I resolve to help the holy souls in purgatory with suffrages as much as I can. And you, infinite Goodness, grant me ever greater fervor, so that after death I may be admitted into heaven to contemplate you forever.

Eternal rest...

> *The above prayers were composed by*
> *the Servant of God, Ven. James Alberione,*
> *Founder of the Pauline Family.*

Daily Prayers for the Souls in Purgatory

Sunday

Father, I implore you by the precious blood your divine Son shed in the garden, deliver the souls in purgatory. Have mercy especially on the one most forsaken and bring that soul into your glory to praise you forever. Amen.

(Our Father, Hail Mary, Eternal rest...)

Monday

Father, I implore you by the precious blood your divine Son shed in his cruel scourging, deliver the souls in purgatory. Have mercy especially on that soul nearest to entrance into your glory.

(Our Father, Hail Mary, Eternal rest...)

Tuesday

Father, I implore you by the precious blood your divine Son shed during his bitter crowning with thorns, deliver the souls in purgatory. Have mercy especially on that soul most in need of our prayers.

(Our Father, Hail Mary, Eternal rest...)

Wednesday

Father, I implore you by the precious blood your divine Son shed while he carried the heaven cross on his shoulders, deliver the souls in purgatory. Have mercy especially on the one richest in merits, so to praise you in glory forever. Amen.

(Our Father, Hail Mary, Eternal rest...)

Thursday

Father, I implore you by the precious Blood of your divine Son which he himself gave as food and drink to his apostles the night before he died, deliver

382

the souls in purgatory. Have mercy especially on that soul most devoted to the Eucharist.

(Our Father, Hail Mary, Eternal rest...)

Friday

Father, I implore you by the precious blood your divine Son shed on the cross, especially from his sacred hands and feet, deliver the souls in purgatory. Have mercy especially on that soul for whom I am particularly bound to pray—spouse, parent, relative, friend, benefactor.

(Our Father, Hail Mary, Eternal rest...)

Saturday

Father, I implore you by the precious blood that gushed forth from the sacred side of your divine Son in the presence of his sorrowful Mother, deliver the souls in purgatory. Have mercy especially on the soul with the greatest devotion to Mary.

(Our Father, Hail Mary, Eternal rest...)

Psalm 130

In our Catholic tradition, Psalm 130 has been a favorite prayer for the dead:

Out of the depths I cry to you, O Lord.
Lord, hear my voice!
Let your ears be attentive to the voice of my
    supplications!
If you, O Lord, should mark iniquities,
    Lord, who could stand?
But there is forgiveness with you, so that you
    may be revered.
I wait for the Lord, my soul waits, and in
    his word I hope;
my soul waits for the Lord more than those
    who watch for the morning, more than those
    who watch for the morning.
O Israel, hope in the Lord!
For with the Lord there is steadfast love, and
    with him is great power to redeem.
It is he who will redeem Israel
    from all its iniquities.

The Heroic Act of Charity

One special way to help the holy souls is the heroic act of charity. Those who make this act freely offer to God, for the holy souls, all the satisfactory value of whatever good they may do, as well as whatever suffrages may be offered for them after death. The satisfactory value of the good works we do can atone for the harmful effects of sin. Whoever makes the heroic act of charity doesn't hold on to this for him or herself, but gives it away for the souls in purgatory. Besides this, all the suffrages offered after death are also given to God to dispose of for whomever he wills. So the heroic act shouldn't be made lightly, but with a full awareness of what one is doing. But God is never outdone in generosity, so we can be sure that if we give away all our suffrages for the holy souls, God will return the favor to us abundantly. "The one who sows bountifully will also reap bountifully. Each of you must give as you have made up your mind, not reluctantly or under compulsion, for God loves a cheerful giver. And God is able to provide you with every blessing in abundance...you will be enriched in every way for your great generosity" (2 Cor 9:6-8, 11).

The following prayer can be used to make the heroic act of charity:

My God, for your greater glory, in union with the merits of Jesus and Mary, I offer and surrender the satisfactory value of all the good I will do, and all the suffrages I will receive after my death, for the holy souls in purgatory. Dispose of everything according to your divine will.

Christmas Novena

Introduction

Father Charles Vachetta, pastor of the Church of the Immaculate in Turin, Italy, wanted to give his parishioners something special for the Advent of 1721. He wanted them to understand the intertwining of the Old and New Testaments so they could see for themselves the love of God unfold from the beginning of time and for all eternity. Father Vachetta decided to give them the gift of a novena—a prayer going deep into the spirit of Advent, leaving one inspired with inexpressible joy. So Father Vachetta began to write his nine day prayer, to stir the hearts of his parishioners to eagerly await the coming of Christ.

Father Vachetta was a poet and scholar, steeped in Biblical theology. Using the Latin Vulgate, he wove the novena from the psalms and prophecies of the Old Testament which foretold the coming of the Messiah, and crowned his masterpiece by retelling the birth of John the Baptist.

Then, taking some of Scripture's lesser known prophecies, he composed a canticle, or prayer-song of incomparable beauty called "Let the Heavens Be

Glad." The canticle is sung after the seven major prophecies and makes a fitting antiphon for the Scripture readings of the day.

The Christmas novena, as it is now known, begins on December 16th, nine days before Christmas, and ends on Christmas Eve. Father Vachetta left us the heritage of a lovely Advent tradition and his work continues to prepare hearts for the coming of Christ through the prophecies, psalms and Gospels. His Christmas novena will inspire people for ages to come.

Christmas Novena

If the novena is led by a priest, the Blessed Sacrament is exposed.

Hymn *(Optional)*
(Sung to the melody of "Creator of the Starry Skies")

> Behold a thrilling voice calls out
> And chides the darkened shades of earth
> Pale dreams are gone, dim shadows fly
> Christ in his might now shines on high!
> The Lamb of God is sent below
> Himself to pay the debt we owe
> O for this gift let every voice
> With songs and prayers to God rejoice.

The Blessed Author of our race
Took human form to bring us grace
Lest lost should be those whom he made
And he with love our sin repaid.
And see! with heavenly grace instilled,
A Mother's loving heart is filled.
Behold a Virgin's body bears
the mystery of endless years!
The Mother makes her spotless breast
A temple for the child to rest
This Virgin loved the Holy One
And she conceived the Eternal Son.
To him who comes the world to free,
To God the Son, all glory be,
To Father, Maker of us all
And Holy Spirit, God, we call.

R. Drop down dew from above you heavens and let the clouds rain the just one.

V. Let the earth be opened and bud forth the Savior.

Christmas Prophecies

R. Our Lord and king is drawing near; O come let us adore him!

V. Our Lord and king is drawing near; O come let us adore him!

Rejoice, Daughter of Sion, and exult Daughter of Jerusalem! Behold the Lord comes, and there will be a great light in that day, and the mountains shall drop down sweetness. The hills shall flow with milk and honey, for in that day the great prophet will come and he will renew Jerusalem (cf. Zeph 3:14-18).

Our Lord and King...

Behold the God-Man of the house of David will come to sit upon the royal throne and you will see him and your heart will rejoice (cf. Jer 23:5-8).

Our Lord and King...

The Lord our protector will come, the Holy One of Israel, wearing a crown upon his royal brow. And he will reign from sea to sea and from the river to the ends of the earth (cf. Is 33:22).

Our Lord and King...

The Lord will appear, and he will not deceive; if he should delay, wait for him to come. He will surely come and will not tarry (cf. Hab 2:3).

Our Lord and King...

The Lord will come down like rain upon the fleece of Gideon. Justice will reign and an abundance of true peace. All the kings of the lands will adore him and every nation will serve him (cf. Jdg 6:38; Ps 72:3-4; Is 2:3).

Our Lord and King...

A child will be born to us, and he will be called God the almighty; he will sit upon the royal throne of David his father, and he will hold sway, the sign of his power on his shoulder (cf. Is 9:6-7).

Our Lord and King...

Bethlehem, city of the Most High God, from you will come forth the king of Israel, and he will proceed forth from his eternity and he will be greatly praised in the midst of the entire universe. And there will be peace in our land when he will have come (cf. Mic 5:2-5).

Our Lord and King...

To be recited or sung on the last day of the novena:

Tomorrow the wickedness of the whole world will be destroyed, and over us will reign the Savior of the world.

R. Our Lord and king is drawing near; O come let us adore him!

V. Near at last is Christ our king; O come let us adore him!

Let the Heavens Be Glad

(Canticle or song-prayer)

Let the heavens be glad and the earth rejoice,
O all you mountains praise the Lord.
Drop down dew from above you heavens,

And let the clouds rain the just one.
Let the earth be opened,
And bud forth the Savior!
Remember us, O Lord,
And visit us in your salvation.
Show your mercy to us, O Lord,
and grant us your salvation.
Send forth, O Lord, the Lamb, the ruler of the earth,
from the rock in the desert to the Mount of Sion.
Come to free us, O Lord God of hosts;
show your face and we shall be saved.
Come, O Lord, and visit us in peace,
so that we may rejoice before you
with a perfect heart.
May we know on earth, O Lord, your way,
your salvation among all nations.
Put forth, O Lord, your strength,
and come to save us.
Come, O Lord, and do not hesitate;
pardon the sins of your people.
O that you would rend the heavens and come down,
the mountains would melt in your presence.
Come and show us your face, O Lord,
you who sit upon the cherubim.

Glory to the Father and to the Son and to the
Holy Spirit; As it was in the beginning, is now and
will be forever. Amen.

Let us pray. Christ the Lamb, who existed before time, in time, and exists for all time, will come to us again. He has been made high priest forever. He is the true king of justice and his reign will have no end.

R. Drop down dew from above you heavens and let the clouds rain the just one.

V. Let the earth be opened and bud forth the Savior.

"O Antiphons"

From December 17 to 23, the liturgy uses seven short prayers that have special richness and importance. Known as the "O antiphons" or the "greater antiphons," these prayers compress and express the Old Testament Messianic hope for Christ. These antiphons are read each day at vespers and are used as the alleluia verse of the Advent Masses.

Each antiphon is a mosaic of biblical references, collected and written in a style called anthological. The unknown author of these beautiful prayers lived around the 6th or 7th century. The author chose seven titles whose first letters are S-A-R-C-O-R-E. Read in reverse order, these letters form two Latin words ero cras, meaning "Tomorrow I shall be."

Note: In this edition we are using a poetic translation of the "O antiphons" from the original Latin.

December 16th

And the foreigners who join themselves to the Lord, to minister to him, to love the name of the Lord, and to be his servants, all who keep the sabbath, and do not profane it, and hold fast my covenant—these I will bring to my holy mountain, and make them joyful in my house of prayer; their burnt offerings and their sacrifices will be accepted on my altar; for my house shall be called a house of prayer for all peoples (Is 56:6-7).

Consideration

Advent prepares our minds and hearts for the coming of the Word of God. It is a gentle time, a time to watch that the word of Scripture does not fall on the rocky ground of distraction, nor by the wayside with our many cares, nor among thorns, caught up in flashy advertisements. It is to fall upon the rich soil of our minds and hearts where the Word of God can bury itself deep and bring forth fruit. The Lord is already near! Let us admit that we need his power and help. Come, Lord Jesus! Give us the gift of yourself.

Antiphon

Behold the king will come, the Lord of the earth, and he will remove from us the yoke of our captivity (cf. Hab 2:3; 1 Cor 4:5).

Magnificat

Intercessions

Jesus, light of the world, we wait in darkness, but also in hope for your coming;
—show yourself to us in mercy and love.

Lord of Israel, you showed yourself to Moses in a burning bush;
—stretch forth your mighty arm and come to save us.

Jesus, born of Mary, we pray with joyful hearts and wait with her in prayer;
—come, Adonai!

Jesus, life of our bodies and souls,
—by your coming let us be immersed in the mystery of your incarnation.

Closing Prayer

(To be said after the intercessions each day of the novena)

Christ goes before us. He is the Lamb without sin who will open to us the gates of heaven. He is the high priest forever according to the order of Melchisedech. He is the king of justice and his reign is eternal.

December 17th

Assemble and hear, O sons of Jacob; listen to Israel your father. Judah, your brothers shall praise you; your hand shall be on the neck of your enemies; your father's sons shall bow down before you. Judah is a lion's whelp; from the prey, my son, you have gone up. He crouches down, he stretches out like a lion, like a lioness—who dares rouse him up? The scepter shall not depart from Judah, nor the ruler's staff from between his feet, until tribute comes to him; and the obedience of the peoples is his (Gen 49:2, 8-10).

Consideration

When we read Scripture and yearn for the coming of the divine, powerful Wisdom who will teach us how to live throughout our life, we think of Mary, the humble Mother of God who always waited upon the Lord as his handmaid.

Let us pray. Father, you spoke, and your Word became man, born of the Virgin Mary. Christ humbled himself to share our human nature. We humble ourselves before the child and ask for faith and love.

Antiphon

O Wisdom eternal, proceeding from the mouth of the Most High, you reach from end to end and order all things mightily and sweetly; come now to direct us in the way of holy prudence (cf. Sir 24; Wis 6-9).

Magnificat

Intercessions

Christ our Redeemer, your law is a light to our path;
—teach us always to walk in the light of your law.

Coming Savior, dawn on us in radiant beauty,
—so that we may receive you with loving devotion at your birth.

God of Jacob, you desire that all might be saved;
—bring all people safely into the kingdom of heaven.

Lord of nations, show us your glory and give us true faith and love;
—protect us from harm and let us live in peace with each other.

Lord of ages, you desired to become one like us;
—may the revelation of your humanity free us from our sinfulness.

Closing Prayer

December 18th

The days are surely coming, says the Lord, when I will raise up for David a righteous Branch, and he shall reign as king and deal wisely, and shall execute justice and righteousness in the land. In his days Judah will be saved and Israel will live in safety. And this is the name by which he will be called: "The Lord is our righteousness." Therefore, the days are surely coming, says the Lord, when it shall no longer be said, "As the Lord lives who brought the people of Israel up out of the land of Egypt," but "As the Lord lives who brought out and led the offspring of the house of Israel out of the land of the north and out of all the lands where he had driven them." Then they shall live in their own land (Jer 23:5-8).

Consideration

God of Israel, you appeared to Moses in the burning bush. You delivered the Israelites from bondage in Egypt by parting the sea, and blessed your people with a covenant as a bridegroom marries his bride. Redeeming Lord, come to save us from the folly of our sins. Give us the blessing of a new covenant written in our hearts for all times. Rescue us with your mighty power!

Antiphon

O Lord and leader of the house of Israel, who once appeared to Moses and spoke to him from a bush aflame, and on the peak of Sinai gave him the law; come now, bring us your redemption with your mighty outstretched arm (cf. Ex 3, 15, 24; Deut 5).

Magnificat

Intercessions

Light of the world, dispel our darkness,
—and make us worthy of your coming.

Key of David, unlock the mystery of your incarnation for all people,
—so that all humanity may praise you together in loving joy.

Eternal Son, let your face shine upon the sick,
—so they may serve you worthily in their infirmity.

Son of David, remember all those who are to die today,
—and bring them into your perfect light.

Closing Prayer

December 19th

In the days of King Herod of Judea, there was a priest named Zechariah, who belonged to the priestly order of Abijah. His wife was a descendant of Aaron, and her name was Elizabeth. Both of them were righteous before God, living blamelessly according to all the commandments and regulations of the Lord. But they had no children, because Elizabeth was barren, and both were getting on in years. Once when he was serving as priest before God and his section was on duty, he was chosen by lot, according to the custom of the priesthood, to enter the sanctuary of the Lord and offer incense. Now at the time of the incense offering, the whole assembly of the people was praying outside. Then there appeared to him an angel of the Lord, standing at the right side of the altar of incense. When Zechariah saw him, he was terrified; and fear overwhelmed him. But the angel said to him, "Do not be afraid, Zechariah, for your prayer has been heard. Your wife Elizabeth will bear you a son, and you will name him John. You will have joy and gladness, and many will rejoice at his birth, for he will be great in the sight of the Lord" (Lk 1:5-14).

Consideration

The infant king will stand as a sign in full view of all the nations. This king will be a sign not only for the Israelites, but also for the Gentiles. All people shall come to him. Our hearts call out, "Come Lord, save your people, do not delay, for we are ready to receive you; we desire to see you face to face."

Antiphon

O root of Jesse, standing an ensign of the people, before whom even kings silent will remain, whom the Gentiles, too, shall beseech, come now to deliver us all; delay no longer (cf. Is 11).

Magnificat

Intercessions

Son of Man, may we celebrate your birth, you who are the Lamb of God;
—you take away our sins and the sins of the world.

Son of Mary, while in your Mother's womb you were welcomed by Elizabeth and her infant son, John;
—though hidden, may we always recognize you and welcome you into our hearts.

God our Counselor, come; tell us that your kingdom is at hand;
—protect the Church and the Pope. Keep the Church as your spotless bride.

Root of Jesse, you humbled yourself to share our human nature;
—come and save us without delay.

Closing Prayer

December 20th

In the sixth month the angel Gabriel was sent by God to a town in Galilee called Nazareth, to a virgin engaged to a man whose name was Joseph, of the house of David. The virgin's name was Mary. And he came to her and said, "Greetings, favored one! The Lord is with you." But she was much perplexed by his words and pondered what sort of greeting this might be. The angel said to her, "Do not be afraid, Mary, for you have found favor with God. And now, you will conceive in your womb and bear a son, and you will name him Jesus. He will be great, and will be called the Son of the Most High, and the Lord God will give to him the throne of his ancestor David. He will reign over the house of Jacob forever, and of his kingdom there will be no end." Mary said to the angel, "How can this be, since I am a virgin?" The angel said to her, "The Holy Spirit will come upon you, and the power of the Most High will overshadow you; therefore the child to be born will be holy; he will be called Son of God. And now, your relative Elizabeth in her old age has also conceived a son; and this is the sixth month for her who was said to be barren. For nothing will be impossible with God."

Then Mary said, "Here am I, the servant of the Lord; let it be with me according to your word." Then the angel departed from her (Lk 1:26-38).

Consideration

The original reference for the fourth "O antiphon" is Isaiah, chapter 22. "Key of David" refers to the one with authority over the royal house of David. The antiphon begs Christ to come and unlock the doors for his people who sit in religious darkness and in the shadows of death. We must wait with longing for our Lord.

Mary's *fiat*—her total acceptance of God's will —brings us the glimmer of light and hope for the coming of Emmanuel, God among us. Mary carries the key of David who will free us forever. Hail, full of grace!

Antiphon

O key of David, royal scepter of Israel, you who open and no one closes; who close and no one can open, come now, and free humanity from its bonds in prison, where it sits in darkness and the shadow of death (cf. Is 22; Rev 3:7).

Magnificat

Intercessions

Adonai! Son of the living God! The day of the Lord draws near;
—he comes as the one who is to save us through his suffering, death and resurrection.

Virgin Mary, Mother of the Savior, we wait with you
quietly for the birth of your Son,
—who will set us free from ignorance and darkness.

Virgin Mother, you placed yourself at God's service
and conceived his Son first in your heart, then in
your womb;
—show us how to open our hearts and receive your
Son, for we have a deep bond with you, Christ's
Mother and our Mother, too.

Mary, our Mother, give doctors and nurses strength
to bring their patients to health,
—that the ill might know the joy of good care in
their infirmities.

Closing Prayer

December 21

In those days Mary set out and went with haste to a
Judean town in the hill country, where she entered
the house of Zechariah and greeted Elizabeth.
When Elizabeth heard Mary's greeting, the child
leaped in her womb. And Elizabeth was filled with
the Holy Spirit and exclaimed with a loud cry,
"Blessed are you among women, and blessed is the
fruit of your womb. And why has this happened
to me, that the mother of my Lord comes to me?
For as soon as I heard the sound of your greeting,

the child in my womb leaped for joy. And blessed is she who believed that there would be a fulfillment of what was spoken to her by the Lord" (Lk 1:39-45).

Consideration

Mary and Elizabeth were deeply rooted in faith and love of God, and both responded wholeheartedly to God's plans. They are a sublime sign of hope for the whole human race. Families all over the world look to their example as they await the blessing of a new baby in their own homes. May they build a foundation of love for the child to come and correspond with joy to God's plans.

Mary, the Morning Star, heralds the coming of her Son; Elizabeth is the first to understand. Her own son leaps for joy in her womb, and the two women embrace because God is in their midst.

Antiphon

O radiant dawn, splendor of eternal light and bright sun of justice, come now and enlighten those who sit in darkness and in the shadow of death (cf. Zech 3:8; 6:12; Is 9:2; 60:1-3; Wis 7:26; Lk 1:78; Heb 1:3).

Magnificat

Intercessions

Ruler of Jacob's house, teach us to guard what is good in ourselves,
—that we may cherish all that you have given to us, for you are our salvation.

God of power and might, help us to be patient and steady our hearts, because the coming of the Lord is at hand;
—drop down dew from above and let the clouds rain down the just one.

Lord, the one foretold by the prophets,
—be mindful of your promises to Abraham and his children.

Messiah, king of glory, you are the fulfillment of the Scriptures,
—grant that all people may recognize you as their Savior and Lord.

Closing Prayer

December 22

My soul magnifies the Lord,
and my spirit rejoices in God my Savior,
for he has looked with favor on the lowliness of his servant.
Surely, from now on all generations will call me blessed;

for the Mighty One has done great things for me,
and holy is his name.
His mercy is for those who fear him
from generation to generation.
He has shown strength with his arm;
he has scattered the proud in the thoughts of their
    hearts.
He has brought down the powerful from their
    thrones,
and lifted up the lowly;
he has filled the hungry with good things,
and sent the rich away empty.
He has helped his servant Israel
in remembrance of his mercy,
according to the promise he made to our
    ancestors,
to Abraham and to his descendants forever
(Lk 1:46-55).

Consideration

In the Magnificat, Mary draws on the Old Testament prophecies and exults in praise of God. Mary's Son is destined to fulfill God's promises to his people. Mary rejoices in the deliverance of God's people and in his care for the poor and destitute of society.

Her song bears another hymn that runs like a golden thread through the readings and antiphons. The expected Messiah will be the Lord of the Gentiles as well as of the Jews. We pray in today's antiphon, "Come, king of all nations." Christ is the peacemaker, the bond of unity among all peoples.

Antiphon

O king of all nations, the one for whom they have been yearning, the cornerstone who unites all of them in perfect union, come now, and rescue poor humanity, which from dust you have fashioned (cf. Jer 10:7; Hg 2:8; Is 28:16, Gen 2:7, Eph 2:14).

Magnificat

Intercessions

Wonderful, Counselor, Prince of Peace! In your great love for us you were born of the Virgin Mary;

—may her prayers for us be our joy and consolation at all times.

Mary has given birth to the Savior, splendor of the rising sun;

—bring those who have died into your light through the intercession of Mary your Mother.

The angels proclaim a mystery today while shepherds hurry to a cave. Mary has given birth to a child in a cold, bare stable;

—we are ready to warm you, holy child, with our hearts. Let us honor you by our lives and deeds, singing glory to God in the highest and peace to all people of goodwill.

Christ, Emmanuel, Mary cared for you in joy and Joseph provided for all the needs of his family;

—help families to love one another and bond them together in love.

Hail, full of grace, the Lord is with you! Blessed are you among women and blessed is the fruit of your womb;

—truly blessed is she who bore the Son of God, and blessed too are those who hear the word of God—and keep it.

Closing Prayer

December 23

See, I am sending my messenger to prepare the way before me, and the Lord whom you seek will suddenly come to his temple. The messenger of the covenant in whom you delight—indeed, he is coming, says the Lord of hosts. But who can endure the day of his coming, and who can stand when he appears? For he is like a refiner's fire and like fullers' soap; he will sit as a refiner and purifier of silver, and he will purify the descendants of Levi and refine them like gold and silver, until they present offerings to the Lord in righteousness.

Then the offering of Judah and Jerusalem will be pleasing to the Lord as in the days of old and as in former years. Lo, I will send you the prophet Elijah before the great and terrible day of the Lord comes. He will turn the hearts of parents to their children and the hearts of children to their parents, so that I will not come and strike the land with a curse (Mal 3:1-4; 4:5-6).

Consideration

Malachi prophecies the birth and mission of John the Baptist. Like a new Elijah, John will go before the Messiah and prepare the people for the Lord's coming. A spirit of joy and wonderment pervades today's prophecy, for the hand of God is active in Israel. The people wonder what it will all mean for their future. What does it mean for us today?

The seventh "O antiphon" climaxes the series. The Messiah is addressed in human form. He is asked to remain with us as Emmanuel. May our hearts be ready to receive the Lord into our small, personal world, as he once came to the little town of Bethlehem. Emmanuel—God is with us! God, stay with us.

Antiphon

O Emmanuel, our ruler and lawgiver, the expected of the nations and the Redeemer of all, come now to deliver us, O our Lord and our master (cf. Is 7:14; Is 33:22; Gen 49:10; Zech 9:9; Jn 20:28).

Magnificat

Intercessions

King of kings, direct the minds and hearts of those who hold authority;
—let justice and peace prevail and let goodwill reign forever.

Lord Jesus, through your saving grace and power,
—may your Church continue to spread until it embraces every nation.

Jesus, prince of peace, you are meek and humble of heart;
—teach us to be thankful for all the blessings you bestow upon us.

Jesus, source of light and growth, increase vocations in your Church, like a gentle rain falling upon the earth;
—the harvest is great and your word must be announced through all the world until your kingdom comes.

Closing Prayer

December 24

And Mary remained with her about three months and then returned to her home.

Then his father Zechariah was filled with the Holy Spirit and spoke this prophecy:

"Blessed be the Lord God of Israel,
for he has looked favorably on his people and
     redeemed them.
He has raised up a mighty savior for us
in the house of his servant David,
as he spoke through the mouth of his holy prophets
     from of old,
that we would be saved from our enemies and
     from the hand of all who hate us.
Thus he has shown the mercy promised to our
     ancestors,
and has remembered his holy covenant,
the oath that he swore to our ancestor Abraham,
to grant us that we, being rescued from the hands
     of our enemies,
might serve him without fear, in holiness and
     righteousness before him all our days.
And you, child, will be called the prophet of the
     Most High;
for you will go before the Lord to prepare his
     ways,
to give knowledge of salvation to his people
by the forgiveness of their sins.
By the tender mercy of our God,
the dawn from on high will break upon us,

to give light to those who sit in darkness and in
   the shadow of death,
to guide our feet into the way of peace."

The child grew and became strong in spirit, and he
was in the wilderness until the day he appeared
publicly to Israel (Lk 1:56; 67-80).

Consideration

Come, O Lord, for the whole world breathlessly
waits for your birth. This one happy moment con-
tains all ages—past, present and future—bonding
eternal peace between heaven and earth through a
newborn child. We bow in adoration and joy. In
calm and peace we look into ourselves and present to
the infant our thoughts and sentiments.

Lord, today your goodness overflows and a
branch springs forth from the root of Jesse. The bud
of salvation unfolds itself from the Virgin's womb in
the dead of winter. The seed entrusted to earth
breaks forth in our cold, frozen hearts and warms
them with the presence of God in human form.

Antiphon

O Emmanuel, our ruler and lawgiver, the expected of the nations and the Redeemer of all, come
now to deliver us, O our Lord and our master.

Magnificat

Intercessions

Father of the Word made flesh, bring us joy and
   peace;
—help us to live united in respect and love for each
   other.

We await the coming of your Son,
—for you are faithful to your promises of salvation
   and eternal life.

May we prepare ourselves for the birth of your Son,
—by meditating upon your word.

Through the Word made flesh may we learn to love
   each other,
—so Christ will find all of us waiting for him in
   joyful prayer at the Second Coming.

Adonai, God of love and mercy, help us follow the
   example of Mary,
—who believed the angel, hastened to help Elizabeth, and welcomed your Son in a cold, bare
   stable, warming him only with her exceeding
   love.

Closing Prayer

   Let us pray. Come to live among us, Lord, so
that we may always receive your forgiveness and
mercy. Jesus our king, clothed in a robe of flesh,
give us love, wisdom and understanding at your

birth. Reveal to us the mystery of your life, then send us forth to reveal your Word over all the earth.

You who live and reign with God the Father in the unity of the Holy Spirit, world without end. Amen.

Magnificat

My soul magnifies the Lord,
and my spirit rejoices in God my Savior,
for he has looked with favor on the lowliness of
    his servant.
Surely, from now on all generations will call me
    blessed;
for the Mighty One has done great things for me,
and holy is his name.
His mercy is for those who fear him
from generation to generation.
He has shown strength with his arm;
he has scattered the proud in the thoughts of
    their hearts.
He has brought down the powerful from their
    thrones,
and lifted up the lowly;
he has filled the hungry with good things,
and sent the rich away empty.
He has helped his servant Israel

in remembrance of his mercy,
according to the promise he made to our
    ancestors,
to Abraham and to his descendants forever
                       (Lk 1:46-55).

Index of Prayers